OSAT
English (107)
Secrets Study Guide

DEAR FUTURE EXAM SUCCESS STORY

First of all, **THANK YOU** for purchasing Mometrix study materials!

Second, congratulations! You are one of the few determined test-takers who are committed to doing whatever it takes to excel on your exam. **You have come to the right place.** We developed these study materials with one goal in mind: to deliver you the information you need in a format that's concise and easy to use.

In addition to optimizing your guide for the content of the test, we've outlined our recommended steps for breaking down the preparation process into small, attainable goals so you can make sure you stay on track.

We've also analyzed the entire test-taking process, identifying the most common pitfalls and showing how you can overcome them and be ready for any curveball the test throws you.

Standardized testing is one of the biggest obstacles on your road to success, which only increases the importance of doing well in the high-pressure, high-stakes environment of test day. Your results on this test could have a significant impact on your future, and this guide provides the information and practical advice to help you achieve your full potential on test day.

Your success is our success

We would love to hear from you! If you would like to share the story of your exam success or if you have any questions or comments in regard to our products, please contact us at **800-673-8175** or **support@mometrix.com**.

Thanks again for your business and we wish you continued success!

Sincerely,
The Mometrix Test Preparation Team

Need more help? Check out our flashcards at:
http://MometrixFlashcards.com/OSAT

TABLE OF CONTENTS

Introduction

Thank you for purchasing this resource! You have made the choice to prepare yourself for a test that could have a huge impact on your future, and this guide is designed to help you be fully ready for test day. Obviously, it's important to have a solid understanding of the test material, but you also need to be prepared for the unique environment and stressors of the test, so that you can perform to the best of your abilities.

For this purpose, the first section that appears in this guide is the **Secret Keys**. We've devoted countless hours to meticulously researching what works and what doesn't, and we've boiled down our findings to the five most impactful steps you can take to improve your performance on the test. We start at the beginning with study planning and move through the preparation process, all the way to the testing strategies that will help you get the most out of what you know when you're finally sitting in front of the test.

We recommend that you start preparing for your test as far in advance as possible. However, if you've bought this guide as a last-minute study resource and only have a few days before your test, we recommend that you skip over the first two Secret Keys since they address a long-term study plan.

If you struggle with **test anxiety**, we strongly encourage you to check out our recommendations for how you can overcome it. Test anxiety is a formidable foe, but it can be beaten, and we want to make sure you have the tools you need to defeat it.

1

Secret Key #1 – Plan Big, Study Small

There's a lot riding on your performance. If you want to ace this test, you're going to need to keep your skills sharp and the material fresh in your mind. You need a plan that lets you review everything you need to know while still fitting in your schedule. We'll break this strategy down into three categories.

Information Organization

Start with the information you already have: the official test outline. From this, you can make a complete list of all the concepts you need to cover before the test. Organize these concepts into groups that can be studied together, and create a list of any related vocabulary you need to learn so you can brush up on any difficult terms. You'll want to keep this vocabulary list handy once you actually start studying since you may need to add to it along the way.

Time Management

Once you have your set of study concepts, decide how to spread them out over the time you have left before the test. Break your study plan into small, clear goals so you have a manageable task for each day and know exactly what you're doing. Then just focus on one small step at a time. When you manage your time this way, you don't need to spend hours at a time studying. Studying a small block of content for a short period each day helps you retain information better and avoid stressing over how much you have left to do. You can relax knowing that you have a plan to cover everything in time. In order for this strategy to be effective though, you have to start studying early and stick to your schedule. Avoid the exhaustion and futility that comes from last-minute cramming!

Study Environment

The environment you study in has a big impact on your learning. Studying in a coffee shop, while probably more enjoyable, is not likely to be as fruitful as studying in a quiet room. It's important to keep distractions to a minimum. You're only planning to study for a short block of time, so make the most of it. Don't pause to check your phone or get up to find a snack. It's also important to **avoid multitasking**. Research has consistently shown that multitasking will make your studying dramatically less effective. Your study area should also be comfortable and well-lit so you don't have the distraction of straining your eyes or sitting on an uncomfortable chair.

 The time of day you study is also important. You want to be rested and alert. Don't wait until just before bedtime. Study when you'll be most likely to comprehend and remember. Even better, if you know what time of day your test will be, set that time aside for study. That way your brain will be used to working on that subject at that specific time and you'll have a better chance of recalling information.

Finally, it can be helpful to team up with others who are studying for the same test. Your actual studying should be done in as isolated an environment as possible, but the work of organizing the information and setting up the study plan can be divided up. In between study sessions, you can discuss with your teammates the concepts that you're all studying and quiz each other on the details. Just be sure that your teammates are as serious about the test as you are. If you find that your study time is being replaced with social time, you might need to find a new team.

Secret Key #2 – Make Your Studying Count

You're devoting a lot of time and effort to preparing for this test, so you want to be absolutely certain it will pay off. This means doing more than just reading the content and hoping you can remember it on test day. It's important to make every minute of study count. There are two main areas you can focus on to make your studying count.

Retention

It doesn't matter how much time you study if you can't remember the material. You need to make sure you are retaining the concepts. To check your retention of the information you're learning, try recalling it at later times with minimal prompting. Try carrying around flashcards and glance at one or two from time to time or ask a friend who's also studying for the test to quiz you.

To enhance your retention, look for ways to put the information into practice so that you can apply it rather than simply recalling it. If you're using the information in practical ways, it will be much easier to remember. Similarly, it helps to solidify a concept in your mind if you're not only reading it to yourself but also explaining it to someone else. Ask a friend to let you teach them about a concept you're a little shaky on (or speak aloud to an imaginary audience if necessary). As you try to summarize, define, give examples, and answer your friend's questions, you'll understand the concepts better and they will stay with you longer. Finally, step back for a big picture view and ask yourself how each piece of information fits with the whole subject. When you link the different concepts together and see them working together as a whole, it's easier to remember the individual components.

Finally, practice showing your work on any multi-step problems, even if you're just studying. Writing out each step you take to solve a problem will help solidify the process in your mind, and you'll be more likely to remember it during the test.

Modality

Modality simply refers to the means or method by which you study. Choosing a study modality that fits your own individual learning style is crucial. No two people learn best in exactly the same way, so it's important to know your strengths and use them to your advantage.

For example, if you learn best by visualization, focus on visualizing a concept in your mind and draw an image or a diagram. Try color-coding your notes, illustrating them, or creating symbols that will trigger your mind to recall a learned concept. If you learn best by hearing or discussing information, find a study partner who learns the same way or read aloud to yourself. Think about how to put the information in your own words. Imagine that you are giving a lecture on the topic and record yourself so you can listen to it later.

For any learning style, flashcards can be helpful. Organize the information so you can take advantage of spare moments to review. Underline key words or phrases. Use different colors for different categories. Mnemonic devices (such as creating a short list in which every item starts with the same letter) can also help with retention. Find what works best for you and use it to store the information in your mind most effectively and easily.

Secret Key #3 – Practice the Right Way

Your success on test day depends not only on how many hours you put into preparing, but also on whether you prepared the right way. It's good to check along the way to see if your studying is paying off. One of the most effective ways to do this is by taking practice tests to evaluate your progress. Practice tests are useful because they show exactly where you need to improve. Every time you take a practice test, pay special attention to these three groups of questions:

- The questions you got wrong
- The questions you had to guess on, even if you guessed right
- The questions you found difficult or slow to work through

This will show you exactly what your weak areas are, and where you need to devote more study time. Ask yourself why each of these questions gave you trouble. Was it because you didn't understand the material? Was it because you didn't remember the vocabulary? Do you need more repetitions on this type of question to build speed and confidence? Dig into those questions and figure out how you can strengthen your weak areas as you go back to review the material.

 Additionally, many practice tests have a section explaining the answer choices. It can be tempting to read the explanation and think that you now have a good understanding of the concept. However, an explanation likely only covers part of the question's broader context. Even if the explanation makes perfect sense, **go back and investigate** every concept related to the question until you're positive you have a thorough understanding.

As you go along, keep in mind that the practice test is just that: practice. Memorizing these questions and answers will not be very helpful on the actual test because it is unlikely to have any of the same exact questions. If you only know the right answers to the sample questions, you won't be prepared for the real thing. **Study the concepts** until you understand them fully, and then you'll be able to answer any question that shows up on the test.

It's important to wait on the practice tests until you're ready. If you take a test on your first day of study, you may be overwhelmed by the amount of material covered and how much you need to learn. Work up to it gradually.

On test day, you'll need to be prepared for answering questions, managing your time, and using the test-taking strategies you've learned. It's a lot to balance, like a mental marathon that will have a big impact on your future. Like training for a marathon, you'll need to start slowly and work your way up. When test day arrives, you'll be ready.

Start with the strategies you've read in the first two Secret Keys—plan your course and study in the way that works best for you. If you have time, consider using multiple study resources to get different approaches to the same concepts. It can be helpful to see difficult concepts from more than one angle. Then find a good source for practice tests. Many times, the test website will suggest potential study resources or provide sample tests.

Practice Test Strategy

If you're able to find at least three practice tests, we recommend this strategy:

UNTIMED AND OPEN-BOOK PRACTICE

Take the first test with no time constraints and with your notes and study guide handy. Take your time and focus on applying the strategies you've learned.

TIMED AND OPEN-BOOK PRACTICE

Take the second practice test open-book as well, but set a timer and practice pacing yourself to finish in time.

TIMED AND CLOSED-BOOK PRACTICE

Take any other practice tests as if it were test day. Set a timer and put away your study materials. Sit at a table or desk in a quiet room, imagine yourself at the testing center, and answer questions as quickly and accurately as possible.

Keep repeating timed and closed-book tests on a regular basis until you run out of practice tests or it's time for the actual test. Your mind will be ready for the schedule and stress of test day, and you'll be able to focus on recalling the material you've learned.

Secret Key #4 – Pace Yourself

Once you're fully prepared for the material on the test, your biggest challenge on test day will be managing your time. Just knowing that the clock is ticking can make you panic even if you have plenty of time left. Work on pacing yourself so you can build confidence against the time constraints of the exam. Pacing is a difficult skill to master, especially in a high-pressure environment, so **practice is vital**.

Set time expectations for your pace based on how much time is available. For example, if a section has 60 questions and the time limit is 30 minutes, you know you have to average 30 seconds or less per question in order to answer them all. Although 30 seconds is the hard limit, set 25 seconds per question as your goal, so you reserve extra time to spend on harder questions. When you budget extra time for the harder questions, you no longer have any reason to stress when those questions take longer to answer.

Don't let this time expectation distract you from working through the test at a calm, steady pace, but keep it in mind so you don't spend too much time on any one question. Recognize that taking extra time on one question you don't understand may keep you from answering two that you do understand later in the test. If your time limit for a question is up and you're still not sure of the answer, mark it and move on, and come back to it later if the time and the test format allow. If the testing format doesn't allow you to return to earlier questions, just make an educated guess; then put it out of your mind and move on.

On the easier questions, be careful not to rush. It may seem wise to hurry through them so you have more time for the challenging ones, but it's not worth missing one if you know the concept and just didn't take the time to read the question fully. Work efficiently but make sure you understand the question and have looked at all of the answer choices, since more than one may seem right at first.

Even if you're paying attention to the time, you may find yourself a little behind at some point. You should speed up to get back on track, but do so wisely. Don't panic; just take a few seconds less on each question until you're caught up. Don't guess without thinking, but do look through the answer choices and eliminate any you know are wrong. If you can get down to two choices, it is often worthwhile to guess from those. Once you've chosen an answer, move on and don't dwell on any that you skipped or had to hurry through. If a question was taking too long, chances are it was one of the harder ones, so you weren't as likely to get it right anyway.

On the other hand, if you find yourself getting ahead of schedule, it may be beneficial to slow down a little. The more quickly you work, the more likely you are to make a careless mistake that will affect your score. You've budgeted time for each question, so don't be afraid to spend that time. Practice an efficient but careful pace to get the most out of the time you have.

Secret Key #5 – Have a Plan for Guessing

When you're taking the test, you may find yourself stuck on a question. Some of the answer choices seem better than others, but you don't see the one answer choice that is obviously correct. What do you do?

The scenario described above is very common, yet most test takers have not effectively prepared for it. Developing and practicing a plan for guessing may be one of the single most effective uses of your time as you get ready for the exam.

In developing your plan for guessing, there are three questions to address:

- When should you start the guessing process?
- How should you narrow down the choices?
- Which answer should you choose?

When to Start the Guessing Process

Unless your plan for guessing is to select C every time (which, despite its merits, is not what we recommend), you need to leave yourself enough time to apply your answer elimination strategies. Since you have a limited amount of time for each question, that means that if you're going to give yourself the best shot at guessing correctly, you have to decide quickly whether or not you will guess.

Of course, the best-case scenario is that you don't have to guess at all, so first, see if you can answer the question based on your knowledge of the subject and basic reasoning skills. Focus on the key words in the question and try to jog your memory of related topics. Give yourself a chance to bring the knowledge to mind, but once you realize that you don't have (or you can't access) the knowledge you need to answer the question, it's time to start the guessing process.

It's almost always better to start the guessing process too early than too late. It only takes a few seconds to remember something and answer the question from knowledge. Carefully eliminating wrong answer choices takes longer. Plus, going through the process of eliminating answer choices can actually help jog your memory.

Summary: Start the guessing process as soon as you decide that you can't answer the question based on your knowledge.

7

How to Narrow Down the Choices

The next chapter in this book (**Test-Taking Strategies**) includes a wide range of strategies for how to approach questions and how to look for answer choices to eliminate. You will definitely want to read those carefully, practice them, and figure out which ones work best for you. Here though, we're going to address a mindset rather than a particular strategy.

Your odds of guessing an answer correctly depend on how many options you are choosing from.

Number of options left	5	4	3	2	1
Odds of guessing correctly	20%	25%	33%	50%	100%

You can see from this chart just how valuable it is to be able to eliminate incorrect answers and make an educated guess, but there are two things that many test takers do that cause them to miss out on the benefits of guessing:

- Accidentally eliminating the correct answer
- Selecting an answer based on an impression

We'll look at the first one here, and the second one in the next section.

To avoid accidentally eliminating the correct answer, we recommend a thought exercise called **the $5 challenge**. In this challenge, you only eliminate an answer choice from contention if you are willing to bet $5 on it being wrong. Why $5? Five dollars is a small but not insignificant amount of money. It's an amount you could afford to lose but wouldn't want to throw away. And while losing $5 once might not

hurt too much, doing it twenty times will set you back $100. In the same way, each small decision you make—eliminating a choice here, guessing on a question there—won't by itself impact your score very much, but when you put them all together, they can make a big difference. By holding each answer choice elimination decision to a higher standard, you can reduce the risk of accidentally eliminating the correct answer.

The $5 challenge can also be applied in a positive sense: If you are willing to bet $5 that an answer choice *is* correct, go ahead and mark it as correct.

Summary: Only eliminate an answer choice if you are willing to bet $5 that it is wrong.

8

Which Answer to Choose

You're taking the test. You've run into a hard question and decided you'll have to guess. You've eliminated all the answer choices you're willing to bet $5 on. Now you have to pick an answer. Why do we even need to talk about this? Why can't you just pick whichever one you feel like when the time comes?

The answer to these questions is that if you don't come into the test with a plan, you'll rely on your impression to select an answer choice, and if you do that, you risk falling into a trap. The test writers know that everyone who takes their test will be guessing on some of the questions, so they intentionally write wrong answer choices to seem plausible. You still have to pick an answer though, and if the wrong answer choices are designed to look right, how can you ever be sure that you're not falling for their trap? The best solution we've found to this dilemma is to take the decision out of your hands entirely. Here is the process we recommend:

Once you've eliminated any choices that you are confident (willing to bet $5) are wrong, select the first remaining choice as your answer.

Whether you choose to select the first remaining choice, the second, or the last, the important thing is that you use some preselected standard. Using this approach guarantees that you will not be enticed into selecting an answer choice that looks right, because you are not basing your decision on how the answer choices look.

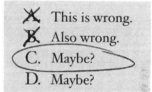

This is not meant to make you question your knowledge. Instead, it is to help you recognize the difference between your knowledge and your impressions. There's a huge difference between thinking an answer is right because of what you know, and thinking an answer is right because it looks or sounds like it should be right.

Summary: To ensure that your selection is appropriately random, make a predetermined selection from among all answer choices you have not eliminated.

Test-Taking Strategies

This section contains a list of test-taking strategies that you may find helpful as you work through the test. By taking what you know and applying logical thought, you can maximize your chances of answering any question correctly!

It is very important to realize that every question is different and every person is different: no single strategy will work on every question, and no single strategy will work for every person. That's why we've included all of them here, so you can try them out and determine which ones work best for different types of questions and which ones work best for you.

Question Strategies

⌀ READ CAREFULLY

Read the question and the answer choices carefully. Don't miss the question because you misread the terms. You have plenty of time to read each question thoroughly and make sure you understand what is being asked. Yet a happy medium must be attained, so don't waste too much time. You must read carefully and efficiently.

⌀ CONTEXTUAL CLUES

Look for contextual clues. If the question includes a word you are not familiar with, look at the immediate context for some indication of what the word might mean. Contextual clues can often give you all the information you need to decipher the meaning of an unfamiliar word. Even if you can't determine the meaning, you may be able to narrow down the possibilities enough to make a solid guess at the answer to the question.

⌀ PREFIXES

If you're having trouble with a word in the question or answer choices, try dissecting it. Take advantage of every clue that the word might include. Prefixes and suffixes can be a huge help. Usually, they allow you to determine a basic meaning. *Pre-* means before, *post-* means after, *pro-* is positive, *de-* is negative. From prefixes and suffixes, you can get an idea of the general meaning of the word and try to put it into context.

⌀ HEDGE WORDS

Watch out for critical hedge words, such as *likely, may, can, sometimes, often, almost, mostly, usually, generally, rarely,* and *sometimes.* Question writers insert these hedge phrases to cover every possibility. Often an answer choice will be wrong simply because it leaves no room for exception. Be on guard for answer choices that have definitive words such as *exactly* and *always.*

⌀ SWITCHBACK WORDS

Stay alert for *switchbacks*. These are the words and phrases frequently used to alert you to shifts in thought. The most common switchback words are *but, although,* and *however.* Others include *nevertheless, on the other hand, even though, while, in spite of, despite,* and *regardless of.* Switchback words are important to catch because they can change the direction of the question or an answer choice.

⌀ FACE VALUE

When in doubt, use common sense. Accept the situation in the problem at face value. Don't read too much into it. These problems will not require you to make wild assumptions. If you have to go beyond creativity and warp time or space in order to have an answer choice fit the question, then you should move on and consider the other answer choices. These are normal problems rooted in reality. The applicable relationship or explanation may not be readily apparent, but it is there for you to figure out. Use your common sense to interpret anything that isn't clear.

Answer Choice Strategies

⊘ ANSWER SELECTION

The most thorough way to pick an answer choice is to identify and eliminate wrong answers until only one is left, then confirm it is the correct answer. Sometimes an answer choice may immediately seem right, but be careful. The test writers will usually put more than one reasonable answer choice on each question, so take a second to read all of them and make sure that the other choices are not equally obvious. As long as you have time left, it is better to read every answer choice than to pick the first one that looks right without checking the others.

⊘ ANSWER CHOICE FAMILIES

An answer choice family consists of two (in rare cases, three) answer choices that are very similar in construction and cannot all be true at the same time. If you see two answer choices that are direct opposites or parallels, one of them is usually the correct answer. For instance, if one answer choice says that quantity x increases and another either says that quantity x decreases (opposite) or says that quantity y increases (parallel), then those answer choices would fall into the same family. An answer choice that doesn't match the construction of the answer choice family is more likely to be incorrect. Most questions will not have answer choice families, but when they do appear, you should be prepared to recognize them.

⊘ ELIMINATE ANSWERS

Eliminate answer choices as soon as you realize they are wrong, but make sure you consider all possibilities. If you are eliminating answer choices and realize that the last one you are left with is also wrong, don't panic. Start over and consider each choice again. There may be something you missed the first time that you will realize on the second pass.

⊘ AVOID FACT TRAPS

Don't be distracted by an answer choice that is factually true but doesn't answer the question. You are looking for the choice that answers the question. Stay focused on what the question is asking for so you don't accidentally pick an answer that is true but incorrect. Always go back to the question and make sure the answer choice you've selected actually answers the question and is not merely a true statement.

⊘ EXTREME STATEMENTS

In general, you should avoid answers that put forth extreme actions as standard practice or proclaim controversial ideas as established fact. An answer choice that states the "process should be used in certain situations, if..." is much more likely to be correct than one that states the "process should be discontinued completely." The first is a calm rational statement and doesn't even make a definitive, uncompromising stance, using a hedge word *if* to provide wiggle room, whereas the second choice is far more extreme.

⊘ BENCHMARK

As you read through the answer choices and you come across one that seems to answer the question well, mentally select that answer choice. This is not your final answer, but it's the one that will help you evaluate the other answer choices. The one that you selected is your benchmark or standard for judging each of the other answer choices. Every other answer choice must be compared to your benchmark. That choice is correct until proven otherwise by another answer choice beating it. If you find a better answer, then that one becomes your new benchmark. Once you've decided that no other choice answers the question as well as your benchmark, you have your final answer.

11

⊘ Predict the Answer

Before you even start looking at the answer choices, it is often best to try to predict the answer. When you come up with the answer on your own, it is easier to avoid distractions and traps because you will know exactly what to look for. The right answer choice is unlikely to be word-for-word what you came up with, but it should be a close match. Even if you are confident that you have the right answer, you should still take the time to read each option before moving on.

General Strategies

⊘ Tough Questions

If you are stumped on a problem or it appears too hard or too difficult, don't waste time. Move on! Remember though, if you can quickly check for obviously incorrect answer choices, your chances of guessing correctly are greatly improved. Before you completely give up, at least try to knock out a couple of possible answers. Eliminate what you can and then guess at the remaining answer choices before moving on.

⊘ Check Your Work

Since you will probably not know every term listed and the answer to every question, it is important that you get credit for the ones that you do know. Don't miss any questions through careless mistakes. If at all possible, try to take a second to look back over your answer selection and make sure you've selected the correct answer choice and haven't made a costly careless mistake (such as marking an answer choice that you didn't mean to mark). This quick double check should more than pay for itself in caught mistakes for the time it costs.

⊘ Pace Yourself

It's easy to be overwhelmed when you're looking at a page full of questions; your mind is confused and full of random thoughts, and the clock is ticking down faster than you would like. Calm down and maintain the pace that you have set for yourself. Especially as you get down to the last few minutes of the test, don't let the small numbers on the clock make you panic. As long as you are on track by monitoring your pace, you are guaranteed to have time for each question.

⊘ Don't Rush

It is very easy to make errors when you are in a hurry. Maintaining a fast pace in answering questions is pointless if it makes you miss questions that you would have gotten right otherwise. Test writers like to include distracting information and wrong answers that seem right. Taking a little extra time to avoid careless mistakes can make all the difference in your test score. Find a pace that allows you to be confident in the answers that you select.

⊘ Keep Moving

Panicking will not help you pass the test, so do your best to stay calm and keep moving. Taking deep breaths and going through the answer elimination steps you practiced can help to break through a stress barrier and keep your pace.

Final Notes

The combination of a solid foundation of content knowledge and the confidence that comes from practicing your plan for applying that knowledge is the key to maximizing your performance on test day. As your foundation of content knowledge is built up and strengthened, you'll find that the strategies included in this chapter become more and more effective in helping you quickly sift through the distractions and traps of the test to isolate the correct answer.

Now that you're preparing to move forward into the test content chapters of this book, be sure to keep your goal in mind. As you read, think about how you will be able to apply this information on the test. If you've already seen sample questions for the test and you have an idea of the question format and style, try to come up with questions of your own that you can answer based on what you're reading. This will give you valuable practice applying your knowledge in the same ways you can expect to on test day.

Good luck and good studying!

Speaking, Listening, and Viewing

Public Speaking

SPEECHES

Speeches are written to be delivered in spoken language in public, to various groups of people, at formal or informal events. Some generic types include welcome speeches, thank-you speeches, keynote addresses, position papers, commemorative and dedication speeches, and farewell speeches. Speeches are commonly written in present tense and usually begin with an introduction greeting the audience. At official functions, specific audience members are named ("Chairperson [name]," "Principal [name], teachers, and students," etc.) and when audiences include a distinguished guest, he or she is often named as well. Then the speaker introduces him or herself by name, position, and department or organization as applicable. After the greeting, the speaker then introduces the topic and states the purpose of the speech. The body of the speech follows, similarly to the body of an essay, stating its main points, an explanation of each point, and supporting evidence. Finally, in the conclusion, the speaker states his or her hope for accomplishing the speech's purpose and thanks the audience for attending and listening to the speech.

CLEARLY WRITTEN PROSE AND SPEECHES

To achieve **clarity**, a writer or speaker must first define his or her purpose carefully. The speech should be organized logically, so that sentences make sense and follow each other in an understandable order. Sentences must also be constructed well, with carefully chosen words and structure. Organizing a speech in advance using an outline provides the writer or speaker with a blueprint, directing and focusing the composition to meet its intended purpose. Organized speeches enable audiences to comprehend and retain the presented information more easily. Humans naturally seek to impose order on the world by seeking patterns. Hence, when ideas in a speech are well-organized and adhere to a consistent pattern, the speaker communicates better with listeners and is more convincing. Speechwriters can use chronological patterns to organize events, sequential patterns to organize processes by their steps, and spatial patterns to help audiences visualize geographical locations and movements or physical scenarios. Also, comparison-contrast patterns give audiences insight about similarities and differences between and among topics, especially when listeners are more familiar with one than the other.

EVALUATING SPEECHES FOR CONCISE INFORMATION

To convince or persuade listeners or reinforce a message, speeches must be succinct. Audiences can become confused by excessive anecdotes and details. If a speaker takes three minutes or more to get to the point, audience members' attention will start to fade and will only worsen when details deviate from the main subject. When answering a question, the asker and speaker may even forget the original question if the speaker takes too long. Speakers should practice not only rehearsing written speeches, but also developing skill for spontaneous question-and-answer sessions after speeches. Speakers should differentiate necessary from simply interesting information because audiences can become overwhelmed by too much information. Speakers should know what points they wish to make. They should not be afraid to pause before responding to questions, which indicates thoughtfulness and control rather than lack of knowledge. Restating questions increases comprehension and appropriate responses, and allows time to form answers mentally.

ORGANIZATIONAL PATTERNS FOR SPEECHES

A speechwriter who uses an **advantages-disadvantages** pattern of organization presents the audience with the pros and cons of a topic. This aids writers in discussing two sides of an issue objectively without an argumentative position, enabling listeners to weigh both aspects. When a speechwriter uses

15

a **cause-and-effect** pattern, it can help to persuade audiences to agree with an action or solution by showing significant relationships between factors. Writers may separate an outline into two main "cause" and "effect" sections or into separate sections for each cause, including the effect for each. Persuasive writing also benefits from **problem-solution** patterns: by establishing the existence of a problem, writers induce audiences to realize a need for change. By supplying a solution and supporting its superiority above other solutions, the writer convinces audiences of the value of that solution. When none of these patterns—or **chronological**, **sequential**, **spatial**, or **comparison-contrast** patterns—applies, speechwriters often use topical patterns. These organize information by various subtopics and types within the main topic or category.

EFFECTIVE SPEECH DELIVERY

Speakers should deliver speeches in a natural, conversational manner rather than being rigidly formal or theatrical. Effective delivery is also supported by confidence. Speakers should be direct, building audience rapport through personal connection and vivid imagery. Speakers should be mindful of the occasion, subject, and audience of their speeches and take care to use appropriate language. Good speakers learn vocal control, including volume, speed, pitch, use of pauses, tonal variety, correct pronunciation, and clear articulation. They can express enthusiasm and emphasize important points with their voices. Nonverbal behaviors, such as eye contact, facial expressions, gestures, good posture, and body movements clarify communication, stress important ideas, and influence perceptions that the speaker is trustworthy, competent, and credible. Nonverbal communications should seem as spontaneous and natural as vocal or verbal ones. Speakers should know their speeches well and practice frequently, taking care to avoid nervous or irrelevant movements such as tapping or pacing.

Classroom Participation

TECHNIQUES TO ENSURE ACTIVE LISTENING AND PRODUCTIVE PARTICIPATION

When assigning students to participate in cooperative learning projects or discussions, teachers should consider their **cognitive, emotional, behavioral, and social developmental levels.** If a teacher assigns a topic for age levels younger than the class, students will be bored and unengaged. If the topic assigned is for older age levels, they will be confused, overwhelmed, or lost. Before initiating class or group discussions, teachers should model and explain appropriate behaviors for discussions—particularly for students unfamiliar or inexperienced with group discussions. For example, teachers can demonstrate active listening, including eye contact, affirming or confirming the speaker's message, and restating the speaker's message for confirmation or correction. Teachers should establish **clear ground rules**, such as not interrupting others when they are speaking, not monopolizing the conversation, not engaging in cross-talk, not insulting classmates verbally, and taking turns and waiting for the appropriate time to make a comment. For young children and students with behavioral issues, this would also include refraining from physical contact like hitting, kicking, and biting.

ACTIVE STUDENT LISTENING

Active listening has multiple dimensions. It involves constructing meaning out of what is heard, being reflective and creative in considering and manipulating information, and making competent decisions rich in ideas. The natural properties of speech and thought enable active listening: the typical speed of speaking is roughly 125 words per minute, whereas the estimated speed of thinking is roughly 500 words per minute. Therefore, students have around 375 words per minute of spare time to think about the speech they hear. Students' minds can wander during this extra time, so teachers should instruct them to use the time instead to summarize lecture information mentally—a form of active listening. Listening and learning are both social and reciprocal. They also both allow and require students to process and consider what they hear and stimulate their curiosity about subsequent information.

INCORPORATING ACTIVE STUDENT LISTENING INTO LESSONS

At the beginning of each day (or class), teachers should clarify the "big picture" and identify the learning objectives incorporated into the day's activities. They should also give students a single word or phrase to summarize the prior day's subject and a single word or phrase to preview the current day's subject. Teachers should not only establish this recall, retrieval, prediction, and planning process as a daily habit, but should also encourage students to develop the same daily habit in their note-taking. Teachers should review main concepts or have students summarize the last lecture's main ideas to make connections with preceding lessons. By encouraging and guiding student listening, teachers supply spoken transitions analogously to those in written research. By cueing students to take notes with questions or summaries at the ends of sections, teachers also help students demonstrate their comprehension.

USING MEDIA TO REVIEW

Teachers can allow students to take photos, videos, and audio recordings of lessons to review as needed. To encourage students to reword and recall instructional input, teachers can let students download class outlines from Google Docs. These outlines may include hard-to-spell terminology or vocabulary words, jargon of specific disciplines, and links reminding students to follow up by accessing resources and readings to inform the notes they take. Teachers should give outlines a two-column format: on the right, a wider column with teacher notes, to which students can add, and on the left, a narrower column for students to record notes and questions about previous lectures and reading. Teachers should advise students to take their own notes in similar formats. Students and teachers alike can learn through speaking, writing, listening, and reading when they contribute narratives to supplement visual graphics (photos, concept maps, charts, advance organizers, illustrations, diagrams, etc.) that support the concepts they analyze and explain.

WHOLE-CLASS LEARNING CIRCLES

Forming **whole classes** into learning circles requires students to apply their skills for listening to lectures, synthesizing information, and summarizing the information. Teachers can prepare students by articulating central discussion points; identifying next steps in thought, question forming, analysis, and action; guiding student analysis and construction of meaning from what they have read, observed, and experienced; and asking students questions beginning with "What?" "Why?" and "Now what?"

Basic ground rules for learning circles include:

1. No student interrupts another.
2. Students may skip a turn until others have taken turns, but no student speaks out of turn.
3. Each student has a certain length of time for speaking.
4. Each student starts by restating what was said previously (e.g., summarizing shared points, differing points, missed points, or points not discussed fully).
5. After every student has had one turn, general discussion is open, possibly guided by teacher-provided questions.

PROCEDURES AND GROUND RULES FOR SMALLER GROUPS

Teachers can develop student discussion skills integrating listening, reading, and speaking skills by assigning small discussion groups to tackle assigned problems. Teachers may use established groups, assign new groups, or allow students to form groups of 4-5 students. Teachers can read a text passage, describe a scenario, or pose a question for discussion. They can then give students several minutes to review homework and notes, briefly read new related material, and review essay drafts. Teachers then give each student in each group a specified number of uninterrupted minutes to speak in turn.

After every student has taken a turn, the teacher opens general discussion, setting the following ground rules:

1. Students can only speak about others' ideas.
2. Teachers and classmates can ask students to clarify their ideas, give examples, connect them more closely to what they read, or elaborate.
3. Small groups can summarize overall points for other groups, including shared points, differences, and potential topics they missed.

EDUCATOR TECHNIQUES FOR CLASSROOM DISCUSSIONS

Students who feel comfortable with the teacher and the class are more likely to engage in open discussion. Teachers can encourage student openness and creativity by learning students' names and by posing questions rather than making comments. Lively discussions with all students participating are evidence that students are comfortable. A variety of student answers is evidence that the questioning technique works. When student discussions stray off the subject, learning goals will not be met. Teachers can redirect discussion by restating topics and questions previously announced, and by introducing new questions related to identified topics. When conversation refocuses on stated topics, teachers can identify specified learning goals/objectives students are meeting in their discussion. In most classes, a few students will dominate conversations. Teachers can pose less challenging questions, which can be answered even without preparation, to engage more reticent students, and then graduate to higher-level questions. They can evaluate all students' participation using checklists generated from attendance sheets.

TEACHING STRATEGIES TO ENCOURAGE DISCUSSION

During class discussions, students often contribute erroneous information. Teachers must be tactful in correcting them. If students withdraw from the conversation or cease further contributions, the teacher has not corrected them appropriately. If corrected students continue to contribute, the teacher has succeeded in providing positive reinforcement rather than punishment with the correction. Some ways to do this include acknowledging how the student came to a conclusion but explaining that it does not apply to the current context, or explaining how the student's response might be correct in another situation. Teachers can also provide incentives for students to contribute to class discussions. They may include participation in the syllabus as part of the grade, keep records to tally when each student contributes to a discussion, or assign different students to lead class discussions in turn. These are some ways teachers can evaluate individual student participation in classroom discussions, as well as their own effectiveness in encouraging such participation.

REDUCING INTIMIDATION

Students often feel intimidated if "put on the spot" to answer questions without warning. Teachers can put them at ease by allowing time to prepare. They can announce topics and questions for class discussion, giving students five minutes to jot down notes for responses and another five minutes for exchanging and reflecting on notes with classmates before beginning whole-class conversation. Teachers may distribute discussion topics at the end of one class for the next day's conversation or post questions online the night before class. One technique for evaluating discussions is asking students early in the term to write papers about the characteristics of good and bad class discussions, and then discuss what they have written. Teachers then compose a list of classroom discussion goals and give copies to all students. Another technique is an informal survey: ask students midway through the semester to evaluate the overall quality of class discussions. Share responses with the class, and inform them of plans incorporating their feedback to enhance discussions.

PROMOTING DISCUSSION OUTSIDE OF CLASS

Teachers can encourage in-class discussion by promoting group meetings and discussions outside the classroom. Interacting with students outside of class also promotes a sense of community. Teachers can demonstrate to students that they care about them as individuals and about their educational development by asking them about their holiday or summer plans, about how they are feeling during midterm and final exam periods, and about their other classes. Teachers can find online articles related to class material and email or text links to these for review. They can allow time at the beginning of each class for announcements. They can also arrange classroom chairs in a semicircle to encourage conversation. These methods are all found effective in promoting a sense of community, which in turn encourages class discussions. To address different student learning styles and abilities, teachers can vary the levels and types of questions they ask their students: asking them to give simple information, describe, compare, analyze, justify, compare, generalize, predict, or apply information.

Writing Process and Applications

Foundations of Grammar

THE EIGHT PARTS OF SPEECH
NOUNS

When you talk about a person, place, thing, or idea, you are talking about a **noun**. The two main types of nouns are **common** and **proper** nouns. Also, nouns can be abstract (i.e., general) or concrete (i.e., specific).

COMMON NOUNS

Common nouns are generic names for people, places, and thing. Common nouns are not usually capitalized. Examples of common nouns:

> *People*: boy, girl, worker, manager

> *Places*: school, bank, library, home

> *Things*: dog, cat, truck, car

PROPER NOUNS

Proper nouns name specific people, places, or things. All proper nouns are capitalized. Examples of proper nouns:

> *People*: Abraham Lincoln; George Washington; Martin Luther King, Jr.

> *Places*: Los Angeles, California; New York; Asia

> *Things*: Statue of Liberty, Earth*, Lincoln Memorial

> Note: When referring to the planet that we live on, capitalize *Earth*. When referring to the dirt, rocks, or land, lowercase *earth*.

GENERAL AND SPECIFIC NOUNS

General nouns are the names of conditions or ideas. **Specific nouns** name people, places, and things that are understood by using your senses.

General nouns:

> *Condition*: beauty, strength

> *Idea*: truth, peace

Specific nouns:

> *People*: baby, friend, father

> *Places*: town, park, city hall

> *Things*: rainbow, cough, apple, silk, gasoline

20

COLLECTIVE NOUNS

Collective nouns are the names for a group of people, places, or things that may act as a whole. The following are examples of collective nouns: *class, company, dozen, group, herd, team,* and *public.* Collective nouns usually require an article, which denotes the noun as being a single unit. For instance, a choir is a group of singers. Even though there are many singers in a choir, the word choir is grammatically treated as a single unit. If we refer to the members of the group, and not the group itself, it is no longer a collective noun.

Incorrect: The **choir are** going to compete nationally this year.

Correct: The **choir is** going to compete nationally this year.

Incorrect: The **members** of the choir **is** competing nationally this year.

Correct: The **members** of the choir **are** competing nationally this year.

PRONOUNS

Pronouns are words that are used to stand in for nouns. A pronoun may be classified as personal, intensive, relative, interrogative, demonstrative, indefinite, and reciprocal.

Personal: *Nominative* is the case for nouns and pronouns that are the subject of a sentence. *Objective* is the case for nouns and pronouns that are an object in a sentence. *Possessive* is the case for nouns and pronouns that show possession or ownership.

Singular.

	Nominative	Objective	Possessive
First Person	I	me	my, mine
Second Person	you	you	your, yours
Third Person	he, she, it	him, her, it	his, her, hers, its

Plural

	Nominative	Objective	Possessive
First Person	we	us	our, ours
Second Person	you	you	your, yours
Third Person	they	them	their, theirs

Intensive: I myself, you yourself, he himself, she herself, the (thing) itself, we ourselves, you yourselves, they themselves

Relative: which, who, whom, whose

Interrogative: what, which, who, whom, whose

Demonstrative: this, that, these, those

Indefinite: all, any, each, everyone, either/neither, one, some, several

Reciprocal: each other, one another

Review Video: **Nouns and Pronouns**
Visit mometrix.com/academy and enter code: 312073

VERBS

If you want to write a sentence, then you need a verb. Without a verb, you have no sentence. The verb of a sentence indicates action or being. In other words, the verb shows something's action or state of being or the action that has been done to something.

TRANSITIVE AND INTRANSITIVE VERBS

A **transitive verb** is a verb whose action (e.g., drive, run, jump) indicates a receiver (e.g., car, dog, kangaroo). **Intransitive verbs** do not indicate a receiver of an action. In other words, the action of the verb does not point to a subject or object.

> **Transitive**: He plays the piano. | The piano was played by him.

> **Intransitive**: He plays. | John plays well.

A dictionary will tell you whether a verb is transitive or intransitive. Some verbs can be transitive and intransitive.

ACTION VERBS AND LINKING VERBS

Action verbs show what the subject is doing. In other words, an action verb shows action. Unlike most types of words, a single action verb, in the right context, can be an entire sentence. **Linking verbs** link the subject of a sentence to a noun or pronoun, or they link a subject with an adjective. You always need a verb if you want a complete sentence. However, linking verbs on their own cannot be a complete sentence.

Common linking verbs include *appear, be, become, feel, grow, look, seem, smell, sound,* and *taste*. However, any verb that shows a condition and connects to a noun, pronoun, or adjective that describes the subject of a sentence is a linking verb.

Action: He sings. | Run! | Go! | I talk with him every day. | She reads.

Linking:

> Incorrect: I am.

> Correct: I am John. | I smell roses. | I feel tired.

Note: Some verbs are followed by words that look like prepositions, but they are a part of the verb and a part of the verb's meaning. These are known as phrasal verbs, and examples include *call off, look up,* and *drop off*.

> **Review Video: Action Verbs and Linking Verbs**
> Visit mometrix.com/academy and enter code: 743142

VOICE

Transitive verbs come in active or passive **voice**. If something does an action or is acted upon, then you will know whether a verb is active or passive. When the subject of the sentence is doing the action, the verb is in **active voice**. When the subject is acted upon, the verb is in **passive voice**.

> **Active**: Jon drew the picture. (The subject *Jon* is doing the action of *drawing a picture*.)

> **Passive**: The picture is drawn by Jon. (The subject *picture* is receiving the action from Jon.)

VERB TENSES

A verb **tense** shows the different form of a verb to point to the time of an action. The present and past tense are indicated the verb's form. An action in the present, *I talk,* can change form for the past: *I talked.* However, for the other tenses, an auxiliary (i.e., helping) verb is needed to show the change in form. These helping verbs include *am, are, is | have, has, had | was, were, will* (or *shall*).

Present: I talk	Present perfect: I have talked
Past: I talked	Past perfect: I had talked
Future: I will talk	Future perfect: I will have talked

Present: The action happens at the current time.

> Example: He *walks* to the store every morning.

To show that something is happening right now, use the progressive present tense: I *am walking.*

Past: The action happened in the past.

> Example: He *walked* to the store an hour ago.

Future: The action is going to happen later.

> Example: I *will walk* to the store tomorrow.

Present perfect: The action started in the past and continues into the present or took place previously at an unspecified time

> Example: I *have walked* to the store three times today.

Past perfect: The second action happened in the past. The first action came before the second.

> Example: Before I walked to the store (Action 2), I *had walked* to the library (Action 1).

Future perfect: An action that uses the past and the future. In other words, the action is complete before a future moment.

> Example: When she comes for the supplies (future moment), I *will have walked* to the store (action completed before the future moment).

CONJUGATING VERBS

When you need to change the form of a verb, you are **conjugating** a verb. The key forms of a verb are singular, present tense (dream); singular, past tense (dreamed); and the past participle (have dreamed). Note: the past participle needs a helping verb to make a verb tense. For example, I *have dreamed* of this day. The following tables demonstrate some of the different ways to conjugate a verb:

Singular

Tense	First Person	Second Person	Third Person
Present	I dream	You dream	He, she, it dreams
Past	I dreamed	You dreamed	He, she, it dreamed
Past Participle	I have dreamed	You have dreamed	He, she, it has dreamed

Plural

Tense	First Person	Second Person	Third Person
Present	We dream	You dream	They dream
Past	We dreamed	You dreamed	They dreamed
Past Participle	We have dreamed	You have dreamed	They have dreamed

MOOD

There are three **moods** in English: the indicative, the imperative, and the subjunctive.

The **indicative mood** is used for facts, opinions, and questions.

> Fact: You can do this.

> Opinion: I think that you can do this.

> Question: Do you know that you can do this?

The **imperative** is used for orders or requests.

> Order: You are going to do this!

> Request: Will you do this for me?

The **subjunctive mood** is for wishes and statements that go against fact.

> Wish: I wish that I were famous.

> Statement against fact: If I were you, I would do this. (This goes against fact because I am not you. You have the chance to do this, and I do not have the chance.)

> **Review Video: Verb Tenses**
> Visit mometrix.com/academy and enter code: 269472

ADJECTIVES

An **adjective** is a word that is used to modify a noun or pronoun. An adjective answers a question: *Which one? What kind?* or *How many?* Usually, adjectives come before the words that they modify, but they may also come after a linking verb.

> Which one? The *third* suit is my favorite.

> What kind? This suit is *navy blue*.

> How many? I am going to buy *four* pairs of socks to match the suit?

ARTICLES

Articles are adjectives that are used to distinguish nouns as definite or indefinite. **Definite** nouns are preceded by the article *the* and indicate a specific person, place, thing, or idea. **Indefinite** nouns are preceded by *a* or *an* and do not indicate a specific person, place, thing, or idea. A, an, and the are the only articles. Note: *An* comes before words that start with a vowel sound. For example, "Are you going to get an **u**mbrella?"

> **Definite**: I lost *the* bottle that belongs to me.

> **Indefinite**: Does anyone have *a* bottle to share?

COMPARISON WITH ADJECTIVES

Some adjectives are relative and other adjectives are absolute. Adjectives that are **relative** can show the comparison between things. **Absolute** adjectives can show comparison. However, they show comparison in a different way. Let's say that you are reading two books. You think that one book is perfect, and the other book is not exactly perfect. It is not possible for one book to be more perfect than the other. Either you think that the book is perfect, or you think that the book is imperfect. In this case, perfect and imperfect are absolute adjectives.

Relative adjectives will show the different **degrees** of something or someone to something else or someone else. The three degrees of adjectives include positive, comparative, and superlative.

The **positive** degree is the normal form of an adjective.

>   Example: This work is *difficult*. | She is *smart*.

The **comparative** degree compares one person or thing to another person or thing.

>   Example: This work is *more difficult* than your work. | She is *smarter* than me.

The **superlative** degree compares more than two people or things.

>   Example: This is the *most difficult* work of my life. | She is the *smartest* lady in school.

Review Video: Adjectives Visit mometrix.com/academy and enter code: 470154

ADVERBS

An **adverb** is a word that is used to **modify** a verb, adjective, or another adverb. Usually, adverbs answer one of these questions: *When?, Where?, How?,* and *Why?* . The negatives *not* and *never* are considered adverbs. Adverbs that modify adjectives or other adverbs **strengthen** or **weaken** the words that they modify.

Examples:

>   He walks *quickly* through the crowd.

>   The water flows *smoothly* on the rocks.

Note: Adverbs are usually indicated by the morpheme -ly, which has been added to the root word. For instance, *quick* can be made into an adverb by adding *-ly* to construct *quickly*. Some words that end in *-ly* do not follow this rule and can behave as other parts of speech. Examples of adjectives ending in *-ly* include: *early, friendly, holy, lonely, silly*, and *ugly*. To know if a word that ends in *-ly* is an adjective or adverb, check your dictionary. Also, while many adverbs end in *-ly*, you need to remember that not all adverbs end in *-ly*.

Examples:

>   He is *never* angry.

>   You walked *across* the bridge.

COMPARISON WITH ADVERBS

The rules for comparing adverbs are the same as the rules for adjectives.

The **positive** degree is the standard form of an adverb.

Example: He arrives *soon*. | She speaks *softly* to her friends.

The **comparative** degree compares one person or thing to another person or thing.

Example: He arrives *sooner* than Sarah. | She speaks *more softly* than him.

The **superlative** degree compares more than two people or things.

Example: He arrives *soonest* of the group. | She speaks the *most softly* of any of her friends.

> **Review Video: Adverbs**
> Visit mometrix.com/academy and enter code: 713951

PREPOSITIONS

A **preposition** is a word placed before a noun or pronoun that shows the relationship between an object and another word in the sentence.

Common prepositions:

about	before	during	on	under
after	beneath	for	over	until
against	between	from	past	up
among	beyond	in	through	with
around	by	of	to	within
at	down	off	toward	without

Examples:

The napkin is *in* the drawer.

The Earth rotates *around* the Sun.

The needle is *beneath* the haystack.

Can you find "me" *among* the words?

> **Review Video: What is a Preposition?**
> Visit mometrix.com/academy and enter code: 946763

CONJUNCTIONS

Conjunctions join words, phrases, or clauses and they show the connection between the joined pieces. **Coordinating conjunctions** connect equal parts of sentences. **Correlative conjunctions** show the connection between pairs. **Subordinating conjunctions** join subordinate (i.e., dependent) clauses with independent clauses.

COORDINATING CONJUNCTIONS

The **coordinating conjunctions** include: *and, but, yet, or, nor, for,* and *so*

Examples:

The rock was small, *but* it was heavy.

She drove in the night, *and* he drove in the day.

<u>CORRELATIVE CONJUNCTIONS</u>

The **correlative conjunctions** are: *either...or | neither...nor | not only...but also*

Examples:

> *Either* you are coming *or* you are staying.

> He *not only* ran three miles *but also* swam 200 yards.

> **Review Video: <u>Coordinating and Correlative Conjunctions</u>**
> Visit mometrix.com/academy and enter code: 390329

<u>SUBORDINATING CONJUNCTIONS</u>

Common **subordinating conjunctions** include:

after	since	whenever
although	so that	where
because	unless	wherever
before	until	whether
in order that	when	while

Examples:

> I am hungry *because* I did not eat breakfast.

> He went home *when* everyone left.

> **Review Video: <u>Subordinating Conjunctions</u>**
> Visit mometrix.com/academy and enter code: 958913

INTERJECTIONS

Interjections are words of exclamation (i.e., audible expression of great feeling) that are used alone or as a part of a sentence. Often, they are used at the beginning of a sentence for an introduction. Sometimes, they can be used in the middle of a sentence to show a change in thought or attitude.

> Common Interjections: Hey! | Oh, | Ouch! | Please! | Wow!

Agreement and Sentence Structure

SUBJECTS AND PREDICATES

SUBJECTS

The **subject** of a sentence names who or what the sentence is about. The subject may be directly stated in a sentence, or the subject may be the implied *you*. The **complete subject** includes the simple subject and all of its modifiers. To find the complete subject, ask *Who* or *What* and insert the verb to complete the question. The answer, including any modifiers (adjectives, prepositional phrases, etc.), is the complete subject. To find the **simple subject**, remove all of the modifiers in the complete subject. Being able to locate the subject of a sentence helps with many problems, such as those involving sentence fragments and subject-verb agreement.

Examples:

The small, red car is the one that he wants for Christmas.

(The simple subject is the *car*, and the complete subject is *the small, red car*.)

The young artist is coming over for dinner.

(The simple subject is the *artist*, and the complete subject is *the young artist*.)

> **Review Video: Subjects**
> Visit mometrix.com/academy and enter code: 444771

In **imperative** sentences, the verb's subject is understood (e.g., [You] Run to the store), but is not actually present in the sentence. Normally, the subject comes before the verb. However, the subject comes after the verb in sentences that begin with *There are* or *There was*.

Direct:

John knows the way to the park.

(Who knows the way to the park? Answer: *John*)

The cookies need ten more minutes.

(What needs ten minutes? Answer: *The cookies*)

By five o'clock, Bill will need to leave.

(Who needs to leave? Answer: *Bill*)

Remember: The subject can come after the verb.

There are five letters on the table for him.

(What is on the table? Answer: *Five letters*)

There were coffee and doughnuts in the house.

(What was in the house? Answer: *Coffee and doughnuts*)

Implied:

Go to the post office for me.

(Who is going to the post office? Answer: *You.*)

Come and sit with me, please?

(Who needs to come and sit? Answer: *You.*)

PREDICATES

In a sentence, you always have a predicate and a subject. The subject tells what the sentence is about, and the **predicate** explains or describes the subject.

Think about the sentence *He sings.* In this sentence, we have a subject (He) and a predicate (sings). This is all that is needed for a sentence to be complete. Most sentences contain more information, but if this is all the information that you are given, then you have a complete sentence.

Now, let's look at another sentence:

John and Jane sing on Tuesday nights at the dance hall.

What is the subject of this sentence?

Answer: John and Jane.

What is the predicate of this sentence?

Answer: sing on Tuesday nights at the dance hall (everything else in the sentence).

SUBJECT-VERB AGREEMENT

Verbs **agree** with their subjects in number. In other words, *singular* subjects need *singular* verbs. *Plural* subjects need *plural* verbs. **Singular** is for **one** person, place, or thing. **Plural** is for **more than one** person, place, or thing. Subjects and verbs must also share the same point of view, as in first, second, or third person. The present tense ending -s is used on a verb if its subject is third person singular; otherwise, the verb' sending is not modified.

> **Review Video: <u>Subject-Verb Agreement</u>**
> Visit mometrix.com/academy and enter code: 479190

NUMBER AGREEMENT EXAMPLES:

Single Subject and Verb: *Dan calls home.*

(Dan is one person. So, the singular verb *calls* is needed.)

Plural Subject and Verb: *Dan and Bob call home.*

(More than one person needs the plural verb *call*.)

PERSON AGREEMENT EXAMPLES:

First Person: I *am* walking.

Second Person: You *are* walking.

Third Person: He *is* walking.

COMPLICATIONS WITH SUBJECT-VERB AGREEMENT
WORDS BETWEEN SUBJECT AND VERB

Words that come between the simple subject and the verb have no bearing on subject-verb agreement.

Examples:

The joy of my life returns home tonight.

(**Singular Subject**: joy **Singular Verb**: returns)

The phrase *of my life* does not influence the verb *returns*.

29

The question that still remains unanswered is "Who are you?"

(**Singular Subject**: question **Singular Verb**: is)

Don't let the phrase "*that still remains...*" trouble you. The subject *question* goes with *is*.

COMPOUND SUBJECTS

A compound subject is formed when two or more nouns joined by *and*, *or*, or *nor* jointly act as the subject of the sentence.

JOINED BY AND

When a compound subject is joined by *and*, it is treated as a plural subject and requires a plural verb.

Examples:

You and Jon are invited to come to my house.

(**Plural Subject**: You and Jon. **Plural Verb**: are)

The pencil and paper belong to me.

(**Plural Subject**: pencil and paper. **Plural Verb**: belong)

JOINED BY OR/NOR

For a compound subject joined by *or* or *nor*, the verb must agree in number with the part of the subject that is closest to the verb (italicized in the examples below).

Examples:

Today or *tomorrow is* the day.

(**Subject**: Today / tomorrow **Verb**: is)

Stan or *Phil wants* to read the book.

(**Subject**: Stan / Phil **Verb**: wants)

Neither the books nor the *pen is* on the desk.

(**Subject**: books / pen **Verb**: is)

Either the blanket or *pillows arrive* this afternoon.

(**Subject**: blanket / pillows **Verb**: arrive)

INDEFINITE PRONOUNS AS SUBJECT

An indefinite pronoun is a pronoun that does not refer to a specific noun. Different indefinite pronouns may only function as a singular noun, only function as a plural noun, or change depending on how they are used.

ALWAYS SINGULAR

Pronouns such as *each*, *either*, *everybody*, *anybody*, *somebody*, and *nobody* are always singular.

Examples:

Each of the runners *has* a different bib number.

(**Singular Subject**: Each **Singular Verb**: has)

Is either of you ready for the game?

(**Singular Subject**: either **Singular Verb**: Is)

Note: The words *each* and *either* can also be used as adjectives (e.g., *each* person is unique). When one of these adjectives modifies the subject of a sentence, it is always a singular subject.

Everybody grows a day older every day.

(**Singular Subject**: Everybody **Singular Verb**: grows)

Anybody is welcome to bring a tent.

(**Singular Subject**: Anybody **Singular Verb**: is)

ALWAYS PLURAL

Pronouns such as *both*, *several*, and *many* are always plural.

Examples:

Both of the siblings *were* too tired to argue.

(**Plural Subject**: Both **Plural Verb**: were)

Many have tried, but none have succeeded.

(**Plural Subject**: Many **Plural Verb**: have tried)

DEPEND ON CONTEXT

Pronouns such as *some*, *any*, *all*, *none*, *more*, and *most* can be either singular or plural depending on what they are representing in the context of the sentence.

Examples:

All of my dog's food *was* still there in his bowl

(**Singular Subject**: All **Singular Verb**: was)

By the end of the night, *all* of my guests *were* already excited about coming to my next party.

(**Plural Subject**: all **Plural Verb**: were)

OTHER CASES INVOLVING PLURAL OR IRREGULAR FORM

Some nouns are **singular in meaning but plural in form**: news, mathematics, physics, and economics.

The *news is* coming on now.

Mathematics is my favorite class.

Some nouns are plural in form and meaning, and have **no singular equivalent**: scissors and pants.

Do these *pants come* with a shirt?

The *scissors are* for my project.

Mathematical operations are **irregular** in their construction, but are normally considered to be **singular in meaning**.

> *One plus one is* two.
>
> *Three times three is* nine.

Note: Look to your **dictionary** for help when you aren't sure whether a noun with a plural form has a singular or plural meaning.

COMPLEMENTS

A complement is a noun, pronoun, or adjective that is used to give more information about the subject or verb in the sentence.

DIRECT OBJECTS

A direct object is a noun or pronoun that takes or receives the **action** of a verb. (Remember: a complete sentence does not need a direct object, so not all sentences will have them. A sentence needs only a subject and a verb.) When you are looking for a direct object, find the verb and ask *who* or *what*.

Examples:

> I took the blanket. (Who or what did I take? *The blanket*)
>
> Jane read books. (Who or what does Jane read? *Books*)

INDIRECT OBJECTS

An indirect object is a word or group of words that show how an action had an **influence** on someone or something. If there is an indirect object in a sentence, then you always have a direct object in the sentence. When you are looking for the indirect object, find the verb and ask *to/for whom or what*.

Examples:

> We taught the old dog a new trick.
>
> (To/For whom or what was taught? *The old dog*)
>
> I gave them a math lesson.
>
> (To/For whom or what was given? *Them*)

> **Review Video: Direct and Indirect Objects**
> Visit mometrix.com/academy and enter code: 817385

PREDICATE NOMINATIVES AND PREDICATE ADJECTIVES

As we looked at previously, verbs may be classified as either action verbs or linking verbs. A linking verb is so named because it links the subject to words in the predicate that describe or define the subject. These words are called predicate nominatives (if nouns or pronouns) or predicate adjectives (if adjectives).

Examples:

> My father is a *lawyer*.
>
> (Father is the **subject**. Lawyer is the **predicate nominative**.)

Your mother is *patient*.

(Mother is the **subject**. Patient is the **predicate adjective**.)

PRONOUN USAGE

The **antecedent** is the noun that has been replaced by a pronoun. A pronoun and its antecedent **agree** when they have the same number (singular or plural) and gender (male, female, or neutral).

Examples:

Singular agreement: *John* came into town, and *he* played for us.

(The word *he* replaces *John*.)

Plural agreement: *John and Rick* came into town, and *they* played for us.

(The word *they* replaces *John and Rick*.)

To determine which is the correct pronoun to use in a compound subject or object, try each pronoun **alone** in place of the compound in the sentence. Your knowledge of pronouns will tell you which one is correct.

Example:

Bob and (I, me) will be going.

Test: (1) *I will be going* or (2) *Me will be going*. The second choice cannot be correct because *me* cannot be used as the subject of a sentence. Instead, *me* is used as an object.

Answer: Bob and I will be going.

When a pronoun is used with a noun immediately following (as in "we boys"), try the sentence **without the added noun**.

Example:

(We/Us) boys played football last year.

Test: (1) *We played football last year* or (2) *Us played football last year*. Again, the second choice cannot be correct because *us* cannot be used as a subject of a sentence. Instead, *us* is used as an object.

Answer: We boys played football last year.

> **Review Video: Pronoun Usage**
> Visit mometrix.com/academy and enter code: 666500

A pronoun should point clearly to the **antecedent**. Here is how a pronoun reference can be unhelpful if it is puzzling or not directly stated.

> **Unhelpful**: Ron and Jim went to the store, and *he* bought soda.
>
> (Who bought soda? Ron or Jim?)
>
> **Helpful**: Jim went to the store, and *he* bought soda.
>
> (The sentence is clear. Jim bought the soda.)

Some pronouns change their form by their placement in a sentence. A pronoun that is a **subject** in a sentence comes in the **subjective case**. Pronouns that serve as **objects** appear in the **objective case**. Finally, the pronouns that are used as **possessives** appear in the **possessive case**.

Examples:

> **Subjective case**: *He* is coming to the show.
>
> (The pronoun *He* is the subject of the sentence.)
>
> **Objective case**: Josh drove *him* to the airport.
>
> (The pronoun *him* is the object of the sentence.)
>
> **Possessive case**: The flowers are *mine*.
>
> (The pronoun *mine* shows ownership of the flowers.)

The word *who* is a subjective-case pronoun that can be used as a **subject**. The word *whom* is an objective-case pronoun that can be used as an **object**. The words *who* and *whom* are common in subordinate clauses or in questions.

Examples:

> **Subject**: He knows who wants to come.
>
> (*Who* is the subject of the verb *wants*.)
>
> **Object**: He knows the man whom we want at the party.
>
> (*Whom* is the object of *we want*.)

CLAUSES

A clause is a group of words that contains both a subject and a predicate (verb). There are two types of clauses: independent and dependent. An **independent clause** contains a complete thought, while a **dependent (or subordinate) clause** does not. A dependent clause includes a subject and a verb, and may also contain objects or complements, but it cannot stand as a complete thought without being joined to an independent clause. Dependent clauses function within sentences as adjectives, adverbs, or nouns.

Example:

> **Independent Clause**: I am running
>
> **Dependent Clause**: because I want to stay in shape
>
> The clause *I am running* is an independent clause: it has a subject and a verb, and it gives a complete thought. The clause *because I want to stay in shape* is a dependent clause: it has a subject and a verb, but it does not express a complete thought. It adds detail to the independent clause to which it is attached.
>
> **Combined**: I am running because I want to stay in shape.

> **Review Video: Independent and Dependent Clauses**
> Visit mometrix.com/academy and enter code: 556903

TYPES OF DEPENDENT CLAUSES
ADJECTIVE CLAUSES

An **adjective clause** is a dependent clause that modifies a noun or a pronoun. Adjective clauses begin with a relative pronoun (*who, whose, whom, which,* and *that*) or a relative adverb (*where, when,* and *why*).

Also, adjective clauses come after the noun that the clause needs to explain or rename. This is done to have a clear connection to the independent clause.

Examples:

> I learned the reason *why I won the award.*
>
> This is the place *where I started my first job.*

An adjective clause can be an essential or nonessential clause. An essential clause is very important to the sentence. **Essential clauses** explain or define a person or thing. **Nonessential clauses** give more information about a person or thing but are not necessary to define them. Nonessential clauses are set off with commas while essential clauses are not.

Examples:

> **Essential**: A person *who works hard at first* can often rest later in life.
>
> **Nonessential**: Neil Armstrong, *who walked on the moon,* is my hero.

> **Review Video: Adjective Clauses and Phrases**
> Visit mometrix.com/academy and enter code: 520888

ADVERB CLAUSES

An **adverb clause** is a dependent clause that modifies a verb, adjective, or adverb. In sentences with multiple dependent clauses, adverb clauses are usually placed immediately before or after the independent clause. An adverb clause is introduced with words such as *after, although, as, before, because, if, since, so, unless, when, where,* and *while.*

Examples:

> *When you walked outside*, I called the manager.

> I will go with you *unless you want to stay*.

NOUN CLAUSES

A **noun clause** is a dependent clause that can be used as a subject, object, or complement. Noun clauses begin with words such as *how, that, what, whether, which, who,* and *why*. These words can also come with an adjective clause. Unless the noun clause is being used as the subject of the sentence, it should come after the verb of the independent clause.

Examples:

> The real mystery is *how you avoided serious injury*.

> *What you learn from each other* depends on your honesty with others.

SUBORDINATION

When two related ideas are not of equal importance, the ideal way to combine them is to make the more important idea an independent clause and the less important idea a dependent or subordinate clause. This is called **subordination**.

Example:

> **Separate ideas**: The team had a perfect regular season. The team lost the championship.

> **Subordinated**: Despite having a perfect regular season, *the team lost the championship*.

PHRASES

A phrase is a group of words that functions as a single part of speech, usually a noun, adjective, or adverb. A phrase is not a complete thought, but it adds **detail** or **explanation** to a sentence, or **renames** something within the sentence.

PREPOSITIONAL PHRASES

One of the most common types of phrases is the prepositional phrase. A **prepositional phrase** begins with a preposition and ends with a noun or pronoun that is the object of the preposition. Normally, the prepositional phrase functions as an **adjective** or an **adverb** within the sentence.

Examples:

> The picnic is *on the blanket*.

> I am sick *with a fever* today.

> *Among the many flowers*, John found a four-leaf clover.

Verbal Phrases

A **verbal** is a word or phrase that is formed from a verb but does not function as a verb. Depending on its particular form, it may be used as a noun, adjective, or adverb. A verbal does **not** replace a verb in a sentence.

Examples:

Correct: *Walk* a mile daily.

(*Walk* is the verb of this sentence. The subject is the implied *you*.)

Incorrect: *To walk* a mile.

(*To walk* is a type of verbal. This is not a sentence since there is no functional verb)

There are three types of verbal: **participles**, **gerunds**, and **infinitives**. Each type of verbal has a corresponding **phrase** that consists of the verbal itself along with any complements or modifiers.

Participles

A **participle** is a type of verbal that always functions as an adjective. The present participle always ends with *-ing*. Past participles end with *-d, -ed, -n,* or *-t.*

Examples: Verb: *dance* | Present Participle: *dancing* | Past Participle: *danced*

Participial phrases most often come right before or right after the noun or pronoun that they modify.

Examples:

Shipwrecked on an island, the boys started to fish for food.

Having been seated for five hours, we got out of the car to stretch our legs.

Praised for their work, the group accepted the first-place trophy.

Gerunds

A **gerund** is a type of verbal that always functions as a **noun**. Like present participles, gerunds always end with *-ing*, but they can be easily distinguished from one another by the part of speech they represent (participles always function as adjectives). Since a gerund or gerund phrase always functions as a noun, it can be used as the subject of a sentence, the predicate nominative, or the object of a verb or preposition.

Examples:

We want to be known for *teaching the poor*. (Object of preposition)

Coaching this team is the best job of my life. (Subject)

We like *practicing our songs* in the basement. (Object of verb)

Infinitives

An **infinitive** is a type of verbal that can function as a noun, an adjective, or an adverb. An infinitive is made of the word *to* and the basic form of the verb. As with all other types of verbal phrases, an infinitive phrase includes the verbal itself and all of its complements or modifiers.

Examples:

> *To join the team* is my goal in life. (Noun)

> The animals have enough food *to eat for the night*. (Adjective)

> People lift weights *to exercise their muscles*. (Adverb)

Review Video: Gerunds, Infinitives, and Participles
Visit mometrix.com/academy and enter code: 634263

APPOSITIVE PHRASES

An **appositive** is a word or phrase that is used to explain or rename nouns or pronouns. Noun phrases, gerund phrases, and infinitive phrases can all be used as appositives.

Examples:

> Terriers, *hunters at heart*, have been dressed up to look like lap dogs.

> (The noun phrase *hunters at heart* renames the noun *terriers*.)

> His plan, *to save and invest his money*, was proven as a safe approach.

> (The infinitive phrase explains what the plan is.)

Appositive phrases can be **essential** or **nonessential**. An appositive phrase is essential if the person, place, or thing being described or renamed is too general for its meaning to be understood without the appositive.

Examples:

> **Essential**: Two of America's Founding Fathers, George Washington and Thomas Jefferson, served as presidents.

> **Nonessential**: George Washington and Thomas Jefferson, two Founding Fathers, served as presidents.

ABSOLUTE PHRASES

An absolute phrase is a phrase that consists of **a noun followed by a participle**. An absolute phrase provides **context** to what is being described in the sentence, but it does not modify or explain any particular word; it is essentially independent.

Examples:

> *The alarm ringing*, he pushed the snooze button.

> *The music paused*, she continued to dance through the crowd.

PARALLELISM

When multiple items or ideas are presented in a sentence in series, such as in a list, the items or ideas must be stated in grammatically equivalent ways. In other words, if one idea is stated in gerund form, the second cannot be stated in infinitive form. For example, to write, *I enjoy reading and to study* would be incorrect. An infinitive and a gerund are not equivalent. Instead, you should write *I enjoy reading and studying*. In lists of more than two, all items must be parallel.

Example:

> **Incorrect**: He stopped at the office, grocery store, and the pharmacy before heading home.
>
> The first and third items in the list of places include the article *the*, so the second item needs it as well.
>
> **Correct**: He stopped at the office, *the* grocery store, and the pharmacy before heading home.

Example:

> **Incorrect**: While vacationing in Europe, she went biking, skiing, and climbed mountains.
>
> The first and second items in the list are gerunds, so the third item must be as well.
>
> **Correct**: While vacationing in Europe, she went biking, skiing, and *mountain climbing*.

> **Review Video: Parallel Construction**
> Visit mometrix.com/academy and enter code: 831988

SENTENCE PURPOSE

There are four types of sentences: declarative, imperative, interrogative, and exclamatory.

A **declarative** sentence states a fact and ends with a period.

> Example: *The football game starts at seven o'clock.*

An **imperative** sentence tells someone to do something and generally ends with a period. (An urgent command might end with an exclamation point instead.)

> Example: *Don't forget to buy your ticket.*

An **interrogative** sentence asks a question and ends with a question mark.

> Example: *Are you going to the game on Friday?*

An **exclamatory** sentence shows strong emotion and ends with an exclamation point.

> Example: *I can't believe we won the game!*

> **Review Video: Functions of a Sentence**
> Visit mometrix.com/academy and enter code: 475974

SENTENCE STRUCTURE

Sentences are classified by structure based on the type and number of clauses present. The four classifications of sentence structure are the following:

Simple: A simple sentence has one independent clause with no dependent clauses. A simple sentence may have **compound elements** (i.e., compound subject or verb).

Examples:

> Judy *watered* the lawn. (single <u>subject</u>, single *verb*)

> Judy and Alan *watered* the lawn. (compound <u>subject</u>, single *verb*)

> Judy *watered* the lawn and *pulled* weeds. (single <u>subject</u>, compound *verb*)

> Judy and Alan *watered* the lawn and *pulled* weeds. (compound <u>subject</u>, compound *verb*)

Compound: A compound sentence has two or more <u>independent clauses</u> with no dependent clauses. Usually, the independent clauses are joined with a comma and a coordinating conjunction or with a semicolon.

Examples:

> <u>The time has come</u>, and <u>we are ready</u>.

> <u>I woke up at dawn</u>; <u>the sun was just coming up</u>.

Complex: A complex sentence has one <u>independent clause</u> and at least one *dependent clause*.

Examples:

> *Although he had the flu,* <u>Harry went to work</u>.

> <u>Marcia got married</u> *after she finished college.*

Compound-Complex: A compound-complex sentence has at least two <u>independent clauses</u> and at least one *dependent clause.*

Examples:

> <u>John is my friend</u> *who went to India,* and <u>he brought back souvenirs</u>.

> <u>You may not realize this</u>, but <u>we heard the music</u> *that you played last night.*

> **Review Video: <u>Sentence Structure</u>**
> Visit mometrix.com/academy and enter code: 700478

Sentence variety is important to consider when writing an essay or speech. A variety of sentence lengths and types creates rhythm, makes a passage more engaging, and gives writers an opportunity to demonstrate their writing style. Writing that uses the same length or type of sentence without variation can be boring or difficult to read. To evaluate a passage for effective sentence variety, it is helpful to note whether the passage contains diverse sentence structures and lengths. It is also important to pay attention to the way each sentence starts and avoid beginning with the same words or phrases.

SENTENCE FRAGMENTS

Recall that a group of words must contain at least one **independent clause** in order to be considered a sentence. If it doesn't contain even one independent clause, it would be called a **sentence fragment**.

The appropriate process for **repairing** a sentence fragment depends on what type of fragment it is. If the fragment is a dependent clause, it can sometimes be as simple as removing a subordinating word (e.g., when, because, if) from the beginning of the fragment. Alternatively, a dependent clause can be

incorporated into a closely related neighboring sentence. If the fragment is missing some required part, like a subject or a verb, the fix might be as simple as adding the missing part.

Examples:

Fragment: Because he wanted to sail the Mediterranean.

Removed subordinating word: He wanted to sail the Mediterranean.

Combined with another sentence: Because he wanted to sail the Mediterranean, he booked a Greek island cruise.

RUN-ON SENTENCES

Run-on sentences consist of multiple independent clauses that have not been joined together properly. Run-on sentences can be corrected in several different ways:

Join clauses properly: This can be done with a comma and coordinating conjunction, with a semicolon, or with a colon or dash if the second clause is explaining something in the first.

Example:

Incorrect: I went on the trip, we visited lots of castles.

Corrected: I went on the trip, and we visited lots of castles.

Split into separate sentences: This correction is most effective when the independent clauses are very long or when they are not closely related.

Example:

Incorrect: The drive to New York takes ten hours, my uncle lives in Boston.

Corrected: The drive to New York takes ten hours. My uncle lives in Boston.

Make one clause dependent: This is the easiest way to make the sentence correct and more interesting at the same time. It's often as simple as adding a subordinating word between the two clauses or before the first clause.

Example:

Incorrect: I finally made it to the store and I bought some eggs.

Corrected: When I finally made it to the store, I bought some eggs.

Reduce to one clause with a compound verb: If both clauses have the same subject, remove the subject from the second clause, and you now have just one clause with a compound verb.

Example:

Incorrect: The drive to New York takes ten hours, it makes me very tired.

Corrected: The drive to New York takes ten hours and makes me very tired.

Note: While these are the simplest ways to correct a run-on sentence, often the best way is to completely reorganize the thoughts in the sentence and rewrite it.

Review Video: Fragments and Run-on Sentences
Visit mometrix.com/academy and enter code: 541989

DANGLING AND MISPLACED MODIFIERS

DANGLING MODIFIERS

A dangling modifier is a dependent clause or verbal phrase that does not have a **clear logical connection** to a word in the sentence.

Example:

> **Dangling**: *Reading each magazine article*, the stories caught my attention.
>
> The word *stories* cannot be modified by *Reading each magazine article*. People can read, but stories cannot read. Therefore, the subject of the sentence must be a person.
>
> **Corrected**: Reading each magazine article, *I* was entertained by the stories.

Example:

> **Dangling**: Ever since childhood, my grandparents have visited me for Christmas.
>
> The speaker in this sentence can't have been visited by her grandparents when *they* were children, since she wouldn't have been born yet. Either the modifier should be **clarified** or the sentence should be **rearranged** to specify whose childhood is being referenced.
>
> **Clarified**: Ever since I was a child, my grandparents have visited for Christmas.
>
> **Rearranged**: I have enjoyed my grandparents visiting for Christmas, ever since childhood.

MISPLACED MODIFIERS

Because modifiers are grammatically versatile, they can be put in many different places within the structure of a sentence. The danger of this versatility is that a modifier can accidentally be placed where it is modifying the wrong word or where it is not clear which word it is modifying.

Example:

> **Misplaced**: She read the book to a crowd *that was filled with beautiful pictures.*
>
> The book was filled with beautiful pictures, not the crowd.
>
> **Corrected**: She read the book *that was filled with beautiful pictures* to a crowd.

Example:

> **Ambiguous**: Derek saw a bus nearly hit a man *on his way to work*.

> Was Derek on his way to work? Or was the other man?

> **Derek**: *On his way to work*, Derek saw a bus nearly hit a man.

> **The other man**: Derek saw a bus nearly hit a man *who was on his way to work*.

SPLIT INFINITIVES

A split infinitive occurs when a modifying word comes between the word *to* and the verb that pairs with *to*.

> Example: To *clearly* explain vs. *To explain* clearly | To *softly* sing vs. *To sing* softly

Though considered improper by some, split infinitives may provide better clarity and simplicity in some cases than the alternatives. As such, avoiding them should not be considered a universal rule.

DOUBLE NEGATIVES

Standard English allows **two negatives** only when a **positive** meaning is intended. For example, *The team was not displeased with their performance*. Double negatives to emphasize negation are not used in standard English.

Negative modifiers (e.g., never, no, and not) should not be paired with other negative modifiers or negative words (e.g., none, nobody, nothing, or neither). The modifiers *hardly, barely*, and *scarcely* are also considered negatives in standard English, so they should not be used with other negatives.

Punctuation

END PUNCTUATION

PERIODS

Use a period to end **all** sentences **except** direct questions and exclamations. Periods are also used for abbreviations.

> Examples: 3 p.m. | 2 a.m. | Mr. Jones | Mrs. Stevens | Dr. Smith | Bill, Jr. | Pennsylvania Ave.

Note: An abbreviation is a shortened form of a word or phrase.

QUESTION MARKS

Question marks should be used following a **direct question**. A polite request can be followed by a period instead of a question mark.

> **Direct Question**: What is for lunch today? | How are you? | Why is that the answer?

> **Polite Requests**: Can you please send me the item tomorrow. | Will you please walk with me on the track.

Review Video: Question Marks
Visit mometrix.com/academy and enter code: 118471

EXCLAMATION MARKS

Exclamation marks are used after a word group or sentence that shows much feeling or has special importance. Exclamation marks should not be overused. They are saved for proper **exclamatory interjections**.

Example: We're going to the finals! | You have a beautiful car! | "That's crazy!" she yelled.

> **Review Video: Exclamation Points**
> Visit mometrix.com/academy and enter code: 199367

COMMAS

The comma is a punctuation mark that can help you understand connections in a sentence. Not every sentence needs a comma. However, if a sentence needs a comma, you need to put it in the right place. A comma in the wrong place (or an absent comma) will make a sentence's meaning unclear. These are some of the rules for commas:

1. Use a comma **before a coordinating conjunction** joining independent clauses.
    Example: Bob caught three fish, and I caught two fish.

2. Use a comma after an introductory phrase or an adverbial clause.
    Examples:
    > *After the final out,* we went to a restaurant to celebrate.
    > *Studying the stars,* I was surprised at the beauty of the sky.

3. Use a comma between items in a series.
    Example: I will bring the turkey, the pie, and the coffee.

4. Use a comma **between coordinate adjectives** not joined with *and*.
    Incorrect: The kind, brown dog followed me home.
    Correct: The *kind, loyal* dog followed me home.
    Not all adjectives are **coordinate** (i.e., equal or parallel). There are two simple ways to know if your adjectives are coordinate. One, you can join the adjectives with *and*: *The kind and loyal dog.* Two, you can change the order of the adjectives: *The loyal, kind dog.*

5. Use commas for **interjections** and **after *yes* and *no*** responses.
    Examples:
    > **Interjection**: Oh, I had no idea. | Wow, you know how to play this game.
    > **Yes and No**: *Yes,* I heard you. | *No,* I cannot come tomorrow.

6. Use commas to separate nonessential modifiers and nonessential appositives.
    Examples:
    > **Nonessential Modifier**: John Frank, who is coaching the team, was promoted today.
    > **Nonessential Appositive**: Thomas Edison, an American inventor, was born in Ohio.

7. Use commas to separate nouns of direct address, interrogative tags, and contrast.
    Examples:
    > **Direct Address**: You, *John,* are my only hope in this moment.
    > **Interrogative Tag**: This is the last time, *correct*?
    > **Contrast**: You are my friend, *not my enemy.*

8. Use commas when writing dates, addresses, geographical names, and titles.

Examples:

> **Date**: *July 4, 1776,* is an important date to remember.
> **Address**: He is meeting me at *456 Delaware Avenue, Washington, D.C.,* tomorrow morning.
> **Geographical Name**: *Paris, France,* is my favorite city.
> **Title**: John Smith, *PhD,* will be visiting your class today.

9. Use commas to **separate expressions like *he said* and *she said*** if they appear between two parts of a quote.

Examples:

> "I want you to know," he began, "that I always wanted the best for you."
> "You can start," Jane said, "with an apology."

> **Review Video: Commas**
> Visit mometrix.com/academy and enter code: 786797

SEMICOLONS

The semicolon is used to connect major sentence pieces of equal value. Some rules for semicolons include:

1. Use a semicolon **between closely connected independent clauses** that are not connected with a coordinating conjunction.

Examples:

> She is outside; we are inside.
> You are right; we should go with your plan.

2. Use a semicolon **between independent clauses linked with a transitional word.**

Examples:

> I think that we can agree on this; *however,* I am not sure about my friends.
> You are looking in the wrong places; *therefore,* you will not find what you need.

3. Use a semicolon **between items in a series that has internal punctuation.**

Example: I have visited New York, New York; Augusta, Maine; and Baltimore, Maryland.

> **Review Video: Semicolon Usage**
> Visit mometrix.com/academy and enter code: 370605

COLONS

The colon is used to call attention to the words that follow it. A colon must come after a **complete independent clause**. The rules for colons are as follows:

1. Use a colon after an independent clause to **make a list.**

Example: I want to learn many languages: Spanish, German, and Italian.

2. Use a colon for **explanations** or to **give a quote.**

Examples:

> **Quote**: He started with an idea: "We are able to do more than we imagine."
> **Explanation**: There is one thing that stands out on your resume: responsibility.

3. Use a colon **after the greeting in a formal letter**, to **show hours and minutes,** and to **separate a title and subtitle.**

Examples:

Greeting in a formal letter: Dear Sir: | To Whom It May Concern:
Time: It is 3:14 p.m.
Title: The essay is titled "America: A Short Introduction to a Modern Country."

Review Video: **Colons**
Visit mometrix.com/academy and enter code: 868673

PARENTHESES

Parentheses are used for additional information. Also, they can be used to put labels for letters or numbers in a series. Parentheses should be not be used very often. If they are overused, parentheses can be a distraction instead of a help.

Examples:

Extra Information: The rattlesnake (see Image 2) is a dangerous snake of North and South America.

Series: Include in the email (1) your name, (2) your address, and (3) your question for the author.

Review Video: **Parentheses**
Visit mometrix.com/academy and enter code: 947743

QUOTATION MARKS

Use quotation marks to close off **direct quotations** of a person's spoken or written words. Do not use quotation marks around indirect quotations. An indirect quotation gives someone's message without using the person's exact words. Use **single quotation marks** to close off a quotation inside a quotation.

Direct Quote: Nancy said, "I am waiting for Henry to arrive."

Indirect Quote: Henry said that he is going to be late to the meeting.

Quote inside a Quote: The teacher asked, "Has everyone read 'The Gift of the Magi'?"

Quotation marks should be used around the titles of **short works**: newspaper and magazine articles, poems, short stories, songs, television episodes, radio programs, and subdivisions of books or websites.

Examples:

"Rip Van Winkle" (short story by Washington Irving)

"O Captain! My Captain!" (poem by Walt Whitman)

Although it is not standard usage, quotation marks are sometimes used to highlight **irony** or the use of words to mean something other than their dictionary definition. This type of usage should be employed sparingly, if at all.

46

Examples:

The boss warned Frank that he was walking on "thin ice."

(Frank is not walking on real ice. Instead, Frank is being warned to avoid mistakes.)

The teacher thanked the young man for his "honesty."

(In this example, the quotation marks around *honesty* show that the teacher does not believe the young man's explanation.)

> **Review Video: Quotation Marks**
> Visit mometrix.com/academy and enter code: 884918

Periods and commas are put **inside** quotation marks. Colons and semicolons are put **outside** the quotation marks. Question marks and exclamation points are placed inside quotation marks when they are part of a quote. When the question or exclamation mark goes with the whole sentence, the mark is left outside of the quotation marks.

Examples:

Period and comma: We read "The Gift of the Magi," "The Skylight Room," and "The Cactus."

Semicolon: They watched "The Nutcracker"; then, they went home.

Exclamation mark that is a part of a quote: The crowd cheered, "Victory!"

Question mark that goes with the whole sentence: Is your favorite short story "The Tell-Tale Heart"?

APOSTROPHES

An apostrophe is used to show **possession** or the **deletion of letters in contractions**. An apostrophe is not needed with the possessive pronouns *his, hers, its, ours, theirs, whose*, and *yours*.

Singular Nouns: David's car | a book's theme | my brother's board game

Plural Nouns that end with -*s*: the scissors' handle | boys' basketball

Plural Nouns that end without -*s*: Men's department | the people's adventure

> **Review Video: Apostrophes**
> Visit mometrix.com/academy and enter code: 213068
>
> **Review Video: Punctuation Errors in Possessive Pronouns**
> Visit mometrix.com/academy and enter code: 221438

HYPHENS

Hyphens are used to **separate compound words**. Use hyphens in the following cases:

1. **Compound numbers** from 21 to 99 when written out in words
   Example: This team needs *twenty-five* points to win the game.

2. **Written-out fractions** that are used as **adjectives**

   Incorrect: *One-fourth* of the road is under construction.
   Correct: The recipe says that we need a *three-fourths* cup of butter.

3. Compound **adjectives that come before a noun**

   Incorrect: The dog was *well-fed* for his nap.
   Correct: The *well-fed* dog took a nap.

4. Unusual compound words that would be **hard to read** or **easily confused with other words**

   Examples: Semi-irresponsible | Anti-itch | Re-sort

Note: This is not a complete set of the rules for hyphens. A dictionary is the best tool for knowing if a compound word needs a hyphen.

> **Review Video: Hyphens**
> Visit mometrix.com/academy and enter code: 981632

DASHES

Dashes are used to show a **break** or a **change in thought** in a sentence or to act as parentheses in a sentence. When typing, use two hyphens to make a dash. Do not put a space before or after the dash. The following are the functions of dashes:

1. to set off **parenthetical statements** or an **appositive with internal punctuation**

   Example: The three trees—oak, pine, and magnolia—are coming on a truck tomorrow.

2. to show a **break or change in tone or thought**

   Example: The first question—how silly of me—does not have a correct answer.

ELLIPSIS MARKS

The ellipsis mark has **three** periods (...) to show when **words have been removed** from a quotation. If a **full sentence or more** is removed from a quoted passage, you need to use **four** periods to show the removed text and the end punctuation mark. The ellipsis mark should not be used at the beginning of a quotation. The ellipsis mark should also not be used at the end of a quotation unless some words have been deleted from the end of the final sentence.

Example:

   "Then he picked up the groceries...paid for them...later he went home."

BRACKETS

There are two main reasons to use brackets:

1. When **placing parentheses inside of parentheses**

   Example: The hero of this story, Paul Revere (a silversmith and industrialist [see Ch. 4]), rode through towns of Massachusetts to warn of advancing British troops.

2. When adding **clarification or detail** to a quotation that is **not part of the quotation**
   Example:

   The father explained, "My children are planning to attend my alma mater [State University]."

Common Usage Mistakes

WORD CONFUSION

WHICH, THAT, AND WHO

Which is used for things only.

Example: John's dog, *which is called Max,* is large and fierce.

That is used for people or things.

Example: Is this the only book *that Louis L'Amour wrote?*

Example: Is Louis L'Amour the author *that wrote Western novels?*

Who is used for people only.

Example: Mozart was the composer *who wrote those operas.*

HOMOPHONES

Homophones are words that sound alike (or similar) but have different **spellings** and **definitions**. A homophone is a type of **homonym**, which is a pair or group of words that are pronounced or spelled the same, but do not mean the same thing.

TO, TOO, AND TWO

To can be an adverb or a preposition for showing direction, purpose, and relationship. See your dictionary for the many other ways to use *to* in a sentence.

Examples: I went to the store. | I want to go with you.

Too is an adverb that means *also, as well, very,* or *in excess.*

Examples: I can walk a mile too. | You have eaten too much.

Two is the second number in the series of numbers (e.g., one (1), two, (2), three (3)...).

Example: You have two minutes left.

THERE, THEIR, AND THEY'RE

There can be an adjective, adverb, or pronoun. Often, *there* is used to show a place or to start a sentence.

Examples: I went there yesterday. | There is something in his pocket.

Their is a pronoun that is used to show ownership.

Examples: He is their father. | This is their fourth apology this week.

They're is a contraction of *they are.*

Example: Did you know that they're in town?

KNEW AND NEW

Knew is the past tense of *know*.

> Example: I knew the answer.

New is an adjective that means something is current, has not been used, or is modern.

> Example: This is my new phone.

THEN AND THAN

Then is an adverb that indicates sequence or order:

> Example: I'm going to run to the library and then come home.

Than is special-purpose word used only for comparisons:

> Example: Susie likes chips more than candy.

ITS AND IT'S

Its is a pronoun that shows ownership.

> Example: The guitar is in its case.

It's is a contraction of *it is*.

> Example: It's an honor and a privilege to meet you.

Note: The *h* in honor is silent, so the sound of the vowel *o* must have the article *an*.

YOUR AND YOU'RE

Your is a pronoun that shows ownership.

> Example: This is your moment to shine.

You're is a contraction of *you are*.

> Example: Yes, you're correct.

SAW AND SEEN

Saw is the past-tense form of *see*.

> Example: I saw a turtle on my walk this morning.

Seen is the past participle of *see*.

> Example: I have seen this movie before.

AFFECT AND EFFECT

There are two main reasons that *affect* and *effect* are so often confused: 1) both words can be used as either a noun or a verb, and 2) unlike most homophones, their usage and meanings are closely related to each other. Here is a quick rundown of the four usage options:

Affect (n): feeling, emotion, or mood that is displayed

> Example: The patient had a flat *affect*. (i.e., his face showed little or no emotion)

Affect (v): to alter, to change, to influence

Example: The sunshine *affects* the plant's growth.

Effect (n): a result, a consequence

Example: What *effect* will this weather have on our schedule?

Effect (v): to bring about, to cause to be

Example: These new rules will *effect* order in the office.

The noun form of *affect* is rarely used outside of technical medical descriptions, so if a noun form is needed on the test, you can safely select *effect*. The verb form of *effect* is not as rare as the noun form of *affect*, but it's still not all that likely to show up on your test. If you need a verb and you can't decide which to use based on the definitions, choosing *affect* is your best bet.

HOMOGRAPHS

Homographs are words that share the same spelling, but have different meanings and sometimes different pronunciations. To figure out which meaning is being used, you should be looking for context clues. The context clues give hints to the meaning of the word. For example, the word *spot* has many meanings. It can mean "a place" or "a stain or blot." In the sentence "After my lunch, I saw a spot on my shirt," the word *spot* means "a stain or blot." The context clues of "After my lunch" and "on my shirt" guide you to this decision. A homograph is another type of homonym.

BANK

(noun): an establishment where money is held for savings or lending

(verb): to collect or pile up

CONTENT

(noun): the topics that will be addressed within a book

(adjective): pleased or satisfied

(verb): to make someone pleased or satisfied

FINE

(noun): an amount of money that acts a penalty for an offense

(adjective): very small or thin

(adverb): in an acceptable way

(verb): to make someone pay money as a punishment

INCENSE

(noun): a material that is burned in religious settings and makes a pleasant aroma

(verb): to frustrate or anger

LEAD

(noun): the first or highest position

(noun): a heavy metallic element

(verb): to direct a person or group of followers

(adjective): containing lead

OBJECT

(noun): a lifeless item that can be held and observed

(verb): to disagree

PRODUCE

(noun): fruits and vegetables

(verb): to make or create something

REFUSE

(noun): garbage or debris that has been thrown away

(verb): to not allow

SUBJECT

(noun): an area of study

(verb): to force or subdue

TEAR

(noun): a fluid secreted by the eyes

(verb): to separate or pull apart

The Writing Process

BRAINSTORMING

Brainstorming is a technique that is used to find a creative approach to a subject. This can be accomplished by simple **free-association** with a topic. For example, with paper and pen, write every thought that you have about the topic in a word or phrase. This is done without critical thinking. You should put everything that comes to your mind about the topic on your scratch paper. Then, you need to read the list over a few times. Next, you look for patterns, repetitions, and clusters of ideas. This allows a variety of fresh ideas to come as you think about the topic.

FREE WRITING

Free writing is a more structured form of brainstorming. The method involves taking a limited amount of time (e.g., 2 to 3 minutes) to write everything that comes to mind about the topic in complete sentences. When time expires, review everything that has been written down. Many of your sentences may make little or no sense, but the insights and observations that can come from free writing make this method a valuable approach. Usually, free writing results in a fuller expression of ideas than brainstorming because thoughts and associations are written in complete sentences. However, both techniques can be used to complement each other.

PLANNING

Planning is the process of planning a piece of writing before composing a draft. Planning can include creating an outline or a graphic organizer, such as a Venn diagram, a spider-map, or a flowchart. These methods should help the writer identify their topic, main ideas, and the general organization of the composition. Preliminary research can also take place during this stage. Planning helps writers organize all of their ideas and decide if they have enough material to begin their first draft. However, writers should remember that the decisions they make during this step will likely change later in the process, so their plan does not have to be perfect.

DRAFTING

Writers may then use their plan, outline, or graphic organizer to compose their first draft. They may write subsequent drafts to improve their writing. Writing multiple drafts can help writers consider different ways to communicate their ideas and address errors that may be difficult to correct without rewriting a section or the whole composition. Most writers will vary in how many drafts they choose to write, as there is no "right" number of drafts. Writing drafts also takes away the pressure to write perfectly on the first try, as writers can improve with each draft they write.

REVISING, EDITING, AND PROOFREADING

Once a writer completes a draft, they can move on to the revising, editing, and proofreading steps to improve their draft. These steps begin with making broad changes that may apply to large sections of a composition and then making small, specific corrections. **Revising** is the first and broadest of these steps. Revising involves ensuring that the composition addresses an appropriate audience, includes all necessary material, maintains focus throughout, and is organized logically. Revising may occur after the first draft to ensure that the following drafts improve upon errors from the first draft. Some revision should occur between each draft to avoid repeating these errors. The **editing** phase of writing is narrower than the revising phase. Editing a composition should include steps such as improving transitions between paragraphs, ensuring each paragraph is on topic, and improving the flow of the text. The editing phase may also include correcting grammatical errors that cannot be fixed without significantly altering the text. **Proofreading** involves fixing misspelled words, typos, other grammatical errors, and any remaining surface-level flaws in the composition.

RECURSIVE WRITING PROCESS

However you approach writing, you may find comfort in knowing that the revision process can occur in any order. The **recursive writing process** is not as difficult as the phrase may make it seem. Simply put, the recursive writing process means that you may need to revisit steps after completing other steps. It also implies that the steps are not required to take place in any certain order. Indeed, you may find that planning, drafting, and revising can all take place at about the same time. The writing process involves moving back and forth between planning, drafting, and revising, followed by more planning, more drafting, and more revising until the writing is satisfactory.

> **Review Video: Recursive Writing Process**
> Visit mometrix.com/academy and enter code: 951611

TECHNOLOGY IN THE WRITING PROCESS

Modern technology has yielded several tools that can be used to make the writing process more convenient and organized. Word processors and online tools, such as databases and plagiarism detectors, allow much of the writing process to be completed in one place, using one device.

TECHNOLOGY FOR PLANNING AND DRAFTING

For the planning and drafting stages of the writing process, word processors are a helpful tool. These programs also feature formatting tools, allowing users to create their own planning tools or create digital outlines that can be easily converted into sentences, paragraphs, or an entire essay draft. Online databases and references also complement the planning process by providing convenient access to information and sources for research. Word processors also allow users to keep up with their work and update it more easily than if they wrote their work by hand. Online word processors often allow users to collaborate, making group assignments more convenient. These programs also allow users to include illustrations or other supplemental media in their compositions.

TECHNOLOGY FOR REVISING, EDITING, AND PROOFREADING

Word processors also benefit the revising, editing, and proofreading stages of the writing process. Most of these programs indicate errors in spelling and grammar, allowing users to catch minor errors and correct them quickly. There are also websites designed to help writers by analyzing text for deeper errors, such as poor sentence structure, inappropriate complexity, lack of sentence variety, and style issues. These websites can help users fix errors they may not know to look for or may have simply missed. As writers finish these steps, they may benefit from checking their work for any plagiarism. There are several websites and programs that compare text to other documents and publications across the internet and detect any similarities within the text. These websites show the source of the similar information, so users know whether or not they referenced the source and unintentionally plagiarized its contents.

TECHNOLOGY FOR PUBLISHING

Technology also makes managing written work more convenient. Digitally storing documents keeps everything in one place and is easy to reference. Digital storage also makes sharing work easier, as documents can be attached to an email or stored online. This also allows writers to publish their work easily, as they can electronically submit it to other publications or freely post it to a personal blog, profile, or website.

Outlining and Organizing Ideas

MAIN IDEAS, SUPPORTING DETAILS, AND OUTLINING A TOPIC

A writer often begins the first paragraph of a paper by stating the **main idea** or point, also known as the **topic sentence**. The rest of the paragraph supplies particular details that develop and support the main point. One way to visualize the relationship between the main point and supporting information is by considering a table: the tabletop is the main point, and each of the table's legs is a supporting detail or group of details. Both professional authors and students can benefit from planning their writing by first making an outline of the topic. Outlines facilitate quick identification of the main point and supporting details without having to wade through the additional language that will exist in the fully developed essay, article, or paper. Outlining can also help readers to analyze a piece of existing writing for the same reason. The outline first summarizes the main idea in one sentence. Then, below that, it summarizes the supporting details in a numbered list. Writing the paper then consists of filling in the outline with detail, writing a paragraph for each supporting point, and adding an introduction and conclusion.

INTRODUCTION

The purpose of the introduction is to capture the reader's attention and announce the essay's main idea. Normally, the introduction contains 50-80 words, or 3-5 sentences. An introduction can begin with an interesting quote, a question, or a strong opinion—something that will **engage** the reader's interest and prompt them to keep reading. If you are writing your essay to a specific prompt, your introduction should include a **restatement or summarization** of the prompt so that the reader will have some context for your essay. Finally, your introduction should briefly state your **thesis or main idea**: the primary thing you hope to communicate to the reader through your essay. Don't try to include all of the details and nuances of your thesis, or all of your reasons for it, in the introduction. That's what the rest of the essay is for!

> **Review Video: Introduction**
> Visit mometrix.com/academy and enter code: 961328

THESIS STATEMENT

The thesis is the main idea of the essay. A temporary thesis, or working thesis, should be established early in the writing process because it will serve to keep the writer focused as ideas develop. This temporary thesis is subject to change as you continue to write.

The temporary thesis has two parts: a topic (i.e., the focus of your essay based on the prompt) and a comment. The comment makes an important point about the topic. A temporary thesis should be interesting and specific. Also, you need to limit the topic to a manageable scope. These three questions are useful tools to measure the effectiveness of any temporary thesis:

- Does the focus of my essay have enough interest to hold an audience?
- Is the focus of my essay specific enough to generate interest?
- Is the focus of my essay manageable for the time limit? Too broad? Too narrow?

The thesis should be a generalization rather than a fact because the thesis prepares readers for facts and details that support the thesis. The process of bringing the thesis into sharp focus may help in outlining major sections of the work. Once the thesis and introduction are complete, you can address the body of the work.

> **Review Video: Thesis Statements**
> Visit mometrix.com/academy and enter code: 691033

SUPPORTING THE THESIS

Throughout your essay, the thesis should be **explained clearly and supported** adequately by additional arguments. The thesis sentence needs to contain a clear statement of the purpose of your essay and a comment about the thesis. With the thesis statement, you have an opportunity to state what is noteworthy of this particular treatment of the prompt. Each sentence and paragraph should build on and support the thesis.

When you respond to the prompt, use parts of the passage to support your argument or defend your position. With supporting evidence from the passage, you strengthen your argument because readers can see your attention to the entire passage and your response to the details and facts within the passage. You can use facts, details, statistics, and direct quotations from the passage to uphold your position. Be sure to point out which information comes from the original passage and base your argument around that evidence.

BODY

In an essay's introduction, the writer establishes the thesis and may indicate how the rest of the piece will be structured. In the body of the piece, the writer **elaborates** upon, **illustrates**, and **explains** the **thesis statement**. How writers arrange supporting details and their choices of paragraph types are development techniques. Writers may give examples of the concept introduced in the thesis statement. If the subject includes a cause-and-effect relationship, the author may explain its causality. A writer will explain or analyze the main idea of the piece throughout the body, often by presenting arguments for the veracity or credibility of the thesis statement. Writers may use development to define or clarify ambiguous terms. Paragraphs within the body may be organized using natural sequences, like space and time. Writers may employ **inductive reasoning**, using multiple details to establish a generalization or causal relationship, or **deductive reasoning**, proving a generalized hypothesis or proposition through a specific example or case.

> **Review Video: Drafting Body Paragraphs**
> Visit mometrix.com/academy and enter code: 724590

PARAGRAPHS

After the introduction of a passage, a series of body paragraphs will carry a message through to the conclusion. Each paragraph should be **unified around a main point**. Normally, a good topic sentence summarizes the paragraph's main point. A topic sentence is a general sentence that gives an introduction to the paragraph.

The sentences that follow support the topic sentence. However, though it is usually the first sentence, the topic sentence can come as the final sentence to the paragraph if the earlier sentences give a clear explanation of the paragraph's topic. This allows the topic sentence to function as a concluding sentence. Overall, the paragraphs need to stay true to the main point. This means that any unnecessary sentences that do not advance the main point should be removed.

The main point of a paragraph requires adequate development (i.e., a substantial paragraph that covers the main point). A paragraph of two or three sentences does not cover a main point. This is especially true when the main point of the paragraph gives strong support to the argument of the thesis. An occasional short paragraph is fine as a transitional device. However, a well-developed argument will have paragraphs with more than a few sentences.

METHODS OF DEVELOPING PARAGRAPHS

Common methods of adding substance to paragraphs include examples, illustrations, analogies, and cause and effect.

- **Examples** are the supporting details to the main idea of a paragraph or a passage. When authors write about something that their audience may not understand, they can provide an example to show their point. When authors write about something that is not easily accepted, they can give examples to prove their point.
- **Illustrations** are extended examples that require several sentences. Well-selected illustrations can be a great way for authors to develop a point that may not be familiar to their audience.
- **Analogies** make comparisons between items that appear to have nothing in common. Analogies are employed by writers to provoke fresh thoughts about a subject. These comparisons may be used to explain the unfamiliar, to clarify an abstract point, or to argue a point. Although analogies are effective literary devices, they should be used carefully in arguments. Two things may be alike in some respects but completely different in others.
- **Cause and effect** is an excellent device used when the cause and effect are accepted as true. One way that authors can use cause and effect is to state the effect in the topic sentence of a paragraph and add the causes in the body of the paragraph. With this method, an author's paragraphs can have structure which always strengthens writing.

> **Review Video: How to Write a Good Paragraph**
> Visit mometrix.com/academy and enter code: 682127

TYPES OF PARAGRAPHS

A **paragraph of narration** tells a story or a part of a story. Normally, the sentences are arranged in chronological order (i.e., the order that the events happened). However, flashbacks (i.e., an anecdote from an earlier time) can be included.

A **descriptive paragraph** makes a verbal portrait of a person, place, or thing. When specific details are used that appeal to one or more of the senses (i.e., sight, sound, smell, taste, and touch), authors give readers a sense of being present in the moment.

A **process paragraph** is related to time order (i.e., First, you open the bottle. Second, you pour the liquid, etc.). Usually, this describes a process or teaches readers how to perform a process.

56

Comparing two things draws attention to their similarities and indicates a number of differences. When authors contrast, they focus only on differences. Both comparing and contrasting may be done point-by-point, noting both the similarities and differences of each point, or in sequential paragraphs, where you discuss the all the similarities and then all the differences, or vice versa.

BREAKING TEXT INTO PARAGRAPHS

For most forms of writing, you will need to use multiple paragraphs. As such, determining when to start a new paragraph is very important. Reasons for starting a new paragraph include:

- To mark off the introduction and concluding paragraphs
- To signal a shift to a new idea or topic
- To indicate an important shift in time or place
- To explain a point in additional detail
- To highlight a comparison, contrast, or cause and effect relationship

PARAGRAPH LENGTH

Most readers find that their comfort level for a paragraph is between 100 and 200 words. Shorter paragraphs cause too much starting and stopping, and give a choppy effect. Paragraphs that are too long often test the attention span of readers. Two notable exceptions to this rule exist. In scientific or scholarly papers, longer paragraphs suggest seriousness and depth. In journalistic writing, constraints are placed on paragraph size by the narrow columns in a newspaper format.

The first and last paragraphs of a text will usually be the introduction and conclusion. These special-purpose paragraphs are likely to be shorter than paragraphs in the body of the work. Paragraphs in the body of the essay follow the subject's outline (e.g., one paragraph per point in short essays and a group of paragraphs per point in longer works). Some ideas require more development than others, so it is good for a writer to remain flexible. A paragraph of excessive length may be divided, and shorter ones may be combined.

COHERENT PARAGRAPHS

A smooth flow of sentences and paragraphs without gaps, shifts, or bumps will lead to paragraph **coherence**. Ties between old and new information can be smoothed using several methods:

- **Linking ideas clearly**, from the topic sentence to the body of the paragraph, is essential for a smooth transition. The topic sentence states the main point, and this should be followed by specific details, examples, and illustrations that support the topic sentence. The support may be direct or indirect. In **indirect support**, the illustrations and examples may support a sentence that in turn supports the topic directly.
- The **repetition of key words** adds coherence to a paragraph. To avoid dull language, variations of the key words may be used.
- **Parallel structures** are often used within sentences to emphasize the similarity of ideas and connect sentences giving similar information.
- Maintaining a **consistent verb tense** throughout the paragraph helps. Shifting tenses affects the smooth flow of words and can disrupt the coherence of the paragraph.

> **Review Video: How to Write a Good Paragraph**
> Visit mometrix.com/academy and enter code: 682127

SEQUENCE WORDS AND PHRASES

When a paragraph opens with the topic sentence, the second sentence may begin with a phrase like "First of all," introducing the first supporting detail or example. The writer may introduce the second supporting item with words or phrases like "Also," "In addition," and "Besides." The writer might introduce succeeding pieces of support with wording like, "Another thing," "Moreover" "Furthermore," or "Not only that, but." The writer may introduce the last piece of support with "Lastly," "Finally," or "Last but not least." Writers get off the point by presenting "off-target" items not supporting the main point. For example, a main point "My dog is not smart" is supported by the statement, "He's six years old and still doesn't answer to his name." But "He cries when I leave for school" is not supportive, as it does not indicate lack of intelligence. Writers stay on point by presenting only supportive statements that are directly relevant to and illustrative of their main point.

TRANSITIONS

Transitions between sentences and paragraphs guide readers from idea to idea. They also indicate relationships between sentences and paragraphs. Writers should be judicious in their use of transitions, inserting them sparingly. They should also be selected to fit the author's purpose—transitions can indicate time, comparison, and conclusion, among other purposes. Tone is also important to consider when using transitional phrases, varying the tone for different audiences. For example, in a scholarly essay, *in summary* would be preferable to the more informal *in short*.

When working with transitional words and phrases, writers usually find a natural flow that indicates when a transition is needed. In reading a draft of the text, it should become apparent where the flow is disrupted. At this point, the writer can add transitional elements during the revision process. Revising can also afford an opportunity to delete transitional devices that seem heavy handed or unnecessary.

> **Review Video: Transitions in Writing**
> Visit mometrix.com/academy and enter code: 233246

TYPES OF TRANSITIONAL WORDS

Time	Afterward, immediately, earlier, meanwhile, recently, lately, now, since, soon, when, then, until, before, etc.
Sequence	too, first, second, further, moreover, also, again, and, next, still, besides, and finally
Comparison	similarly, in the same way, likewise, also, again, and once more
Contrasting	but, although, despite, however, instead, nevertheless, on the one hand... on the other hand, regardless, yet, and in contrast.
Cause and Effect	because, consequently, thus, therefore, then, to this end, since, so, as a result, if... then, and accordingly
Examples	for example, for instance, such as, to illustrate, indeed, in fact, and specifically
Place	near, far, here, there, to the left/right, next to, above, below, beyond, opposite, and beside
Concession	granted that, naturally, of course, it may appear, and although it is true that
Repetition, Summary, or Conclusion	as mentioned earlier, as noted, in other words, in short, on the whole, to summarize, therefore, as a result, to conclude, and in conclusion
Addition	and, also, furthermore, moreover
Generalization	in broad terms, broadly speaking, in general

> **Review Video: Transitional Words and Phrases**
> Visit mometrix.com/academy and enter code: 197796
>
> **Review Video: Transitions**
> Visit mometrix.com/academy and enter code: 707563

CONCLUSION

Two important principles to consider when writing a conclusion are strength and closure. A strong conclusion gives the reader a sense that the author's main points are meaningful and important, and that the supporting facts and arguments are convincing, solid, and well developed. When a conclusion achieves closure, it gives the impression that the writer has stated all necessary information and points and completed the work, rather than simply stopping after a specified length. Some things to avoid when writing concluding paragraphs include:

- Introducing a completely new idea
- Beginning with obvious or unoriginal phrases like "In conclusion" or "To summarize"
- Apologizing for one's opinions or writing
- Repeating the thesis word for word rather than rephrasing it
- Believing that the conclusion must always summarize the piece

> **Review Video: Drafting Conclusions**
> Visit mometrix.com/academy and enter code: 209408

Organization within a Passage

ORGANIZATION OF THE TEXT

The way a text is organized can help readers understand the author's intent and his or her conclusions. There are various ways to organize a text, and each one has a purpose and use. Usually, authors will organize information logically in a passage so the reader can follow and locate the information within the text. However, since not all passages are written with the same logical structure, you need to be familiar with several different types of passage structure.

> **Review Video: Organizational Methods to Structure Text**
> Visit mometrix.com/academy and enter code: 606263

CHRONOLOGICAL

When using **chronological** order, the author presents information in the order that it happened. For example, biographies are typically written in chronological order. The subject's birth and childhood are presented first, followed by their adult life, and lastly the events leading up to the person's death.

CAUSE AND EFFECT

One of the most common text structures is **cause and effect**. A **cause** is an act or event that makes something happen, and an **effect** is the thing that happens as a result of the cause. A cause-and-effect relationship is not always explicit, but there are some terms in English that signal causes, such as *since*, *because*, and *due to*. Furthermore, terms that signal effects include *consequently, therefore, this leads to*. As an example, consider the sentence *Because the sky was clear, Ron did not bring an umbrella*. The cause is the clear sky, and the effect is that Ron did not bring an umbrella. However, readers may find that sometimes the cause-and-effect relationship will not be clearly noted. For instance, the sentence *He was late and missed the meeting* does not contain any signaling words, but the sentence still contains a cause (he was late) and an effect (he missed the meeting).

> **Review Video: Cause and Effect**
> Visit mometrix.com/academy and enter code: 868099

MULTIPLE EFFECTS

Be aware of the possibility for a single cause to have **multiple effects.** (e.g., *Single cause*: Because you left your homework on the table, your dog engulfed the assignment. *Multiple effects*: As a result, you receive a failing grade, your parents do not allow you to go out with your friends, you miss out on the new movie, and one of your classmates spoils it for you before you have another chance to watch it).

MULTIPLE CAUSES

Also, there is the possibility for a single effect to have **multiple causes.** (e.g., *Single effect*: Alan has a fever. *Multiple causes*: An unexpected cold front came through the area, and Alan forgot to take his multi-vitamin to avoid getting sick.) Additionally, an effect can in turn be the cause of another effect, in what is known as a cause-and-effect chain. (e.g., As a result of her disdain for procrastination, Lynn prepared for her exam. This led to her passing her test with high marks. Consequently, her resume was accepted and her application was approved.)

CAUSE AND EFFECT IN PERSUASIVE ESSAYS

Persuasive essays, in which an author tries to make a convincing argument and change the minds of readers, usually include cause-and-effect relationships. However, these relationships should not always be taken at face value. Frequently, an author will assume a cause or take an effect for granted. To read a persuasive essay effectively, readers need to judge the cause-and-effect relationships that the author is presenting. For instance, imagine an author wrote the following: *The parking deck has been unprofitable because people would prefer to ride their bikes.* The relationship is clear: the cause is that people prefer to ride their bikes, and the effect is that the parking deck has been unprofitable. However, readers should consider whether this argument is conclusive. Perhaps there are other reasons for the failure of the parking deck: a down economy, excessive fees, etc. Too often, authors present causal relationships as if they are fact rather than opinion. Readers should be on the alert for these dubious claims.

PROBLEM-SOLUTION

Some nonfiction texts are organized to **present a problem** followed by a solution. For this type of text, the problem is often explained before the solution is offered. In some cases, as when the problem is well known, the solution may be introduced briefly at the beginning. Other passages may focus on the solution, and the problem will be referenced only occasionally. Some texts will outline multiple solutions to a problem, leaving readers to choose among them. If the author has an interest or an allegiance to one solution, he or she may fail to mention or describe accurately some of the other solutions. Readers should be careful of the author's agenda when reading a problem-solution text. Only by understanding the author's perspective and interests can one develop a proper judgment of the proposed solution.

COMPARE AND CONTRAST

Many texts follow the **compare-and-contrast** model in which the similarities and differences between two ideas or things are explored. Analysis of the similarities between ideas is called **comparison**. In an ideal comparison, the author places ideas or things in an equivalent structure, i.e., the author presents the ideas in the same way. If an author wants to show the similarities between cricket and baseball, then he or she may do so by summarizing the equipment and rules for each game. Be mindful of the similarities as they appear in the passage and take note of any differences that are mentioned. Often, these small differences will only reinforce the more general similarity.

Review Video: **Compare and Contrast Essays**
Visit mometrix.com/academy and enter code: 798319

Thinking critically about ideas and conclusions can seem like a daunting task. One way to ease this task is to understand the basic elements of ideas and writing techniques. Looking at the way different ideas relate to each other can be a good way for readers to begin their analysis. For instance, sometimes authors will write about two ideas that are in opposition to each other. Or, one author will provide his or her ideas on a topic, and another author may respond in opposition. The analysis of these opposing ideas is known as **contrast**. Contrast is often marred by the author's obvious partiality to one of the ideas. A discerning reader will be put off by an author who does not engage in a fair fight. In an analysis of opposing ideas, both ideas should be presented in clear and reasonable terms. If the author does prefer a side, you need to read carefully to determine the areas where the author shows or avoids this preference. In an analysis of opposing ideas, you should proceed through the passage by marking the major differences point by point with an eye that is looking for an explanation of each side's view. For instance, in an analysis of capitalism and communism, there is an importance in outlining each side's view on labor, markets, prices, personal responsibility, etc. Additionally, as you read through the passages, you should note whether the opposing views present each side in a similar manner.

SEQUENCE

Readers must be able to identify a text's **sequence**, or the order in which things happen. Often, when the sequence is very important to the author, the text is indicated with signal words like *first, then, next*, and *last*. However, a sequence can be merely implied and must be noted by the reader. Consider the sentence *He walked through the garden and gave water and fertilizer to the plants*. Clearly, the man did not walk through the garden before he collected water and fertilizer for the plants. So, the implied sequence is that he first collected water, then he collected fertilizer, next he walked through the garden, and last he gave water or fertilizer as necessary to the plants. Texts do not always proceed in an orderly sequence from first to last. Sometimes they begin at the end and start over at the beginning. As a reader, you can enhance your understanding of the passage by taking brief notes to clarify the sequence.

Style and Form

WRITING STYLE AND LINGUISTIC FORM

Linguistic form encodes the literal meanings of words and sentences. It comes from the phonological, morphological, syntactic, and semantic parts of a language. **Writing style** consists of different ways of encoding the meaning and indicating figurative and stylistic meanings. An author's writing style can also be referred to as his or her **voice**.

Writers' stylistic choices accomplish three basic effects on their audiences:

- They **communicate meanings** beyond linguistically dictated meanings,
- They communicate the **author's attitude**, such as persuasive or argumentative effects accomplished through style, and
- They communicate or **express feelings**.

Within style, component areas include: narrative structure; viewpoint; focus; sound patterns; meter and rhythm; lexical and syntactic repetition and parallelism; writing genre; representational, realistic, and mimetic effects; representation of thought and speech; meta-representation (representing representation); irony; metaphor and other indirect meanings; representation and use of historical and dialectal variations; gender-specific and other group-specific speech styles, both real and fictitious; and analysis of the processes for inferring meaning from writing.

LEVEL OF FORMALITY

The relationship between writer and reader is important in choosing a **level of formality** as most writing requires some degree of formality. **Formal writing** is for addressing a superior in a school or work environment. Business letters, textbooks, and newspapers use a moderate to high level of formality. **Informal writing** is appropriate for private letters, personal emails, and business correspondence between close associates.

For your exam, you will want to be aware of informal and formal writing. One way that this can be accomplished is to watch for shifts in point of view in the essay. For example, unless writers are using a personal example, they will rarely refer to themselves (e.g., "*I* think that *my* point is very clear.") to avoid being informal when they need to be formal.

Also, be mindful of an author who addresses his or her audience **directly** in their writing (e.g., "Readers, *like you*, will understand this argument.") as this can be a sign of informal writing. Good writers understand the need to be consistent with their level of formality. Shifts in levels of formality or point of view can confuse readers and cause them to discount the message.

CLICHÉS

Clichés are phrases that have been **overused** to the point that the phrase has no importance or has lost the original meaning. These phrases have no originality and add very little to a passage. Therefore, most writers will avoid the use of clichés. Another option is to make changes to a cliché so that it is not predictable and empty of meaning.

Examples:

> When life gives you lemons, make lemonade.

> Every cloud has a silver lining.

JARGON

Jargon is a **specialized vocabulary** that is used among members of a trade or profession. Since jargon is understood by only a small audience, writers will use jargon in passages that will only be read by a specialized audience. For example, medical jargon should be used in a medical journal but not in a New York Times article. Jargon includes exaggerated language that tries to impress rather than inform. Sentences filled with jargon are not precise and are difficult to understand.

Examples:

> "He is going to *toenail* these frames for us." (Toenail is construction jargon for nailing at an angle.)

> "They brought in a *kip* of material today." (Kip refers to 1000 pounds in architecture and engineering.)

SLANG

Slang is an **informal** and sometimes private language that is understood by some individuals. Slang terms have some usefulness, but they can have a small audience. So, most formal writing will not include this kind of language.

Examples:

> "Yes, the event was a blast!" (In this sentence, *blast* means that the event was a great experience.)

> "That attempt was an epic fail." (By *epic fail*, the speaker means that his or her attempt was not a success.)

COLLOQUIALISM

A colloquialism is a word or phrase that is found in informal writing. Unlike slang, **colloquial language** will be familiar to a greater range of people. However, colloquialisms are still considered inappropriate for formal writing. Colloquial language can include some slang, but these are limited to contractions for the most part.

Examples:

> "Can *y'all* come back another time?" (Y'all is a contraction of "you all.")

"Will you stop him from building this *castle in the air*?" (A "castle in the air" is an improbable or unlikely event.)

ACADEMIC LANGUAGE

In educational settings, students are often expected to use academic language in their schoolwork. Academic language is also commonly found in dissertations and theses, texts published by academic journals, and other forms of academic research. Academic language conventions may vary between fields, but general academic language is free of slang, regional terminology, and noticeable grammatical errors. Specific terms may also be used in academic language, and it is important to understand their proper usage. A writer's command of academic language impacts their ability to communicate in an academic or professional context. While it is acceptable to use colloquialisms, slang, improper grammar, or other forms of informal speech in social settings or at home, it is inappropriate to practice academic language in academic contexts.

TONE

Tone may be defined as the writer's **attitude** toward the topic, and to the audience. This attitude is reflected in the language used in the writing. The tone of a work should be **appropriate to the topic** and to the intended audience. Some texts should not contain slang or jargon, while it may be fine to use such terms in a different piece. Tone can range from humorous to serious and any level in between. It may be more or less formal, depending on the purpose of the writing and its intended audience. All these nuances in tone can flavor the entire writing and should be kept in mind as the work evolves.

WORD SELECTION

A writer's choice of words is a signature of their style. Careful thought about the use of words can improve a piece of writing. A passage can be an exciting piece to read when attention is given to the use of vivid or specific nouns rather than general ones.

Example:

General: His kindness will never be forgotten.

Specific: His thoughtful gifts and bear hugs will never be forgotten.

Attention should also be given to the kind of verbs that are used in sentences. Active verbs (e.g., run, swim) should be about an action. Whenever possible, an **active verb should replace a linking verb** to provide clear examples for arguments and to strengthen a passage overall. When using an active verb, one should be sure that the verb is used in the active voice instead of the passive voice. Verbs are in the active voice when the subject is the one doing the action. A verb is in the passive voice when the subject is the recipient of an action.

Example:

Passive: The winners were called to the stage by the judges.

Active: The judges called the winners to the stage.

> **Review Video: Word Usage**
> Visit mometrix.com/academy and enter code: 197863

CONCISENESS

Conciseness is writing that communicates a message in the fewest words possible. Writing concisely is valuable because short, uncluttered messages allow the reader to understand the author's message more easily and efficiently. Planning is important in writing concise messages. If you have in mind what you need to write beforehand, it will be easier to make a message short and to the point. Do not state the obvious.

Revising is also important. After the message is written, make sure you have effective, pithy sentences that efficiently get your point across. When reviewing the information, imagine a conversation taking place, and concise writing will likely result.

APPROPRIATE KINDS OF WRITING FOR DIFFERENT TASKS, PURPOSES, AND AUDIENCES

When preparing to write a composition, consider the audience and purpose to choose the best type of writing. Three common types of writing are persuasive, expository, and narrative. **Persuasive**, or argumentative writing, is used to convince the audience to take action or agree with the author's claims. **Expository** writing is meant to inform the audience of the author's observations or research on a topic. **Narrative** writing is used to tell the audience a story and often allows more room for creativity. While task, purpose, and audience inform a writer's mode of writing, these factors also impact elements such as tone, vocabulary, and formality.

For example, students who are writing to persuade their parents to grant them some additional privilege, such as permission for a more independent activity, should use more sophisticated vocabulary and diction that sounds more mature and serious to appeal to the parental audience. However, students who are writing for younger children should use simpler vocabulary and sentence structure, as well as choose words that are more vivid and entertaining. They should treat their topics more lightly, and include humor when appropriate. Students who are writing for their classmates may use language that is more informal, as well as age-appropriate.

> **Review Video: Writing Purpose and Audience**
> Visit mometrix.com/academy and enter code: 146627

Modes of Writing

ESSAYS

Essays usually focus on one topic, subject, or goal. There are several types of essays, including informative, persuasive, and narrative. An essay's structure and level of formality depend on the type of essay and its goal. While narrative essays typically do not include outside sources, other types of essays often require some research and the integration of primary and secondary sources.

The basic format of an essay typically has three major parts: the introduction, the body, and the conclusion. The body is further divided into the writer's main points. Short and simple essays may have three main points, while essays covering broader ranges and going into more depth can have almost any number of main points, depending on length.

An essay's introduction should answer three questions:

1. What is the **subject** of the essay?

   If a student writes an essay about a book, the answer would include the title and author of the book and any additional information needed—such as the subject or argument of the book.

2. How does the essay **address** the subject?

   To answer this, the writer identifies the essay's organization by briefly summarizing main points and the evidence supporting them.

3. What will the essay **prove**?

   This is the thesis statement, usually the opening paragraph's last sentence, clearly stating the writer's message.

The body elaborates on all the main points related to the thesis, introducing one main point at a time, and includes supporting evidence with each main point. Each body paragraph should state the point in a topic sentence, which is usually the first sentence in the paragraph. The paragraph should then explain the point's meaning, support it with quotations or other evidence, and then explain how this point and the evidence are related to the thesis. The writer should then repeat this procedure in a new paragraph for each additional main point.

The conclusion reiterates the content of the introduction, including the thesis, to remind the reader of the essay's main argument or subject. The essay writer may also summarize the highlights of the argument or description contained in the body of the essay, following the same sequence originally used in the body. For example, a conclusion might look like: Point 1 + Point 2 + Point 3 = Thesis, or Point 1 → Point 2 → Point 3 → Thesis Proof. Good organization makes essays easier for writers to compose and provides a guide for readers to follow. Well-organized essays hold attention better and are more likely to get readers to accept their theses as valid.

INFORMATIVE VS. PERSUASIVE WRITING

Informative writing, also called explanatory or expository writing, begins with the basis that something is true or factual, while **persuasive** writing strives to prove something that may or may not be true or factual. Whereas argumentative text is written to **persuade** readers to agree with the author's position, informative text merely **provides information and insight** to readers. Informative writing concentrates on **informing** readers about why or how something is as it is. This can include offering new information, explaining how a process works, and developing a concept for readers. To accomplish these objectives, the essay may name and distinguish various things within a category; provide definitions; provide details about the parts of something; explain a particular function or behavior; and give readers explanations for why a fact, object, event, or process exists or occurs.

> **Review Video: Informative Text**
> Visit mometrix.com/academy and enter code: 924964
>
> **Review Video: Argumentative Writing**
> Visit mometrix.com/academy and enter code: 561544

NARRATIVE WRITING

Put simply, **narrative** writing tells a story. The most common examples of literary narratives are novels. Non-fictional biographies, autobiographies, memoirs, and histories are also narratives. Narratives should tell stories in such a way that the readers learn something or gain insight or understanding. Students can write more interesting narratives by describing events or experiences that were meaningful to them. Narratives should start with the story's actions or events, rather than begin with long descriptions or introductions. Students should ensure that there is a point to each story by describing what they learned from the experience they narrate. To write an effective description, students should include sensory details, asking themselves what they saw, heard, felt or touched, smelled, and tasted during the experiences they describe. In narrative writing, the details should be **concrete** rather than **abstract**. Using concrete details enables readers to imagine everything that the writer describes.

Review Video: Narratives
Visit mometrix.com/academy and enter code: 280100

SENSORY DETAILS

Students need to use vivid descriptions when writing descriptive essays. Narratives should also include descriptions of characters, things, and events. Students should remember to describe not only the visual detail of what someone or something looks like, but details from other senses, as well. For example, they can contrast the feeling of a sea breeze to that of a mountain breeze, describe how they think something inedible would taste, and compare sounds they hear in the same location at different times of day and night. Readers have trouble visualizing images or imagining sensory impressions and feelings from abstract descriptions, so concrete descriptions make these more real.

CONCRETE VS. ABSTRACT DESCRIPTIONS IN NARRATIVE

Concrete language provides information that readers can grasp and may empathize with, while **abstract language**, which is more general, can leave readers feeling disconnected, empty, or even confused. "It was a lovely day" is abstract, but "The sun shone brightly, the sky was blue, the air felt warm, and a gentle breeze wafted across my skin" is concrete. "Ms. Couch was a good teacher" uses abstract language, giving only a general idea of the writer's opinion. But "Ms. Couch is excellent at helping us take our ideas and turn them into good essays and stories" uses concrete language, giving more specific examples of what makes Ms. Couch a good teacher. "I like writing poems but not essays" gives readers a general idea that the student prefers one genre over another, but not why. But by reading, "I like writing short poems with rhythm and rhyme, but I hate writing five-page essays that go on and on about the same ideas," readers understand that the student prefers the brevity, rhyme, and meter of short poetry over the length and redundancy of longer prose.

AUTOBIOGRAPHICAL NARRATIVES

Autobiographical narratives are narratives written by an author about an event or period in their life. Autobiographical narratives are written from one person's perspective, in first person, and often include the author's thoughts and feelings alongside their description of the event or period. Structure, style, or theme varies between different autobiographical narratives, since each narrative is personal and specific to its author and their experience.

REFLECTIVE ESSAY

A less common type of essay is the reflective essay. **Reflective essays** allow the author to reflect, or think back on, an experience and analyze what they recall. They should consider what they learned from the experience, what they could have done differently, what would have helped them during the experience, or anything else that they have realized from looking back on the experience. Reflection essays incorporate both objective reflection on one's own actions and subjective explanation of thoughts and feelings. These essays can be written for a number of experiences in a formal or informal context.

JOURNALS AND DIARIES

A **journal** is a personal account of events, experiences, feelings, and thoughts. Many people write journals to express their feelings and thoughts or to help them process experiences they have had. Since journals are **private documents** not meant to be shared with others, writers may not be concerned with grammar, spelling, or other mechanics. However, authors may write journals that they expect or hope to publish someday; in this case, they not only express their thoughts and feelings and process their experiences, but they also attend to their craft in writing them. Some authors compose journals to record a particular time period or a series of related events, such as a cancer diagnosis, treatment, surviving the disease, and how these experiences have changed or affected them. Other experiences someone might include in a journal are recovering from addiction, journeys of spiritual exploration and discovery, time spent in another country, or anything else someone wants to personally document. Journaling can also be therapeutic, as some people use journals to work through feelings of grief over loss or to wrestle with big decisions.

EXAMPLES OF DIARIES IN LITERATURE

The Diary of a Young Girl by Dutch Jew Anne Frank (1947) contains her life-affirming, nonfictional diary entries from 1942-1944 while her family hid in an attic from World War II's genocidal Nazis. *Go Ask Alice* (1971) by Beatrice Sparks is a cautionary, fictional novel in the form of diary entries by Alice, an unhappy, rebellious teen who takes LSD, runs away from home and lives with hippies, and eventually returns home. Frank's writing reveals an intelligent, sensitive, insightful girl, raised by intellectual European parents—a girl who believes in the goodness of human nature despite surrounding atrocities. Alice, influenced by early 1970s counterculture, becomes less optimistic. However, similarities can be found between them: Frank dies in a Nazi concentration camp while the fictitious Alice dies from a drug overdose. Both young women are also unable to escape their surroundings. Additionally, adolescent searches for personal identity are evident in both books.

> **Review Video: Journals, Diaries, Letters, and Blogs**
> Visit mometrix.com/academy and enter code: 432845

LETTERS

Letters are messages written to other people. In addition to letters written between individuals, some writers compose letters to the editors of newspapers, magazines, and other publications, while some write "Open Letters" to be published and read by the general public. Open letters, while intended for everyone to read, may also identify a group of people or a single person whom the letter directly addresses. In everyday use, the most-used forms are business letters and personal or friendly letters. Both kinds share common elements: business or personal letterhead stationery; the writer's return address at the top; the addressee's address next; a salutation, such as "Dear [name]" or some similar opening greeting, followed by a colon in business letters or a comma in personal letters; the body of the letter, with paragraphs as indicated; and a closing, like "Sincerely/Cordially/Best regards/etc." or "Love," in intimate personal letters.

EARLY LETTERS

The Greek word for "letter" is *epistolē*, which became the English word "epistle." The earliest letters were called epistles, including the New Testament's epistles from the apostles to the Christians. In ancient Egypt, the writing curriculum in scribal schools included the epistolary genre. Epistolary novels frame a story in the form of letters. Examples of noteworthy epistolary novels include:

- *Pamela* (1740), by 18th-century English novelist Samuel Richardson
- *Shamela* (1741), Henry Fielding's satire of *Pamela* that mocked epistolary writing.
- *Lettres persanes* (1721) by French author Montesquieu
- *The Sorrows of Young Werther* (1774) by German author Johann Wolfgang von Goethe
- *The History of Emily Montague* (1769), the first Canadian novel, by Frances Brooke
- *Dracula* (1897) by Bram Stoker
- *Frankenstein* (1818) by Mary Shelley
- *The Color Purple* (1982) by Alice Walker

67

Copyright © Mometrix Media. You have been licensed one copy of this document for personal use only. Any other reproduction or redistribution is strictly prohibited. All rights reserved.

BLOGS

The word "blog" is derived from "weblog" and refers to writing done exclusively on the internet. Readers of reputable newspapers expect quality content and layouts that enable easy reading. These expectations also apply to blogs. For example, readers can easily move visually from line to line when columns are narrow, while overly wide columns cause readers to lose their places. Blogs must also be posted with layouts enabling online readers to follow them easily. However, because the way people read on computer, tablet, and smartphone screens differs from how they read print on paper, formatting and writing blog content is more complex than writing newspaper articles. Two major principles are the bases for blog-writing rules: The first is while readers of print articles skim to estimate their length, online they must scroll down to scan; therefore, blog layouts need more subheadings, graphics, and other indications of what information follows. The second is onscreen reading can be harder on the eyes than reading printed paper, so legibility is crucial in blogs.

RULES AND RATIONALES FOR WRITING BLOGS

1. Format all posts for smooth page layout and easy scanning.
2. Column width should not be too wide, as larger lines of text can be difficult to read
3. Headings and subheadings separate text visually, enable scanning or skimming, and encourage continued reading.
4. Bullet-pointed or numbered lists enable quick information location and scanning.
5. Punctuation is critical, so beginners should use shorter sentences until confident.
6. Blog paragraphs should be far shorter—two to six sentences each—than paragraphs written on paper to enable "chunking" because reading onscreen is more difficult.
7. Sans-serif fonts are usually clearer than serif fonts, and larger font sizes are better.
8. Highlight important material and draw attention with **boldface**, but avoid overuse. Avoid hard-to-read *italics* and ALL CAPITALS.
9. Include enough blank spaces: overly busy blogs tire eyes and brains. Images not only break up text but also emphasize and enhance text and can attract initial reader attention.
10. Use background colors judiciously to avoid distracting the eye or making it difficult to read.
11. Be consistent throughout posts, since people read them in different orders.
12. Tell a story with a beginning, middle, and end.

SPECIALIZED MODES OF WRITING

EDITORIALS

Editorials are articles in newspapers, magazines, and other serial publications. Editorials express an opinion or belief belonging to the majority of the publication's leadership. This opinion or belief generally refers to a specific issue, topic, or event. These articles are authored by a member, or a small number of members, of the publication's leadership and are often written to affect their readers, such as persuading them to adopt a stance or take a particular action.

RESUMES

Resumes are brief, but formal, documents that outline an individual's experience in a certain area. Resumes are most often used for job applications. Such resumes will list the applicant's work experience, certification, and achievements or qualifications related to the position. Resumes should only include the most pertinent information. They should also use strategic formatting to highlight the applicant's most impressive experiences and achievements, ensure the document can be read quickly and easily, and to eliminate both visual clutter and excessive negative space.

REPORTS

Reports summarize the results of research, new methodology, or other developments in an academic or professional context. Reports often include details about methodology and outside influences and

factors. However, a report should focus primarily on the results of the research or development. Reports are objective and deliver information efficiently, sacrificing style for clear and effective communication.

MEMORANDA

A memorandum, also called a memo, is a formal method of communication used in professional settings. Memoranda are printed documents that include a heading listing the sender and their job title, the recipient and their job title, the date, and a specific subject line. Memoranda often include an introductory section explaining the reason and context for the memorandum. Next, a memorandum includes a section with details relevant to the topic. Finally, the memorandum will conclude with a paragraph that politely and clearly defines the sender's expectations of the recipient.

Research

RESEARCH WRITING

Writing for research is essentially writing to answer a question or a problem about a particular **research topic**. A **problem statement** is written to clearly define what a problem with the topic is before asking about how to solve the problem. A **research question** serves to ask what can be done to address the problem. Before a researcher should try to solve a problem, the researcher should spend significant time performing a **literature review** to find out what has already been learned about the topic and if there are already solutions in place. The literature review can help to re-evaluate the research question as well. If the question has not been thoroughly answered, then it is proper to do more broad research to learn about the topic and build up the body of literature. If the literature review provides plenty of background, but no practical solutions to the problem, then the research question should be targeted at solving a problem more directly. After the research has been performed, a **thesis** can act as a proposal for a solution or as a recommendation to future researchers to continue to learn more about the topic. The thesis should then be supported by significant contributing evidence to help support the proposed solution.

EXAMPLE OF RESEARCH WRITING ELEMENTS

Topic	The general idea the research is about. This is usually broader than the problem itself. <u>Example</u>: Clean Water
Problem Statement	A problem statement is a brief, clear description of a problem with the topic. <u>Example</u>: Not all villages in third-world countries have ready access to clean water.
Research Question	A research question asks a specific question about what needs to be learned or done about the problem statement. <u>Example</u>: What can local governments do to improve access to clean water?
Literature Review	A review of the body of literature by the researcher to show what is already known about the topic and the problem. If the literature review shows that the research question has already been thoroughly answered, the researcher should consider changing problem statements to something that has not been solved.
Thesis	A brief proposal of a solution to a problem. Theses do not include their own support, but are supported by later evidence. <u>Example</u>: Local governments can improve access to clean water by installing sealed rain-water collection units.
Body Paragraphs	Paragraphs focused on the primary supporting evidence for the main idea of the thesis. There are usually three body paragraphs, but there can be more if needed.
Conclusion	A final wrap-up of the research research project. The conclusion should reiterate the problem, question, thesis, and briefly mention how the main evidences support the thesis.

THE RESEARCH PROCESS

Researchers should prepare some information before gathering sources. Researchers who have chosen a **research question** should choose key words or names that pertain to their question. They should also identify what type of information and sources they are looking for. Researchers should consider whether secondary or primary sources will be most appropriate for their research project. As researchers find credible and appropriate sources, they should be prepared to adjust the scope of their research question or topic in response to the information and insights they gather.

USING SOURCES AND SYNTHESIZING INFORMATION

As researchers find potential sources for their research project, it is important to keep a **record** of the material they find and note how each source may impact their work. When taking these notes, researchers should keep their research question or outline in mind and consider how their chosen references would complement their discussion. **Literature reviews** and **annotated bibliographies** are helpful tools for evaluating sources, as they require the researcher to consider the qualities and offerings of the sources they choose to use. These tools also help researchers synthesize the information they find.

SYNTHESIZING INFORMATION

Synthesizing information requires the researcher to integrate sources and their own thoughts by quoting, paraphrasing, or summarizing outside information in their research project. Synthesizing information indicates that the research complements the writer's claims, ensures that the ideas in the composition flow logically, and makes including small details and quotes easier. Paraphrasing is one of the simplest ways to integrate a source. **Paraphrasing** allows the writer to support their ideas with research while presenting the information in their own words, rather than using the source's original wording. Paraphrasing also allows the writer to reference the source's main ideas instead of specific details. While paraphrasing does not require the writer to quote the source, it still entails a direct reference to the source, meaning that any paraphrased material still requires a citation.

CITING SOURCES

While researchers should combine research with their own ideas, the information and ideas that come from outside sources should be attributed to the author of the source. When conducting research, it is helpful to record the publication information for each source so that **citations** can be easily added within the composition. Keeping a close record of the source of each idea in a composition or project is helpful for avoiding plagiarism, as both direct and indirect references require documentation.

PLAGIARISM

Understanding what is considered to be plagiarism is important to preventing unintentional plagiarism. Using another person's work in any way without proper attribution is **plagiarism**. However, it is easy to mistakenly commit plagiarism by improperly citing a source or creating a citation that is not intended for the way the source was used. Even when an honest attempt to attribute information is made, small errors can still result in plagiarized content. For this reason, it is important to create citations carefully and review citations before submitting or publishing research. It is also possible to plagiarize one's own work. This occurs when a writer has published work with one title and purpose and then attempts to publish it again as new material under a new title or purpose.

LITERATURE REVIEW

One of the two main parts of a literature review is searching through existing literature. The other is actually writing the review. Researchers must take care not to get lost in the information and inhibit progress toward their research goal. A good precaution is to write out the research question and keep it nearby. It is also wise to make a search plan and establish a time limit in advance. Finding a seemingly endless number of references indicates a need to revisit the research question because the topic is too broad. Finding too little material means that the research topic is too narrow. With new or cutting-edge research, one may find that nobody has investigated this particular question. This requires systematic searching, using abstracts in periodicals for an overview of available literature, research papers or other specific sources to explore its reference, and references in books and other sources.

When searching published literature on a research topic, one must take thorough notes. It is common to find a reference that could be useful later in the research project, but is not needed yet. In situations like this, it is helpful to make a note of the reference so it will be easy to find later. These notes can be grouped in a word processing document, which also allows for easy compiling of links and quotes from internet research. Researchers should explore the internet regularly, view resources for their research often, learn how to use resources correctly and efficiently, experiment with resources available within the disciplines, open and examine databases, become familiar with reference desk materials, find publications with abstracts of articles and books on one's topic, use papers' references to locate the most utile journals and important authors, identify keywords for refining and narrowing database searches, and peruse library catalogues online for available sources—all while taking notes.

As one searches for references, one will gradually develop an overview of the body of literature available for his or her subject. This signals the time to prepare for writing the literature review. The researcher should assemble his or her notes along with copies of all the journal articles and all the books he or she has acquired. Then one should write the research question again at the top of a page and list below it all of the author names and keywords discovered while searching. It is also helpful to observe whether any groups or pairs of these stand out. These activities are parts of structuring one's literature review—the first step for writing a thesis, dissertation, or research paper. Writers should rewrite their work as necessary rather than expecting to write only one draft. However, stopping to edit along the way can distract from the momentum of writing the first draft. If the writer is dissatisfied with a certain part of the draft, it may be better to skip to a later portion of the paper and revisit the problem section at another time.

BODY AND CONCLUSION IN LITERATURE REVIEW

The first step of a literature review paper is to create a rough draft. The next step is to edit: rewrite for clarity, eliminate unnecessary verbiage, and change terminology that could confuse readers. After editing, a writer should ask others to read and give feedback. Additionally, the writer should read the paper aloud to hear how it sounds, editing as needed. Throughout a literature review, the writer should not only summarize and comment on each source reviewed, but should also relate these findings to the original research question. The writer should explicitly state in the conclusion how the research question and pertinent literature interaction is developed throughout the body, reflecting on insights gained through the process.

> **Review Video: Drafting Conclusions**
> Visit mometrix.com/academy and enter code: 209408

SUMMARIES AND ABSTRACTS

When preparing to submit or otherwise publish research, it may be necessary to compose a summary or abstract to accompany the research composition.

A summary is a brief description of the contents of a longer work that provides an overview of the work and may include its most important details. One common type of summary is an abstract. Abstracts are specialized summaries that are most commonly used in the context of research. Abstracts may include details such as the purpose for the research, the researcher's methodology, and the most significant results of the research. Abstracts sometimes include sections and headings, where most summaries are limited to one or a few paragraphs with no special groupings.

EDITING AND REVISING

After composing a rough draft of a research paper, the writer should **edit** it. The purpose of the paper is to communicate the answer to one's research question in an efficient and effective manner. The writing should be as **concise** and **clear** as possible, and the style should also be consistent. Editing is often easier to do after writing the first draft rather than during it, as taking time between writing and editing allows writers to be more objective. If the paper includes an abstract and an introduction, the writer should compose these after writing the rest, when he or she will have a better grasp of the theme and arguments. Not all readers understand technical terminology or long words, so writers should use these sparingly. Finally, writers should consult a writing and style guide address any industry- or institution-specific issues that may arise as they edit.

> **Review Video: Revising and Editing**
> Visit mometrix.com/academy and enter code: 674181

Sources for Research

PRIMARY SOURCES

In literature review, one may examine both primary and secondary sources. Primary sources contain original information that was witnessed, gathered, or otherwise produced by the source's author. Primary sources can include firsthand accounts, found in sources such as books, autobiographies, transcripts, speeches, videos, photos, and personal journals or diaries. Primary sources may also include records of information, such as government documents, or personally-conducted research in sources like reports and essays. They may be found in academic books, journals and other periodicals, and authoritative databases. Using primary sources allows researchers to develop their own conclusions about the subject. Primary sources are also reliable for finding information about a person or their personal accounts and experiences. Primary sources such as photos, videos, audio recordings, transcripts, and government documents are often reliable, as they are usually objective and can be used to confirm information from other sources.

SECONDARY SOURCES

Secondary sources are sources that reference information originally provided by another source. The original source may be cited, quoted, paraphrased, or described in a secondary source. Secondary sources may be articles, essays, videos, or books found in periodicals, magazines, newspapers, films, databases, or websites. A secondary source can be used to reference another researcher's analysis or conclusion from a primary source. This information can inform the researcher of the existing discussions regarding their subject. These types of sources may also support the researcher's claims by providing a credible argument that contributes to the researcher's argument. Secondary sources may also highlight connections between primary sources or criticize both primary and other secondary sources. These types of secondary sources are valuable because they provide information and conclusions the researcher may not have considered or found, otherwise.

> **Review Video: Primary and Secondary Sources**
> Visit mometrix.com/academy and enter code: 383328

TYPES OF SOURCES

- **Textbooks** are specialized materials that are designed to thoroughly instruct readers on a particular topic. Textbooks often include features such as a table of contents, visuals, an index, a glossary, headings, and practice questions and exercises.
- **Newspapers** are collections of several written pieces and are primarily used to distribute news stories to their audience. In addition to news articles, newspapers may also include advertisements or pieces meant to entertain their audience, such as comic strips, columns, and letters from readers. Newspapers are written for a variety of audiences, as they are published on both the local and national levels.
- **Manuals** are instructional documents that accompany a product or explain an important procedure. Manuals include a table of contents, guidelines, and instructional content. Instructional manuals often include information about safe practices, risks, and product warranty. The instructions in manuals are often presented as step-by-step instructions, as they are meant to help users properly use a product or complete a task.
- **Electronic texts** are written documents that are read digitally and are primarily accessed online or through a network. Many electronic texts have characteristics similar to printed texts, such as a table of contents, publication information, a main text, and supplemental materials. However, electronic texts are more interactive and can be navigated more quickly. Electronic texts can also provide more accessibility, as they can be easily resized or narrated by text-to-speech software.

FINDING SOURCES

Finding sources for a research project may be intimidating or difficult. There are numerous sources available, and several research tools to help researchers find them. Starting with one of these tools can help narrow down the number of sources a researcher is working with at one time.

- **Libraries** house independent, printed publications that are organized by subject. This makes finding sources easy, since researchers can visit sections with sources relevant to their topic and immediately see what sources are available. Many libraries also offer printed journals and collections that include sources related to a common subject or written by the same author.

- **Databases** offer digital access to sources from a wide variety of libraries and online containers. To use a database, users search for keywords related to their topic or the type of source they want to use. The database then lists results related to or featuring those key words. Users can narrow their results using filters that will limit their results based on factors such as publication year, source type, or whether the sources are peer-reviewed. Database search results also list individual articles and methods of accessing the article directly. While databases help users find sources, they do not guarantee users access to each source.
- **Academic Journals** are collections of articles that cover a particular topic or fit within a certain category. These journals are often offered both online and in print. Academic journals typically contain peer-reviewed works or works that have undergone another type of reviewing process.

CREDIBILITY

There are innumerable primary and secondary sources available in print and online. However, not every published or posted source is appropriate for a research project. When finding sources, the researcher must know how to evaluate each source for credibility and relevance. Not only must the sources be reliable and relevant to the research subject, but they must also be appropriate and help form an answer to the research question. As researchers progress in their research and composition, the relevance of each source will become clear. Appropriate sources will contribute valuable information and arguments to the researcher's own thoughts and conclusions, providing useful evidence to bolster the researcher's claims. The researcher has the freedom to choose which sources they reference or even change their research topic and question in response to the sources they find. However, the researcher should not use unreliable sources, and determining a source's credibility is not always easy.

CONSIDERATIONS FOR EVALUATING THE CREDIBILITY OF A SOURCE
- The author and their purpose for writing the source
- The author's qualifications to write on the topic
- Whether the source is peer-reviewed or included in a scholarly publication
- The publisher
- The target audience
- The jargon or dialect the source is written in (e.g., academic, technical)
- The presence of bias or manipulation of information
- The date of publication
- The author's use of other sources to support their claims
- Whether any outside sources are cited appropriately in the source
- The accuracy of information presented

AUTHOR'S PURPOSE AND CREDIBILITYF

Knowing who wrote a source and why they wrote it is important to determining whether a source is appropriate for a research project. The author should be qualified to write on the subject of the material. Their purpose may be to inform their audience of information, to present and defend an analysis, or even to criticize a work or other argument. The researcher must decide whether the author's purpose makes the source appropriate to use. The source's container and publisher are important to note because they indicate the source's reputability and whether other qualified individuals have reviewed the information in the source. Credible secondary sources should also reference other sources, primary or secondary, that support or inform the source's content. Evaluating the accuracy of the information or the presence of bias in a source will require careful reading and critical thinking on the part of the researcher. However, a source with excellent credentials may still contain pieces of inaccurate information or bias, so it is the researcher's responsiblilty to be careful in their use of each source.

INTEGRATING REFERENCES AND QUOTATIONS

In research papers, one can include studies whose conclusions agree with one's position (Reed 284; Becker and Fagen 93), as well as studies that disagree (Limbaugh 442, Beck 69) by including parenthetical citations as demonstrated in this sentence. Quotations should be selective: writers should compose an original sentence and incorporate only a few words from a research source. If students cannot use more original words than quotation, they are likely padding their compositions. However, including quotations appropriately increases the credibility of the writer and their argument.

PROPERLY INTEGRATING QUOTATIONS

When using sources in a research paper, it is important to integrate information so that the flow of the composition is not interrupted as the two compositions are combined. When quoting outside sources, it is necessary to lead into the quote and ensure that the whole sentence is logical, is grammatically correct, and flows well. Below is an example of an incorrectly integrated quote.

> During the Industrial Revolution, many unions organized labor strikes "child labor, unregulated working conditions, and excessive working hours" in America.

Below is the same sentence with a properly integrated quote.

> During the Industrial Revolution, many unions organized labor strikes to protest the presence of "child labor, unregulated working conditions, and excessive working hours" in America.

In the first example, the connection between "strikes" and the quoted list is unclear. In the second example, the phrase "to protest the presence of" link the ideas together and successfully creates a suitable place for the quotation.

When quoting sources, writers should work quotations and references seamlessly into their sentences instead of interrupting the flow of their own argument to summarize a source. Summarizing others' content is often a ploy to bolster word counts. Writing that analyzes the content, evaluates it, and synthesizes material from various sources demonstrates critical thinking skills and is thus more valuable.

PROPERLY INCORPORATING OUTSIDE SOURCES

Writers do better to include short quotations rather than long. For example, quoting six to eight long passages in a 10-page paper is excessive. It is also better to avoid wording like "This quotation shows," "As you can see from this quotation," or "It talks about." These are amateur, feeble efforts to interact with other authors' ideas. Also, writing about sources and quotations wastes words that should be used to develop one's own ideas. Quotations should be used to stimulate discussion rather than taking its place. Ending a paragraph, section, or paper with a quotation is not incorrect per se, but using it to prove a point, without including anything more in one's own words regarding the point or subject, suggests a lack of critical thinking about the topic and consideration of multiple alternatives. It can also be a tactic to dissuade readers from challenging one's propositions. Writers should include references and quotations that challenge as well as support their thesis statements. Presenting evidence on both sides of an issue makes it easier for reasonably skeptical readers to agree with a writer's viewpoint.

CITING SOURCES

Formal research writers must **cite all sources** used—books, articles, interviews, conversations, and anything else that contributed to the research. One reason is to **avoid plagiarism** and give others credit for their ideas. Another reason is to help readers find the sources consulted in the research and access more information about the subject for further reading and research. Additionally, citing sources helps to make a paper academically authoritative. To prepare, research writers should keep a running list of sources consulted, in an electronic file or on file cards. For every source used, the writer needs specific information. For books, a writer needs to record the author's and editor's name, book title, publication date, city, and publisher name. For articles, one needs the author name, article title, journal (or magazine or newspaper) name, volume and issue number, publication date, and page numbers. For electronic resources, a writer will need the author's name, article information plus the URL, database name, name of the database's publisher, and the date of access.

COMMON REFERENCE STYLES

Three common reference styles are **MLA** (Modern Language Association), **APA** (American Psychological Association), and **Turabian** (created by author Kate Turabian, also known as the Chicago Manual of Style). Each style formats citation information differently. Professors and instructors often specify that students use one of these. Generally, APA style is used in psychology and sociology papers, and MLA style is used in English literature papers and similar scholarly projects. To understand how these styles differ, consider an imaginary article cited in each of these styles. This article is titled "Ten Things You Won't Believe Dragons Do," written by author Andra Gaines, included in the journal *Studies in Fantasy Fiction*, and published by Quest for Knowledge Publishing.

MLA:

Gaines, Andra. "Ten Things You Won't Believe Dragons Do". *Studies in Fantasy Fiction*, vol. 3, no. 8, Quest for Knowledge Publishing, 21 Aug. 2019.

APA:

Gaines, A. (2019). Ten Things You Won't Believe Dragons Do. *Studies in Fantasy Fiction*, *3(8)*, 42-65.

CHICAGO:

Gaines, Andra. "Ten Things You Won't Believe Dragons Do," *Studies in Fantasy Fiction* 3, no. 8 (2019): 42-65.

Within each of these styles, citations, though they vary according to the type of source and how its used, generally follow a structure and format similar to those above. For example, citations for whole books will probably not include a container title or a volume number, but will otherwise look very similar.

> **Review Video: Citing Sources**
> Visit mometrix.com/academy and enter code: 993637

Reading Process and Comprehension

Prose

COMMON FORMS OF PROSE FICTION

HISTORICAL FICTION

Historical fiction is set in particular historical periods, including prehistoric and mythological. Examples include Walter Scott's *Rob Roy* and *Ivanhoe*; Leo Tolstoy's *War and Peace*; Robert Graves' *I, Claudius*; Mary Renault's *The King Must Die* and *The Bull from the Sea* (an historical novel using Greek mythology); Virginia Woolf's *Orlando* and *Between the Acts*; and John Dos Passos's *U.S.A* trilogy. **Picaresque** novels recount episodic adventures of a rogue protagonist or *pícaro*, like Miguel de Cervantes' *Don Quixote* or Henry Fielding's *Tom Jones*. **Gothic** novels originated as a reaction against 18th-century Enlightenment rationalism, featuring horror, mystery, superstition, madness, supernatural elements, and revenge. Early examples include Horace Walpole's *Castle of Otranto*, Matthew Gregory Lewis' *Monk*, Mary Shelley's *Frankenstein*, and Bram Stoker's *Dracula*. In America, Edgar Allan Poe wrote many Gothic works. Contemporary novelist Anne Rice has penned many Gothic novels under the pseudonym A. N. Roquelaure. **Psychological** novels, originating in 17th-century France, explore characters' motivations. Examples include Abbé Prévost's *Manon Lescaut*; George Eliot's novels; Fyodor Dostoyevsky's *Crime and Punishment*; Tolstoy's *Anna Karenina*; Gustave Flaubert's *Madame Bovary*; and the novels of Henry James, James Joyce, and Vladimir Nabokov.

NOVELS OF MANNERS

Novels of manners are fictional stories that observe, explore, and analyze the social behaviors of a specific time and place. While deep psychological themes are more universal across different historical periods and countries, the manners of a particular society are shorter-lived and more varied; the novel of manners captures these societal details. Novels of manners can also be regarded as symbolically representing, in artistic form, certain established and secure social orders. Characteristics of novels of manners include descriptions of a society with defined behavioral codes; language that uses standardized, impersonal formulas; and inhibition of emotional expression, as contrasted with the strong emotions expressed in romantic or sentimental novels. Jane Austen's detailed descriptions of English society and characters struggling with the definitions and restrictions placed on them by society are excellent models of the novel of manners. In the 20th century, Evelyn Waugh's *Handful of Dust* is a novel of social manners, and his *Sword of Honour* trilogy contains novels of military manners. Another 20th-century example is *The Unbearable Bassington* by Saki (the pen name of writer H. H. Munro), focusing on Edwardian society.

WESTERN-WORLD SENTIMENTAL NOVELS

Sentimental love novels originated in the movement of Romanticism. Eighteenth-century examples of novels that emphasize the emotional aspect of love include Samuel Richardson's *Pamela* (1740) and Jean-Jacques Rousseau's *Nouvelle Héloïse* (1761). Also in the 18th century, Laurence Sterne's novel *Tristram Shandy* (1760-1767) is an example of a novel with elements of sentimentality. The Victorian era's rejection of emotionalism caused the term "sentimental" to have undesirable connotations. However, even non-sentimental novelists such as William Makepeace Thackeray and Charles Dickens incorporated sentimental elements in their writing. A 19th-century author of genuinely sentimental novels was Mrs. Henry Wood (e.g., *East Lynne,* 1861). In the 20th century, Erich Segal's sentimental novel *Love Story* (1970) was a popular bestseller.

EPISTOLARY NOVELS

Epistolary novels are told in the form of letters written by their characters rather than in typical narrative form. Samuel Richardson, the best-known author of epistolary novels like *Pamela* (1740) and *Clarissa* (1748), widely influenced early Romantic epistolary novels throughout Europe that freely expressed emotions. Richardson, a printer, published technical manuals on letter-writing for young gentlewomen; his epistolary novels were fictional extensions of those nonfictional instructional books. Nineteenth-century English author Wilkie Collins' *The Moonstone* (1868) was a mystery written in epistolary form. By the 20th century, the format of well-composed written letters came to be regarded as artificial and outmoded. A 20th-century evolution of letters was tape-recording transcripts, such as in French playwright Samuel Beckett's drama *Krapp's Last Tape.* Though evoking modern alienation, Beckett still created a sense of fictional characters' direct communication without author intervention as Richardson had.

PASTORAL NOVELS

Pastoral novels lyrically idealize country life as idyllic and utopian, akin to the Garden of Eden. *Daphnis and Chloe*, written by Greek novelist Longus around the second or third century, influenced Elizabethan pastoral romances like Thomas Lodge's *Rosalynde* (1590), which inspired Shakespeare's *As You Like It*, and Philip Sidney's *Arcadia* (1590). Jacques-Henri Bernardin de St. Pierre's French work *Paul et Virginie* (1787) demonstrated the early Romantic view of the innocence and goodness of nature. Though the style lost popularity by the 20th century, pastoral elements can still be seen in novels like *The Rainbow* (1915) and *Lady Chatterley's Lover* (1928), both by D. H. Lawrence. Growing realism transformed pastoral writing into less ideal and more dystopian, distasteful and ironic depictions of country life in George Eliot's and Thomas Hardy's novels. Saul Bellow's novel *Herzog* (1964) may demonstrate how urban ills highlight an alternative pastoral ideal. The pastoral style is commonly thought to be overly idealized and outdated today, as seen in Stella Gibbons' pastoral satire, Cold Comfort Farm (1932).

BILDUNGSROMAN

Bildungsroman is German for "education novel." This term is also used in English to describe "apprenticeship" novels focusing on coming-of-age stories, including youth's struggles and searches for things such as identity, spiritual understanding, or the meaning in life. Johann Wolfgang von Goethe's *Wilhelm Meisters Lehrjahre* (1796) is credited as the origin of this genre. Two of Charles Dickens' novels, *David Copperfield* (1850) and *Great Expectations* (1861), also fit this form. H. G. Wells wrote *bildungsromans* about questing for apprenticeships to address the complications of modern life in *Joan and Peter* (1918) and from a Utopian perspective in *The Dream* (1924). School *bildungsromans* include Thomas Hughes' *Tom Brown's School Days* (1857) and Alain-Fournier's *Le Grand Meaulnes* (1913). Many Hermann Hesse novels, including *Demian, Steppenwolf, Siddhartha, Magister Ludi,* and *Beneath the Wheel* are *bildungsromans* about a struggling, searching youth. Samuel Butler's *The Way of All Flesh* (1903) and James Joyce's *A Portrait of the Artist as a Young Man* (1916) are two modern examples. Variations include J. D. Salinger's *The Catcher in the Rye* (1951), set both within and beyond school, and William Golding's *Lord of the Flies* (1955), a novel not set in a school but one that is a coming-of-age story nonetheless.

ROMAN À CLEF

Roman à clef, French for "novel with a key," refers to books that require a real-life frame of reference, or key, for full comprehension. In Geoffrey Chaucer's *Canterbury Tales,* the Nun's Priest's Tale contains details that confuse readers unaware of history about the Earl of Bolingbroke's involvement in an assassination plot. Other literary works fitting this form include John Dryden's political satirical poem "Absalom and Achitophel" (1681), Jonathan Swift's satire "A Tale of a Tub" (1704), and George Orwell's political allegory *Animal Farm* (1945), all of which cannot be understood completely without knowing their camouflaged historical contents. *Roman à clefs* disguise truths too dangerous for authors to state directly. Readers must know about the enemies of D. H. Lawrence and Aldous Huxley to appreciate their respective novels: *Aaron's Rod* (1922) and *Point Counter Point* (1928). Marcel Proust's *Remembrance of*

Things Past (À la recherché du temps perdu, 1871-1922) is informed by his social context. James Joyce's *Finnegans Wake* is an enormous *roman à clef* containing multitudinous personal references.

> **Review Video: Major Forms of Prose**
> Visit mometrix.com/academy and enter code: 565543

OTHER COMMON TYPES OF PROSE

- A **narrative** is any composition that tells a story. Narratives have characters, settings, and a structure. Narratives may be fiction or nonfiction stories and may follow a linear or nonlinear structure. The purpose of a narrative is generally to entertain, but nonfiction narratives can be informative, as well. Narratives also appear in a variety of structures and formats.
- **Biographies** are books written about another person's life. Biographies can be valuable historical resources. Though they provide a narrow view of the relevant time period and culture, their specificity can also provide a unique context for that period or culture. Biographies, especially those whose subject was a well-known and influential figure, can provide a more complete picture of the figure's life or contributions. Biographies can also serve as a source of inspiration or communicate a moral because of their focus on one person over an extended period of time.
- **Myths**, or stories from mythology, exist in most ancient cultures and continue to influence modern cultures. Mythology is so influential that it has even inspired numerous pieces of modern literature and media in popular culture. While popular culture most clearly references mythology from the Ancient Greek and Roman cultures, literature has been influenced by mythologies from around the entire world. Since mythology is so prevalent in ancient literature, it makes sense that universal themes and morals often appear in mythology and even drive some myths. This suggests connections between cultures through the stories they pass down.
- **Fables** are short, didactic stories that typically feature imaginary creatures or talking animals. The famous story "The Tortoise and the Hare" is a fable. Fables are still told and used today because of their universally understandable morals and characters, making them suitable for children's literature and media.
- **Fairy tales** are stories that involve fictional creatures or realistic characters with fantastical traits and abilities. Fairy tales often end happily and depict the victory of good over evil. The plots and characters in fairy tales are often far-fetched and whimsical.
- **Folk Tales** are stories that have withstood time and are usually popular in a particular region or culture. Folk tales often depict the clever success of a common person, though the story may, alternatively, end poorly for the protagonist. Folk tales are easily confused with fairytales because fairytales can be a type of folk tale.
- **Legends** are stories that typically focus on one character and highlight their victory over a particular enemy or obstacle. Legends often feature some facts or are inspired by true events, but are still understood to be either exaggerated or partially fictional. Heroes are often the protagonists of legends as they often save or protect others as they conquer enemies and obstacles.
- A **short story** is a fictional narrative that is shorter than a novel. However, there is not a definite page or word count that defines the short story category. Short stories tend to focus on one or few elements of a story in order to efficiently tell the story. Though they are often brief, short stories may still contain a moral or impact their readers.

COMMON GENRES IN PROSE

- The **mystery** genre includes stories with plots that follow a protagonist as they work to solve an unexplained situation, such as a murder, disappearance, or robbery. Protagonists of mysteries may be hired professionals or amateurs who solve the mystery despite their lack of experience and resources. Mysteries allow the reader to solve the case along with the protagonist, and often grant the reader an advantageous perspective, creating dramatic irony. The *Sherlock Holmes* novels by Sir Arthur Conan Doyle are examples of mystery novels.
- **Science Fiction** is a genre that is based on the manipulation and exaggeration of real scientific discoveries and processes. These works are speculative and frequently depict a world where scientific discoveries and society have progressed beyond the point reached at the time of the work's creation. Works of science fiction often take place in a distant location or time, allowing for the dramatic advancements and conveniences they often depict. *Dune*, written by Frank Herbert, is an example of a science-fiction novel.
- The **fantasy** genre includes stories that feature imaginary creatures and supernatural abilities, but often take place in settings that resemble real places and cultures in history. Fantasy novels usually follow a gifted protagonist from humble beginnings as they embark on a quest, journey, or adventure and encounter mystical beings and personally challenging obstacles. Common themes in the fantasy genre include personal growth, good versus evil, and the value of the journey. J.R.R. Tolkien's *The Lord of the Rings* trilogy belongs to the fantasy genre.
- **Realistic fiction** describes fictional narratives that include events and characters that do not exist, but could appear in reality. Within the narrative, these characters and events may be depicted in real places. For example, Pip, the protagonist of Charles Dickens's *Great Expectations*, was not a real person, but the novel shows him living in London, England for much of his young adulthood. Realistic fiction contains no far-fetched or impossible elements and presents situations that can or do occur in real life. A contemporary example of realistic fiction is *Wonder* by R.J. Palacio.
- **Historical fiction** includes works that take place in the past and model their setting after real historical cultures, societies, and time periods. These works may include real historical figures and events, but they also may not. Works of historical fiction must be fully informed by the period and location they are set in, meaning both the major and minor details of the work must be historically compatible with the work's setting. Examples of historical fiction include Kathryn Stockett's *The Help* and Markus Zusak's *The Book Thief*.
- The phrase **Literary Nonfiction** describes nonfiction narratives that present true facts and events in a way that entertains readers and displays creativity. Literary nonfiction, also called creative nonfiction, may resemble fiction in its style and flow, but the truth of the events it describes sets it apart from fictional literature. Different types of books may be considered literary nonfiction, such as biographies, if they appear to employ creativity in their writing. An example of literary nonfiction is *The Immortal Life of Henrietta Lacks* by Rebecca Skloot.

REALISM AND SATIRE

REALISM

Realism is a literary form with the goal of representing reality as faithfully as possible. Its genesis in Western literature was a reaction against the sentimentality and extreme emotionalism of the works written during the Romantic literary movement, which championed feelings and emotional expression. Realists focused in great detail on immediacy of time and place, on specific actions of their characters, and the justifiable consequences of those actions. Some techniques of realism include writing in vernacular (conversational language), using specific dialects, and placing an emphasis on character rather than plot. Realistic literature also often addresses ethical issues. Historically, realistic works have often concentrated on the middle classes of the authors' societies. Realists eschew treatments that are too dramatic or sensationalistic as exaggerations of the reality that they strive to portray as closely as they are able. Influenced by his own bleak past, Fyodor Dostoevsky wrote several novels, such as *Crime and Punishment* (1866) that shunned romantic ideals and sought to portray a stark reality. Henry James was a prominent writer of realism in novels such as *Daisy Miller* (1879). Samuel Clemens (Mark Twain) skillfully represented the language and culture of lower-class Mississippi in his novel *The Adventures of Huckleberry Finn* (1885).

SATIRE

Satire uses sarcasm, irony, and humor as social criticism to lampoon human folly. Unlike realism, which intends to depict reality as it exists without exaggeration, satire often involves creating situations or ideas that deliberately exaggerate reality to appear ridiculous to illuminate flawed behaviors. Ancient Roman satirists included Horace and Juvenal. Alexander Pope's poem "The Rape of the Lock" satirized the values of fashionable members of the 18th-century upper-middle class, which Pope found shallow and trivial. The theft of a lock of hair from a young woman is blown out of proportion: the poem's characters regard it as seriously as they would a rape. Irishman Jonathan Swift satirized British society, politics, and religion in works like "A Modest Proposal" and *Gulliver's Travels*. In "A Modest Proposal," Swift used essay form and mock-serious tone, satirically "proposing" cannibalism of babies and children as a solution to poverty and overpopulation. He satirized petty political disputes in *Gulliver's Travels*.

Poetry

POETRY TERMINOLOGY

Unlike prose, which traditionally (except in forms like stream of consciousness) consists of complete sentences connected into paragraphs, poetry is written in **verses**. These may form complete sentences, clauses, or phrases. Poetry may be written with or without rhyme. It can be metered, following a particular rhythmic pattern such as iambic, dactylic, spondaic, trochaic, or **anapestic**, or may be without regular meter. The terms **iamb** and **trochee**, among others, identify stressed and unstressed syllables in each verse. Meter is also described by the number of beats or stressed syllables per verse: **dimeter** (2), **trimeter** (3), **tetrameter** (4), **pentameter** (5), and so forth. Using the symbol ◡ to denote unstressed and / to denote stressed syllables, **iambic** = ◡/; **trochaic** = /◡; **spondaic** =//; **dactylic** =/◡◡; **anapestic** =◡◡/. **Rhyme schemes** identify which lines rhyme, such as ABAB, ABCA, AABA, and so on. Poetry with neither rhyme nor meter is called **free verse**. Poems may be in free verse, metered but unrhymed, rhymed but without meter, or using both rhyme and meter. In English, the most common meter is iambic pentameter. Unrhymed iambic pentameter is called **blank verse**.

MAJOR FORMS OF POETRY

From man's earliest days, he expressed himself with poetry. A large percentage of the surviving literature from ancient times is in **epic poetry**, utilized by Homer and other Greco-Roman poets. Epic poems typically recount heroic deeds and adventures, using stylized language and combining dramatic and lyrical conventions. **Epistolary poems**, poems that are written and read as letters, also developed in ancient times. In the fourteenth and fifteenth centuries, the **ballad** became a popular convention. Ballads often follow a rhyme scheme and meter and focus on subjects such as love, death, and religion. Many ballads tell stories, and several modern ballads are put to music. From these early conventions, numerous other poetic forms developed, such as **elegies**, **odes**, and **pastoral poems**. Elegies are mourning poems written in three parts: lament, praise of the deceased, and solace for loss. Odes evolved from songs to the typical poem of the Romantic time period, expressing strong feelings and contemplative thoughts. Pastoral poems idealize nature and country living. Poetry can also be used to make short, pithy statements. **Epigrams** (memorable rhymes with one or two lines) and **limericks** (two lines of iambic dimeter followed by two lines of iambic dimeter and another of iambic trimeter) are known for humor and wit.

HAIKU

Haiku was originally a Japanese poetry form. In the 13th century, haiku was the opening phrase of renga, a 100-stanza oral poem. By the 16th century, haiku diverged into a separate short poem. When Western writers discovered haiku, the form became popular in English, as well as other languages. A haiku has 17 syllables, traditionally distributed across three lines as 5/7/5, with a pause after the first or second line. Haiku are syllabic and unrhymed. Haiku philosophy and technique are that brevity's compression forces writers to express images concisely, depict a moment in time, and evoke illumination and enlightenment. An example is 17th-century haiku master Matsuo Basho's classic: "An old silent pond... / A frog jumps into the pond, / splash! Silence again." Modern American poet Ezra Pound revealed the influence of haiku in his two-line poem "In a Station of the Metro." In this poem, line 1 has 12 syllables (combining the syllable count of the first two lines of a haiku) and line 2 has 7, but it still preserves haiku's philosophy and imagistic technique: "The apparition of these faces in the crowd; / Petals on a wet, black bough."

SONNETS

The sonnet traditionally has 14 lines of iambic pentameter, tightly organized around a theme. The Petrarchan sonnet, named for 14th-century Italian poet Petrarch, has an eight-line stanza, the octave, and a six-line stanza, the sestet. There is a change or turn, known as the volta, between the eighth and ninth verses, setting up the sestet's answer or summary. The rhyme scheme is ABBA/ABBA/CDECDE or CDCDCD. The English or Shakespearean sonnet has three quatrains and one couplet, with the rhyme scheme ABAB/CDCD/EFEF/GG. This format better suits English, which has fewer rhymes than Italian. The final couplet often contrasts sharply with the preceding quatrains, as in Shakespeare's sonnets—for example, Sonnet 130, "My mistress' eyes are nothing like the sun...And yet, by heaven, I think my love as rare / As any she belied with false compare." Variations on the sonnet form include Edmund Spenser's Spenserian sonnet in the 16th century, John Milton's Miltonic sonnet in the 17th century, and sonnet sequences. Sonnet sequences are seen in works such as John Donne's *La Corona* and Elizabeth Barrett Browning's *Sonnets from the Portuguese*.

> **Review Video: Structural Elements of Poetry**
> Visit mometrix.com/academy and enter code: 265216

Poetic Themes and Devices

CARPE DIEM TRADITION IN POETRY

Carpe diem is Latin for "seize the day." A long poetic tradition, it advocates making the most of time because it passes swiftly and life is short. It is found in multiple languages, including Latin, Torquato Tasso's Italian, Pierre de Ronsard's French, and Edmund Spenser's English, and is often used in seduction to argue for indulging in earthly pleasures. Roman poet Horace's Ode 1.11 tells a younger woman, Leuconoe, to enjoy the present, not worrying about inevitable aging. Two Renaissance Metaphysical Poets, Andrew Marvell and Robert Herrick, treated *carpe diem* more as a call to action. In "To His Coy Mistress," Marvell points out that time is fleeting, arguing for love, and concluding that because they cannot stop time, they may as well defy it, getting the most out of the short time they have. In "To the Virgins, to Make Much of Time," Herrick advises young women to take advantage of their good fortune in being young by getting married before they become too old to attract men and have babies.

"To His Coy Mistress" begins, "Had we but world enough, and time, / This coyness, lady, were no crime." Using imagery, Andrew Marvell describes leisure they could enjoy if time were unlimited. Arguing for seduction, he continues famously, "But at my back I always hear/Time's winged chariot hurrying near; / And yonder all before us lie / Deserts of vast eternity." He depicts time as turning beauty to death and decay. Contradictory images in "amorous birds of prey" and "tear our pleasures with rough strife / Through the iron gates of life" overshadow romance with impending death, linking present pleasure with mortality and spiritual values with moral considerations. Marvell's concluding couplet summarizes *carpe diem*: "Thus, though we cannot make our sun / Stand still, yet we will make him run." "To the Virgins, to Make Much of Time" begins with the famous "Gather ye rosebuds while ye may." Rather than seduction to live for the present, Robert Herrick's experienced persona advises young women's future planning: "Old time is still a-flying / And this same flower that smiles today, / Tomorrow will be dying."

EFFECT OF STRUCTURE ON MEANING IN POETRY

The way a poem is structured can affect its meaning. Different structural choices can change the way a reader understands a poem, so poets are careful to ensure that the form they use reflects the message they want to convey. The main structural elements in poetry include lines and stanzas. The number of lines within a stanza and the number of stanzas vary between different poems, but some poetic forms require a poem to have a certain number of lines and stanzas. Some of these forms also require each line to conform to a certain meter, or number and pattern of syllables. Many forms are associated with a certain topic or tone because of their meter. Poetic forms include sonnets, concrete poems, haiku, and villanelles. Another popular form of poetry is free verse, which is poetry that does not conform to a particular meter or rhyme scheme.

The arrangement of lines and stanzas determines the speed at which a poem is read. Long lines are generally read more quickly since the reader is often eager to reach the end of the line and does not have to stop to find the next word. Short lines cause the reader to briefly pause and look to the next line, so their reading is slowed. These effects often contribute to the meaning a reader gleans from a poem, so poets aim to make the line length compatible with the tone of their message.

For example, Edgar Allan Poe's poem "The Raven" is written with mostly long lines. The poem's speaker experiences troubling events and becomes paranoid throughout the poem, and he narrates his racing thoughts. Poe's use of long lines leads the reader to read each line quickly, allowing their reading experience to resemble the thoughts of the narrator:

> Deep into that darkness peering, long I stood there wondering, fearing,
> Doubting, dreaming dreams no mortal ever dared to dream before;
>   But the silence was unbroken, and the stillness gave no token,
>   And the only word there spoken was the whispered word, "Lenore?"
> This I whispered, and an echo murmured back the word, "Lenore!"—
>   Merely this and nothing more.

The poem's meter also contributes to its tone, but consider the same stanza written using shorter lines:

> Deep into that darkness peering,
> long I stood there wondering, fearing,
> Doubting, dreaming dreams no mortal
> ever dared to dream before;
>   But the silence was unbroken,
> and the stillness gave no token,
>   And the only word there spoken
> was the whispered word, "Lenore?"
> This I whispered, and an echo
> murmured back the word, "Lenore!"—
>   Merely this and nothing more.

Breaking the lines apart creates longer pauses and a slower, more suspenseful experience for the reader. While the tone of the poem is dark and suspense is appropriate, the longer lines allow Poe to emphasize and show the narrator's emotions. The narrator's emotions are more important to the poem's meaning than the creation of suspense, making longer lines more suitable in this case.

CONCRETE POETRY

A less common form of poetry is concrete poetry, also called shape poetry. **Concrete poems** are arranged so the full poem takes a shape that is relevant to the poem's message. For example, a concrete poem about the beach may be arranged to look like a palm tree. This contributes to a poem's meaning by influencing which aspect of the poem or message that the reader focuses on. In the beach poem example, the image of the palm tree leads the reader to focus on the poem's setting and visual imagery. The reader may also look for or anticipate the mention of a palm tree in the poem. This technique allows the poet to direct the reader's attention and emphasize a certain element of their work.

FREE VERSE

Free verse is a very common form of poetry. Because **free verse** poetry does not always incorporate meter or rhyme, it relies more heavily on punctuation and structure to influence the reader's experience and create emphasis. Free verse poetry makes strategic use of the length and number of both lines and stanzas. While meter and rhyme direct the flow and tone of other types of poems, poets of free verse pieces use the characteristics of lines and stanzas to establish flow and tone, instead.

Free verse also uses punctuation in each line to create flow and tone. The punctuation in each line directs the reader to pause after certain words, allowing the poet to emphasize specific ideas or images to clearly communicate their message. Similar to the effects of line length, the presence of punctuation at the end of a line can create pauses that affect a reader's pace. **End-stopped** lines, or lines with a punctuation mark at the end, create a pause that can contribute to the poem's flow or create emphasis. **Enjambed** lines, or lines that do not end with a punctuation mark, carry a sentence to the next line and create an effect similar to long lines. The use of enjambment can speed up a poem's flow and reflect an idea within the poem or contribute to tone.

POETIC STRUCTURE TO ENHANCE MEANING

The opening stanza of Romantic English poet, artist and printmaker William Blake's famous poem "The Tyger" demonstrates how a poet can create tension by using line length and punctuation independently of one another: "Tyger! Tyger! burning bright / In the forests of the night, / What immortal hand or eye / Could frame thy fearful symmetry?" The first three lines of this stanza are **trochaic** (/$\cup$), with "masculine" endings—that is, strongly stressed syllables at the ends of each of the lines. But Blake's punctuation contradicts this rhythmic regularity by not providing any divisions between the words "bright" and "In" or between "eye" and "Could." This irregular punctuation foreshadows how Blake disrupts the meter at the end of this first stanza by using a contrasting **dactyl** (/$\cup\cup$), with a "feminine" (unstressed) ending syllable in the last word, "symmetry." Thus Blake uses structural contrasts to heighten the intrigue of his work.

In enjambment, one sentence or clause in a poem does not end at the end of its line or verse, but runs over into the next line or verse. Clause endings coinciding with line endings give readers a feeling of completion, but enjambment influences readers to hurry to the next line to finish and understand the sentence. In his blank-verse epic religious poem "Paradise Lost," John Milton wrote: "Anon out of the earth a fabric huge / Rose like an exhalation, with the sound / Of dulcet symphonies and voices sweet, / Built like a temple, where pilasters round / Were set, and Doric pillars overlaid / With golden architrave." Only the third line is end-stopped. Milton, describing the palace of Pandemonium bursting from Hell up through the ground, reinforced this idea through phrases and clauses bursting through the boundaries of the lines. A **caesura** is a pause in mid-verse. Milton's commas in the third and fourth lines signal caesuras. They interrupt flow, making the narration jerky to imply that Satan's glorious-seeming palace has a shaky and unsound foundation.

COUPLETS AND METER TO ENHANCE MEANING IN POETRY

When a poet uses a couplet—a stanza of two lines, rhymed or unrhymed—it can function as the answer to a question asked earlier in the poem, or the solution to a problem or riddle. Couplets can also enhance the establishment of a poem's mood, or clarify the development of a poem's theme. Another device to enhance thematic development is irony, which also communicates the poet's tone and draws the reader's attention to a point the poet is making. The use of meter gives a poem a rhythmic context, contributes to the poem's flow, makes it more appealing to the reader, can represent natural speech rhythms, and produces specific effects. For example, in "The Song of Hiawatha," Henry Wadsworth Longfellow uses trochaic (/ ⌣) tetrameter (four beats per line) to evoke for readers the rhythms of Native American chanting: "*By* the *shores* of *Gitche Gum*ee, / *By* the *shin*ing *Big*-Sea-*Wat*er / *Stood* the *wig*wam *of* No*ko*mis." (Italicized syllables are stressed; non-italicized syllables are unstressed.)

REFLECTION OF CONTENT THROUGH STRUCTURE

Wallace Stevens' short yet profound poem "The Snow Man" is reductionist: the snow man is a figure without human biases or emotions. Stevens begins, "One must have a mind of winter," the criterion for realizing nature and life does not inherently possess subjective qualities; we only invest it with these. Things are not as we see them; they simply are. The entire poem is one long sentence of clauses connected by conjunctions and commas, and modified by relative clauses and phrases. The successive phrases lead readers continually to reconsider as they read. Stevens' construction of the poem mirrors the meaning he conveys. With a mind of winter, the snow man, Stevens concludes, "nothing himself, beholds nothing that is not there, and the nothing that is."

CONTRAST OF CONTENT AND STRUCTURE

Robert Frost's poem "Stopping by Woods on a Snowy Evening" (1923) is deceptively short and simple, with only four stanzas, each of only four lines, and short and simple words. Reinforcing this is Frost's use of regular rhyme and meter. The rhythm is iambic tetrameter throughout; the rhyme scheme is AABA in the first three stanzas and AAAA in the fourth. In an additional internal subtlety, B ending "here" in the first stanza is rhymed with A endings "queer," "near," and "year" of the second; B ending "lake" in the second is rhymed in A endings "shake", "mistake," and "flake" of the third. The final stanza's AAAA endings reinforce the ultimate darker theme. Though the first three stanzas seem to describe quietly watching snow fill the woods, the last stanza evokes the seductive pull of mysterious death: "The woods are lovely, dark and deep," countered by the obligations of living life: "But I have promises to keep, / And miles to go before I sleep, / And miles to go before I sleep." The last line's repetition strengthens Frost's message that despite death's temptation, life's course must precede it.

EFFECTS OF FIGURATIVE DEVICES ON MEANING IN POETRY

Through exaggeration, hyperbole communicates the strength of a poet's or persona's feelings and enhances the mood of the poem. Imagery appeals to the reader's senses, creating vivid mental pictures, evoking reader emotions and responses, and helping to develop themes. Irony also aids thematic development by drawing the reader's attention to the poet's point and communicating the poem's tone. Thematic development is additionally supported by the comparisons of metaphors and similes, which emphasize similarities, enhance imagery, and affect readers' perceptions. The use of mood communicates the atmosphere of a poem, builds a sense of tension, and evokes the reader's emotions. Onomatopoeia appeals to the reader's auditory sense and enhances sound imagery even when the poem is visual (read silently) rather than auditory (read aloud). Rhyme connects and unites verses, gives the rhyming words emphasis, and makes poems more fluent. Symbolism communicates themes, develops imagery, evokes readers' emotions, and elicits a response from the reader.

REPETITION TO ENHANCE MEANING

A **villanelle** is a nineteen-line poem composed of five tercets and one quatrain. The defining characteristic is the repetition: two lines appear repeatedly throughout the poem. In Theodore Roethke's "The Waking," the two repeated lines are "I wake to sleep, and take my waking slow," and "I learn by going where I have to go." At first these sound paradoxical, but the meaning is gradually revealed through the poem. The repetition also fits with the theme of cycle: the paradoxes of waking to sleep, learning by going, and thinking by feeling represent a constant cycle through life. They also symbolize abandoning conscious rationalism to embrace spiritual vision. We wake from the vision to "Great Nature," and "take the lively air." "This shaking keeps me steady"—another paradox—juxtaposes and balances fear of mortality with ecstasy in embracing experience. The transcendent vision of all life's interrelationship demonstrates, "What falls away is always. And is near." Readers experience the poem holistically, like music, through Roethke's integration of theme, motion, and sound.

Sylvia Plath's villanelle "Mad Girl's Love Song" narrows the scope from universal to personal but keeps the theme of cycle. The two repeated lines, "I shut my eyes and all the world drops dead" and "(I think I made you up inside my head.)" reflect the existential viewpoint that nothing exists in any absolute reality outside of our own perceptions. In the first stanza, the middle line, "I lift my lids and all is born again," in its recreating the world, bridges between the repeated refrain statements—one of obliterating reality, the other of having constructed her lover's existence. Unlike other villanelles wherein key lines are subtly altered in their repetitions, Plath repeats these exactly each time. This reflects the young woman's love, constant throughout the poem as it neither fades nor progresses.

> **Review Video: Structural Elements of Poetry**
> Visit mometrix.com/academy and enter code: 265216

Drama

EARLY DEVELOPMENT

English **drama** originally developed from religious ritual. Early Christians established traditions of presenting pageants or mystery plays, traveling on wagons and carts through the streets to depict Biblical events. Medieval tradition assigned responsibility for performing specific plays to the different guilds. In Middle English, "mystery" referred to craft, or trade, and religious ritual and truth. Historically, mystery plays were to be reproduced exactly the same every time they were performed, like religious rituals. However, some performers introduced individual interpretations of roles and even improvised. Thus, drama was born. Narrative detail and nuanced acting were evident in mystery cycles by the Middle Ages. As individualized performance evolved, plays on other subjects also developed. Middle English mystery plays extant include the York Cycle, Coventry Cycle, Chester Mystery Plays, N-Town Plays, and Towneley/Wakefield Plays. In recent times, these plays began to draw interest again, and several modern actors such as Dame Judi Dench began their careers with mystery plays.

> **Review Video: Dramas**
> Visit mometrix.com/academy and enter code: 216060

DEFINING CHARACTERISTICS

In the Middle Ages, plays were commonly composed in **verse**. By the time of the Renaissance, Shakespeare and other dramatists wrote plays that mixed **prose**, **rhymed verse**, and **blank verse**. The traditions of costumes and masks were seen in ancient Greek drama, medieval mystery plays, and Renaissance drama. Conventions like **asides**, in which actors make comments directly to the audience unheard by other characters, and **soliloquies** were also common during Shakespeare's Elizabethan dramatic period. **Monologues** date back to ancient Greek drama. Elizabethan dialogue tended to use colloquial prose for lower-class characters' speech and stylized verse for upper-class characters. Another Elizabethan convention was the play-within-a-play, as in *Hamlet*. As drama moved toward realism, dialogue became less poetic and more conversational, as in most modern English-language plays. Contemporary drama, both onstage and onscreen, includes a convention of **breaking the fourth wall**, as actors directly face and address audiences.

COMEDY

Today, most people equate the idea of **comedy** with something funny, and of **tragedy** with something sad. However, the ancient Greeks defined these differently. Comedy needed not be humorous or amusing; it needed only a happy ending. The classical definition of comedy, as included in Aristotle's works, is any work that tells the story of a sympathetic main character's rise in fortune. According to Aristotle, protagonists need not be heroic or exemplary, nor evil or worthless, but ordinary people of unremarkable morality. Comic figures who were sympathetic were usually of humble origins, proving their "natural nobility" through their actions as they were tested. Characters born into nobility were often satirized as self-important or pompous.

SHAKESPEAREAN COMEDY

William Shakespeare lived in England from 1564-1616. He was a poet and playwright of the Renaissance period in Western culture. He is generally considered the foremost dramatist in world literature and the greatest author to write in the English language. He wrote many poems, particularly sonnets, of which 154 survive today, and approximately 38 plays. Though his sonnets are greater in number and are very famous, he is best known for his plays, including comedies, tragedies, tragicomedies and historical plays. His play titles include: *All's Well That Ends Well, As You Like It, The Comedy of Errors, Love's Labour's Lost, Measure for Measure, The Merchant of Venice, The Merry Wives of Windsor, A Midsummer Night's Dream, Much Ado About Nothing, The Taming of the Shrew, The Tempest, Twelfth Night, The Two Gentlemen of Verona, The Winter's Tale, King John, Richard II, Henry IV, Henry V, Richard III, Romeo and Juliet, Coriolanus, Titus Andronicus, Julius Caesar, Macbeth, Hamlet, Troilus and Cressida, King Lear, Othello, Antony and Cleopatra,* and *Cymbeline.* Some scholars have suggested that Christopher Marlowe wrote several of Shakespeare's works. While most scholars reject this theory, Shakespeare did pay homage to Marlowe, alluding to several of his characters, themes, or verbiage, as well as borrowing themes from several of his plays (e.g., Marlowe's *Jew of Malta* influenced Shakespeare's *Merchant of Venice*).

When Shakespeare was writing, during the Elizabethan period of the Renaissance, Aristotle's version of comedies was popular. While some of Shakespeare's comedies were humorous and others were not, all had happy endings. *A Comedy of Errors* is a farce. Based and expanding on a Classical Roman comedy, it is lighthearted and includes slapstick humor and mistaken identity. *Much Ado About Nothing* is a romantic comedy. It incorporates some more serious themes, including social mores, perceived infidelity, marriage's duality as both trap and ideal, honor and its loss, public shame, and deception, but also much witty dialogue and a happy ending.

DRAMATIC COMEDY

Three types of dramas classified as comedy include the farce, the romantic comedy, and the satirical comedy.

FARCE

The **farce** is a zany, goofy type of comedy that includes pratfalls and other forms of slapstick humor. The characters in a farce tend to be ridiculous or fantastical in nature. The plot also tends to contain highly improbable events, featuring complications and twists that continue throughout, and incredible coincidences that would likely never occur in reality. Mistaken identity, deceptions, and disguises are common devices used in farcical comedies. Shakespeare's play *The Comedy of Errors,* with its cases of accidental mistaken identity and slapstick, is an example of farce. Contemporary examples of farce include the Marx Brothers' movies, the Three Stooges movies and TV episodes, and the *Pink Panther* movie series.

ROMANTIC COMEDY

Romantic comedies are probably the most popular of the types of comedy, in both live theater performances and movies. They include not only humor and a happy ending, but also love. In the typical plot of a romantic comedy, two people well suited to one another are either brought together for the first time, or reconciled after being separated. They are usually both sympathetic characters and seem destined to be together, yet they are separated by some intervening complication, such as ex-lovers, interfering parents or friends, or differences in social class. The happy ending is achieved through the lovers overcoming all these obstacles. William Shakespeare's *Much Ado About Nothing*, Walt Disney's version of *Cinderella* (1950), and Broadway musical *Guys and Dolls* (1955) are example of romantic comedies. Many live-action movies are also examples of romantic comedies, such as *The Princess Bride* (1987), *Sleepless in Seattle* (1993), *You've Got Mail* (1998), and *Forget Paris* (1995).

SATIRICAL COMEDY AND BLACK COMEDY

Satires generally mock and lampoon human foolishness and vices. **Satirical comedies** fit the classical definition of comedy by depicting a main character's rise in fortune, but they also fit the definition of satire by making that main character either a fool, morally corrupt, or cynical in attitude. All or most of the other characters in the satirical comedy display similar foibles. These include cuckolded spouses, dupes, and other gullible types; tricksters, con artists, and criminals; hypocrites; fortune seekers; and other deceptive types who prey on the gullible, who are their willing and unwitting victims. Some classical examples of satirical comedies include *The Birds* by ancient Greek comedic playwright Aristophanes, and *Volpone* by 17th-century poet and playwright Ben Jonson, who made the comedy of humors popular. When satirical comedy is extended to extremes, it becomes **black comedy**, wherein the comedic occurrences are grotesque or terrible.

TRAGEDY

The opposite of comedy is tragedy, portraying a hero's fall in fortune. While by classical definitions, tragedies could be sad, Aristotle went further, requiring that they depict suffering and pain to cause "terror and pity" in audiences. Additionally, he decreed that tragic heroes can be basically good, admirable, or noble, and that their downfalls result from personal action, choice, or error, not by bad luck or accident.

ARISTOTLE'S CRITERIA FOR TRAGEDY

In his *Poetics,* Aristotle defined five critical terms relative to tragedy:

- *Anagnorisis:* Meaning tragic insight or recognition, this is a moment of realization by a tragic hero or heroine that he or she has become enmeshed in a "web of fate."
- *Hamartia:* This is often called a "tragic flaw," but is better described as a tragic error. *Hamartia* is an archery term meaning a shot missing the bull's eye, used here as a metaphor for a mistake—often a simple one—which results in catastrophe.
- *Hubris:* While often called "pride," this is actually translated as "violent transgression," and signifies an arrogant overstepping of moral or cultural bounds—the sin of the tragic hero who over-presumes or over-aspires.
- *Nemesis:* translated as "retribution," this represents the cosmic punishment or payback that the tragic hero ultimately receives for committing hubristic acts.
- *Peripateia:* Literally "turning," this is a plot reversal consisting of a tragic hero's pivotal action, which changes his or her status from safe to endangered.

HEGEL'S THEORY OF TRAGEDY

Georg Wilhelm Friedrich Hegel (1770-1831) proposed a different theory of tragedy than Aristotle (384-322 BCE), which was also very influential. Whereas Aristotle's criteria involved character and plot, Hegel defined tragedy as a dynamic conflict of opposite forces or rights. For example, if an individual believes in the moral philosophy of the conscientious objector (i.e., that fighting in wars is morally wrong, but is confronted with being drafted into military service), this conflict would fit Hegel's definition of a tragic plot premise. Hegel theorized that a tragedy must involve some circumstance in which two values, or two rights, are fatally at odds with one another and conflict directly. Hegel did not view this as good triumphing over evil, or evil winning out over good, but rather as one good fighting against another good unto death. He saw this conflict of two goods as truly tragic. In ancient Greek playwright Sophocles' tragedy *Antigone,* the main character experiences this tragic conflict between her public duties and her family and religious responsibilities.

REVENGE TRAGEDY

Along with Aristotelian definitions of comedy and tragedy, ancient Greece was the origin of the **revenge tragedy**. This genre became highly popular in Renaissance England, and is still popular today in contemporary movies. In a revenge tragedy, the protagonist has suffered a serious wrong, such as the murder of a family member. However, the wrongdoer has not been punished. In contemporary plots, this often occurs when some legal technicality has interfered with the miscreant's conviction and sentencing, or when authorities are unable to locate and apprehend the criminal. The protagonist then faces the conflict of suffering this injustice, or exacting his or her own justice by seeking revenge. Greek revenge tragedies include *Agamemnon* and *Medea.* Playwright Thomas Kyd's *The Spanish Tragedy* (1582-1592) is credited with beginning the Elizabethan genre of revenge tragedies. Shakespearean revenge tragedies include *Hamlet* (1599-1602) and *Titus Andronicus* (1588-1593). A Jacobean example is Thomas Middleton's *The Revenger's Tragedy* (1606, 1607).

HAMLET'S "TRAGIC FLAW"

Despite virtually limitless interpretations, one way to view Hamlet's tragic error generally is as indecision. He suffers the classic revenge tragedy's conflict of whether to suffer with his knowledge of his mother's and uncle's assassination of his father, or to exact his own revenge and justice against Claudius, who has assumed the throne after his crime went unknown and unpunished. Hamlet's famous soliloquy, "To be or not to be" reflects this dilemma. Hamlet muses "Whether 'tis nobler in the mind to suffer the slings and arrows of outrageous fortune, / Or to take arms against a sea of troubles, / And by opposing end them?" Hamlet both longs for and fears death, as "the dread of something after death ... makes us rather bear those ills we have / Than fly to others that we know not ... Thus, conscience does make cowards of us all." For most of the play, Hamlet struggles with his responsibility to avenge his father, who was killed by Hamlet's uncle, Claudius. So, Hamlet's tragic error at first might be considered a lack of action. But he then makes several attempts at revenge, each of which end in worse tragedy, until his efforts are ended by the final tragedy – Hamlet's own death.

Informational Texts

TEXT FEATURES IN INFORMATIONAL TEXTS

The **title of a text** gives readers some idea of its content. The **table of contents** is a list near the beginning of a text, showing the book's sections and chapters and their coinciding page numbers. This gives readers an overview of the whole text, and helps them find specific chapters easily. An **appendix**, at the back of the book or document, includes important information that is not present in the main text. Also at the back, an **index** lists the book's important topics alphabetically with their page numbers to help readers find them easily. **Glossaries**, usually found at the backs of books, list technical terms alphabetically with their definitions to aid vocabulary learning and comprehension. Boldface print is used to emphasize certain words, often identifying words included in the text's glossary where readers can look up their definitions. **Headings** separate sections of text and show the topic of each. **Subheadings** divide subject headings into smaller, more specific categories to help readers organize information. **Footnotes**, at the bottom of the page, give readers more information, such as citations or links. **Bullet points** list items separately, making facts and ideas easier to see and understand. A **sidebar** is a box of information to one side of the main text giving additional information, often on a more focused or in-depth example of a topic.

Illustrations and **photographs** are pictures that visually emphasize important points in text. The captions below the illustrations explain what those images show. Charts and tables are visual forms of information that make something easier to understand quickly. Diagrams are drawings that show relationships or explain a process. Graphs visually show the relationships among multiple sets of information plotted along vertical and horizontal axes. Maps show geographical information visually to help readers understand the relative locations of places covered in the text. Timelines are visual graphics that show historical events in chronological order to help readers see their sequence.

> **Review Video: Informative Text**
> Visit mometrix.com/academy and enter code: 924964

LANGUAGE USE

LITERAL AND FIGURATIVE LANGUAGE

As in fictional literature, informational text also uses both **literal language**, which means just what it says, and **figurative language**, which imparts more than literal meaning. For example, an informational text author might use a simile or direct comparison, such as writing that a racehorse "ran like the wind." Informational text authors also use metaphors or implied comparisons, such as "the cloud of the Great Depression." Imagery may also appear in informational texts to increase the reader's understanding of ideas and concepts discussed in the text.

> **Review Video: Figurative Language**
> Visit mometrix.com/academy and enter code: 584902

EXPLICIT AND IMPLICIT INFORMATION

When informational text states something explicitly, the reader is told by the author exactly what is meant, which can include the author's interpretation or perspective of events. For example, a professor writes, "I have seen students go into an absolute panic just because they weren't able to complete the exam in the time they were allotted." This explicitly tells the reader that the students were afraid, and by using the words "just because," the writer indicates their fear was exaggerated out of proportion relative to what happened. However, another professor writes, "I have had students come to me, their faces drained of all color, saying 'We weren't able to finish the exam.'" This is an example of implicit meaning: the second writer did not state explicitly that the students were panicked. Instead, he wrote a description of their faces being "drained of all color." From this description, the reader can infer that the students were so frightened that their faces paled.

> **Review Video: Explicit and Implicit Information**
> Visit mometrix.com/academy and enter code: 735771

TECHNICAL LANGUAGE

Technical language is more impersonal than literary and vernacular language. Passive voice makes the tone impersonal. For example, instead of writing, "We found this a central component of protein metabolism," scientists write, "This was found a central component of protein metabolism." While science professors have traditionally instructed students to avoid active voice because it leads to first-person ("I" and "we") usage, science editors today find passive voice dull and weak. Many journal articles combine both. Tone in technical science writing should be detached, concise, and professional. While one may normally write, "This chemical has to be available for proteins to be digested," professionals write technically, "The presence of this chemical is required for the enzyme to break the covalent bonds of proteins." The use of technical language appeals to both technical and non-technical audiences by displaying the author or speaker's understanding of the subject and suggesting their credibility regarding the message they are communicating.

TECHNICAL MATERIAL FOR NON-TECHNICAL READERS

Writing about **technical subjects** for **non-technical readers** differs from writing for colleagues because authors place more importance on delivering a critical message than on imparting the maximum technical content possible. Technical authors also must assume that non-technical audiences do not have the expertise to comprehend extremely scientific or technical messages, concepts, and terminology. They must resist the temptation to impress audiences with their scientific knowledge and expertise and remember that their primary purpose is to communicate a message that non-technical readers will understand, feel, and respond to. Non-technical and technical styles include similarities. Both should formally cite any references or other authors' work utilized in the text. Both must follow intellectual property and copyright regulations. This includes the author's protecting his or her own rights, or a public domain statement, as he or she chooses.

Non-Technical Audiences

Writers of technical or scientific material may need to write for many non-technical audiences. Some readers have no technical or scientific background, and those who do may not be in the same field as the authors. Government and corporate policymakers and budget managers need technical information they can understand for decision-making. Citizens affected by technology or science are a different audience. Non-governmental organizations can encompass many of the preceding groups. Elementary and secondary school programs also need non-technical language for presenting technical subject matter. Additionally, technical authors will need to use non-technical language when collecting consumer responses to surveys, presenting scientific or para-scientific material to the public, writing about the history of science, and writing about science and technology in developing countries.

Use of Everyday Language

Authors of technical information sometimes must write using non-technical language that readers outside their disciplinary fields can comprehend. They should use not only non-technical terms, but also use normal, everyday language to accommodate readers whose native language is different than the language the text is written in. For example, instead of writing that "eustatic changes like thermal expansion are causing hazardous conditions in the littoral zone," an author would do better to write that "a rising sea level is threatening the coast." When technical terms cannot be avoided, authors should also define or explain them using non-technical language. Although authors must cite references and acknowledge their use of others' work, they should avoid the kinds of references or citations that they would use in scientific journals—unless they reinforce author messages. They should not use endnotes, footnotes, or any other complicated referential techniques because non-technical journal publishers usually do not accept them. Including high-resolution illustrations, photos, maps, or satellite images and incorporating multimedia into digital publications will enhance non-technical writing about technical subjects. Technical authors may publish using non-technical language in e-journals, trade journals, specialty newsletters, and daily newspapers.

Making Inferences About Informational Text

With informational text, reader comprehension depends not only on recalling important statements and details, but also on reader inferences based on examples and details. Readers add information from the text to what they already know to draw inferences about the text. These inferences help the readers to fill in the information that the text does not explicitly state, enabling them to understand the text better. When reading a nonfictional autobiography or biography, for example, the most appropriate inferences might concern the events in the book, the actions of the subject of the autobiography or biography, and the message the author means to convey. When reading a nonfictional expository (informational) text, the reader would best draw inferences about problems and their solutions, and causes and their effects. When reading a nonfictional persuasive text, the reader will want to infer ideas supporting the author's message and intent.

Structures or Organizational Patterns in Informational Texts

Informational text can be descriptive, appealing to the five senses and answering the questions what, who, when, where, and why. Another method of structuring informational text is sequence and order. Chronological texts relate events in the sequence that they occurred, from start to finish, while how-to texts organize information into a series of instructions in the sequence in which the steps should be followed. Comparison-contrast structures of informational text describe various ideas to their readers by pointing out how things or ideas are similar and how they are different. Cause and effect structures of informational text describe events that occurred and identify the causes or reasons that those events occurred. Problem and solution structures of informational text introduce and describe problems and offer one or more solutions for each problem described.

> **Review Video: Organizational Methods to Structure Text**
> Visit mometrix.com/academy and enter code: 606263

DETERMINING AN INFORMATIONAL AUTHOR'S PURPOSE

Informational authors' purposes are why they write texts. Readers must determine authors' motivations and goals. Readers gain greater insight into a text by considering the author's motivation. This develops critical reading skills. Readers perceive writing as a person's voice, not simply printed words. Uncovering author motivations and purposes empowers readers to know what to expect from the text, read for relevant details, evaluate authors and their work critically, and respond effectively to the motivations and persuasions of the text. The main idea of a text is what the reader is supposed to understand from reading it; the purpose of the text is why the author has written it and what the author wants readers to do with its information. Authors state some purposes clearly, while other purposes may be unstated but equally significant. When stated purposes contradict other parts of a text, the author may have a hidden agenda. Readers can better evaluate a text's effectiveness, whether they agree or disagree with it, and why they agree or disagree through identifying unstated author purposes.

IDENTIFYING AUTHOR'S POINT OF VIEW OR PURPOSE

In some informational texts, readers find it easy to identify the author's point of view and purpose, such as when the author explicitly states his or her position and reason for writing. But other texts are more difficult, either because of the content or because the authors give neutral or balanced viewpoints. This is particularly true in scientific texts, in which authors may state the purpose of their research in the report, but never state their point of view except by interpreting evidence or data.

To analyze text and identify point of view or purpose, readers should ask themselves the following four questions:

1. With what main point or idea does this author want to persuade readers to agree?
2. How does this author's word choice affect the way that readers consider this subject?
3. How do this author's choices of examples and facts affect the way that readers consider this subject?
4. What is it that this author wants to accomplish by writing this text?

> **Review Video: Purpose**
> Visit mometrix.com/academy and enter code: 511819

EVALUATING ARGUMENTS MADE BY INFORMATIONAL TEXT WRITERS

When evaluating an informational text, the first step is to identify the argument's conclusion. Then identify the author's premises that support the conclusion. Try to paraphrase premises for clarification and make the conclusion and premises fit. List all premises first, sequentially numbered, then finish with the conclusion. Identify any premises or assumptions not stated by the author but required for the stated premises to support the conclusion. Read word assumptions sympathetically, as the author might. Evaluate whether premises reasonably support the conclusion. For inductive reasoning, the reader should ask if the premises are true, if they support the conclusion, and if so, how strongly. For deductive reasoning, the reader should ask if the argument is valid or invalid. If all premises are true, then the

Copyright © Mometrix Media. You have been licensed one copy of this document for personal use only. Any other reproduction or redistribution is strictly prohibited. All rights reserved.

argument is valid unless the conclusion can be false. If it can, then the argument is invalid. An invalid argument be made valid through alterations such as the addition of needed premises.

USE OF RHETORIC IN INFORMATIONAL TEXTS

There are many ways authors can support their claims, arguments, beliefs, ideas, and reasons for writing in informational texts. For example, authors can appeal to readers' sense of **logic** by communicating their reasoning through a carefully sequenced series of logical steps to help "prove" the points made. Authors can appeal to readers' **emotions** by using descriptions and words that evoke feelings of sympathy, sadness, anger, righteous indignation, hope, happiness, or any other emotion to reinforce what they express and share with their audience. Authors may appeal to the **moral** or **ethical values** of readers by using words and descriptions that can convince readers that something is right or wrong. By relating personal anecdotes, authors can supply readers with more accessible, realistic examples of points they make, as well as appealing to their emotions. They can provide supporting evidence by reporting case studies. They can also illustrate their points by making analogies to which readers can better relate.

Vocabulary and Word Relationships

SYNONYMS AND ANTONYMS

When you understand how words relate to each other, you will discover more in a passage. This is explained by understanding **synonyms** (e.g., words that mean the same thing) and **antonyms** (e.g., words that mean the opposite of one another). As an example, *dry* and *arid* are synonyms, and *dry* and *wet* are antonyms.

There are many pairs of words in English that can be considered synonyms, despite having slightly different definitions. For instance, the words *friendly* and *collegial* can both be used to describe a warm interpersonal relationship, and one would be correct to call them synonyms. However, *collegial* (kin to *colleague*) is often used in reference to professional or academic relationships, and *friendly* has no such connotation.

If the difference between the two words is too great, then they should not be called synonyms. *Hot* and *warm* are not synonyms because their meanings are too distinct. A good way to determine whether two words are synonyms is to substitute one word for the other word and verify that the meaning of the sentence has not changed. Substituting *warm* for *hot* in a sentence would convey a different meaning. Although warm and hot may seem close in meaning, warm generally means that the temperature is moderate, and hot generally means that the temperature is excessively high.

Antonyms are words with opposite meanings. *Light* and *dark*, *up* and *down*, *right* and *left*, *good* and *bad*: these are all sets of antonyms. Be careful to distinguish between antonyms and pairs of words that are simply different. *Black* and *gray*, for instance, are not antonyms because gray is not the opposite of black. *Black* and *white*, on the other hand, are antonyms.

Not every word has an antonym. For instance, many nouns do not. What would be the antonym of *chair*? During your exam, the questions related to antonyms are more likely to concern adjectives. You will recall that adjectives are words that describe a noun. Some common adjectives include *purple, fast, skinny*, and *sweet*. From those four adjectives, *purple* is the item that lacks a group of obvious antonyms.

> **Review Video: Synonyms and Antonyms**
> Visit mometrix.com/academy and enter code: 105612

AFFIXES

Affixes in the English language are morphemes that are added to words to create related but different words. Derivational affixes form new words based on and related to the original words. For example, the affix –ness added to the end of the adjective *happy* forms the noun *happiness*. Inflectional affixes form different grammatical versions of words. For example, the plural affix –s changes the singular noun *book* to the plural noun *books*, and the past tense affix –ed changes the present tense verb *look* to the past tense *looked*. Prefixes are affixes placed in front of words. For example, *heat* means to make hot; *preheat* means to heat in advance. Suffixes are affixes placed at the ends of words. The *happiness* example above contains the suffix –ness. Circumfixes add parts both before and after words, such as how *light* becomes *enlighten* with the prefix *en-* and the suffix –en. Interfixes create compound words via central affixes: *speed* and *meter* become *speedometer* via the interfix –o–.

> **Review Video: Affixes**
> Visit mometrix.com/academy and enter code: 782422

WORD ROOTS, PREFIXES, AND SUFFIXES TO HELP DETERMINE MEANINGS OF WORDS

Many English words were formed from combining multiple sources. For example, the Latin *habēre* means "to have," and the prefixes *in-* and *im-* mean a lack or prevention of something, as in *insufficient* and *imperfect*. Latin combined *in-* with *habēre* to form *inhibēre*, whose past participle was *inhibitus*. This is the origin of the English word *inhibit*, meaning to prevent from having. Hence by knowing the meanings of both the prefix and the root, one can decipher the word meaning. In Greek, the root *enkephalo-* refers to the brain. Many medical terms are based on this root, such as encephalitis and hydrocephalus. Understanding the prefix and suffix meanings (-itis means inflammation; *hydro-* means water) allows a person to deduce that encephalitis refers to brain inflammation and hydrocephalus refers to water (or other fluid) on the brain.

> **Review Video: Determining Word Meanings**
> Visit mometrix.com/academy and enter code: 894894

PREFIXES

While knowing prefix meanings helps ESL and beginning readers learn new words, other readers take for granted the meanings of known words. However, prefix knowledge will also benefit them for determining meanings or definitions of unfamiliar words. For example, native English speakers and readers familiar with recipes know what *preheat* means. Knowing that *pre-* means in advance can also inform them that *presume* means to assume in advance, that *prejudice* means advance judgment, and that this understanding can be applied to many other words beginning with *pre-*. Knowing that the prefix *dis-* indicates opposition informs the meanings of words like *disbar, disagree, disestablish,* and many more. Knowing *dys-* means bad, impaired, abnormal, or difficult informs *dyslogistic, dysfunctional, dysphagia,* and *dysplasia*.

SUFFIXES

In English, certain suffixes generally indicate both that a word is a noun, and that the noun represents a state of being or quality. For example, -ness is commonly used to change an adjective into its noun form, as with *happy* and *happiness, nice* and *niceness,* and so on. The suffix –tion is commonly used to transform a verb into its noun form, as with *converse* and *conversation or move* and *motion*. Thus, if readers are unfamiliar with the second form of a word, knowing the meaning of the transforming suffix can help them determine meaning.

DENOTATIVE VS. CONNOTATIVE MEANING

The **denotative** meaning of a word is the literal meaning. The **connotative** meaning goes beyond the denotative meaning to include the emotional reaction that a word may invoke. The connotative meaning often takes the denotative meaning a step further due to associations the reader makes with the denotative meaning. Readers can differentiate between the denotative and connotative meanings by first recognizing how authors use each meaning. Most non-fiction, for example, is fact-based and authors do not use flowery, figurative language. The reader can assume that the writer is using the denotative meaning of words. In fiction, the author may use the connotative meaning. Readers can determine whether the author is using the denotative or connotative meaning of a word by implementing context clues.

> **Review Video: Denotation and Connotation**
> Visit mometrix.com/academy and enter code: 310092

NUANCES OF WORD MEANING RELATIVE TO CONNOTATION, DENOTATION, DICTION, AND USAGE

A word's denotation is simply its objective dictionary definition. However, its connotation refers to the subjective associations, often emotional, that specific words evoke in listeners and readers. Two or more words can have the same dictionary meaning, but very different connotations. Writers use diction (word choice) to convey various nuances of thought and emotion by selecting synonyms for other words that best communicate the associations they want to trigger for readers. For example, a car engine is naturally greasy; in this sense, "greasy" is a neutral term. But when a person's smile, appearance, or clothing is described as "greasy," it has a negative connotation. Some words have even gained additional or different meanings over time. For example, *awful* used to be used to describe things that evoked a sense of awe. When *awful* is separated into its root word, awe, and suffix, -ful, it can be understood to mean "full of awe." However, the word is now commonly used to describe things that evoke repulsion, terror, or another intense, negative reaction.

> **Review Video: Denotation and Connotation**
> Visit mometrix.com/academy and enter code: 310092
>
> **Review Video: Word Usage**
> Visit mometrix.com/academy and enter code: 197863

CONTEXT CLUES

Readers of all levels will encounter words that they have either never seen or have encountered only on a limited basis. The best way to define a word in **context** is to look for nearby words that can assist in revealing the meaning of the word. For instance, unfamiliar nouns are often accompanied by examples that provide a definition. Consider the following sentence: *Dave arrived at the party in hilarious garb: a leopard-print shirt, buckskin trousers, and bright green sneakers.* If a reader was unfamiliar with the meaning of garb, he or she could read the examples (i.e., a leopard-print shirt, buckskin trousers, and high heels) and quickly determine that the word means *clothing*. Examples will not always be this obvious. Consider this sentence: *Parsley, lemon, and flowers were just a few of the items he used as garnishes.* Here, the word *garnishes* is exemplified by parsley, lemon, and flowers. Readers who have eaten in a variety of restaurants will probably be able to identify a garnish as something used to decorate a plate.

> **Review Video: Context**
> Visit mometrix.com/academy and enter code: 613660

USING CONTRAST IN CONTEXT CLUES

In addition to looking at the context of a passage, readers can use contrast to define an unfamiliar word in context. In many sentences, the author will not describe the unfamiliar word directly; instead, he or she will describe the opposite of the unfamiliar word. Thus, you are provided with some information that will bring you closer to defining the word. Consider the following example: *Despite his intelligence,*

Hector's low brow and bad posture made him look obtuse. The author writes that Hector's appearance does not convey intelligence. Therefore, *obtuse* must mean unintelligent. Here is another example: *Despite the horrible weather, we were beatific about our trip to Alaska.* The word *despite* indicates that the speaker's feelings were at odds with the weather. Since the weather is described as *horrible*, then *beatific* must mean something positive.

SUBSTITUTION TO FIND MEANING

In some cases, there will be very few contextual clues to help a reader define the meaning of an unfamiliar word. When this happens, one strategy that readers may employ is **substitution**. A good reader will brainstorm some possible synonyms for the given word, and he or she will substitute these words into the sentence. If the sentence and the surrounding passage continue to make sense, then the substitution has revealed at least some information about the unfamiliar word. Consider the sentence: *Frank's admonition rang in her ears as she climbed the mountain.* A reader unfamiliar with *admonition* might come up with some substitutions like *vow, promise, advice, complaint,* or *compliment.* All of these words make general sense of the sentence though their meanings are diverse. However, this process has suggested that an admonition is some sort of message. The substitution strategy is rarely able to pinpoint a precise definition, but this process can be effective as a last resort.

Occasionally, you will be able to define an unfamiliar word by looking at the descriptive words in the context. Consider the following sentence: *Fred dragged the recalcitrant boy kicking and screaming up the stairs.* The words *dragged, kicking,* and *screaming* all suggest that the boy does not want to go up the stairs. The reader may assume that *recalcitrant* means something like unwilling or protesting. In this example, an unfamiliar adjective was identified.

Additionally, using description to define an unfamiliar noun is a common practice compared to unfamiliar adjectives, as in this sentence: *Don's wrinkled frown and constantly shaking fist identified him as a curmudgeon of the first order.* Don is described as having a *wrinkled frown and constantly shaking fist,* suggesting that a *curmudgeon* must be a grumpy person. Contrasts do not always provide detailed information about the unfamiliar word, but they at least give the reader some clues.

WORDS WITH MULTIPLE MEANINGS

When a word has more than one meaning, readers can have difficulty determining how the word is being used in a given sentence. For instance, the verb *cleave,* can mean either *join* or *separate.* When readers come upon this word, they will have to select the definition that makes the most sense. Consider the following sentence: *Hermione's knife cleaved the bread cleanly.* Since a knife cannot join bread together, the word must indicate separation. A slightly more difficult example would be the sentence: *The birds cleaved to one another as they flew from the oak tree.* Immediately, the presence of the words *to one another* should suggest that in this sentence *cleave* is being used to mean *join.* Discovering the intent of a word with multiple meanings requires the same tricks as defining an unknown word: look for contextual clues and evaluate the substituted words.

CONTEXT CLUES TO HELP DETERMINE MEANINGS OF WORDS

If readers simply bypass unknown words, they can reach unclear conclusions about what they read. However, looking for the definition of every unfamiliar word in the dictionary can slow their reading progress. Moreover, the dictionary may list multiple definitions for a word, so readers must search the word's context for meaning. Hence context is important to new vocabulary regardless of reader methods. Four types of context clues are examples, definitions, descriptive words, and opposites. Authors may use a certain word, and then follow it with several different examples of what it describes. Sometimes authors actually supply a definition of a word they use, which is especially true in informational and technical texts. Authors may use descriptive words that elaborate upon a vocabulary word they just used. Authors may also use opposites with negation that help define meaning.

EXAMPLES AND DEFINITIONS

An author may use a word and then give examples that illustrate its meaning. Consider this text: "Teachers who do not know how to use sign language can help students who are deaf or hard of hearing understand certain instructions by using gestures instead, like pointing their fingers to indicate which direction to look or go; holding up a hand, palm outward, to indicate stopping; holding the hands flat, palms up, curling a finger toward oneself in a beckoning motion to indicate 'come here'; or curling all fingers toward oneself repeatedly to indicate 'come on', 'more', or 'continue.'" The author of this text has used the word "gestures" and then followed it with examples, so a reader unfamiliar with the word could deduce from the examples that "gestures" means "hand motions." Readers can find examples by looking for signal words "for example," "for instance," "like," "such as," and "e.g.."

While readers sometimes have to look for definitions of unfamiliar words in a dictionary or do some work to determine a word's meaning from its surrounding context, at other times an author may make it easier for readers by defining certain words. For example, an author may write, "The company did not have sufficient capital, that is, available money, to continue operations." The author defined "capital" as "available money," and heralded the definition with the phrase "that is." Another way that authors supply word definitions is with appositives. Rather than being introduced by a signal phrase like "that is," "namely," or "meaning," an appositive comes after the vocabulary word it defines and is enclosed within two commas. For example, an author may write, "The Indians introduced the Pilgrims to pemmican, cakes they made of lean meat dried and mixed with fat, which proved greatly beneficial to keep settlers from starving while trapping." In this example, the appositive phrase following "pemmican" and preceding "which" defines the word "pemmican."

DESCRIPTIONS

When readers encounter a word they do not recognize in a text, the author may expand on that word to illustrate it better. While the author may do this to make the prose more picturesque and vivid, the reader can also take advantage of this description to provide context clues to the meaning of the unfamiliar word. For example, an author may write, "The man sitting next to me on the airplane was obese. His shirt stretched across his vast expanse of flesh, strained almost to bursting." The descriptive second sentence elaborates on and helps to define the previous sentence's word "obese" to mean extremely fat. A reader unfamiliar with the word "repugnant" can decipher its meaning through an author's accompanying description: "The way the child grimaced and shuddered as he swallowed the medicine showed that its taste was particularly repugnant."

OPPOSITES

Text authors sometimes introduce a contrasting or opposing idea before or after a concept they present. They may do this to emphasize or heighten the idea they present by contrasting it with something that is the reverse. However, readers can also use these context clues to understand familiar words. For example, an author may write, "Our conversation was not cheery. We sat and talked very solemnly about his experience and a number of similar events." The reader who is not familiar with the word "solemnly" can deduce by the author's preceding use of "not cheery" that "solemn" means the opposite of cheery or happy, so it must mean serious or sad. Or if someone writes, "Don't condemn his entire project because you couldn't find anything good to say about it," readers unfamiliar with "condemn" can understand from the sentence structure that it means the opposite of saying anything good, so it must mean reject, dismiss, or disapprove. "Entire" adds another context clue, meaning total or complete rejection.

SYNTAX TO DETERMINE PART OF SPEECH AND MEANINGS OF WORDS

Syntax refers to sentence structure and word order. Suppose that a reader encounters an unfamiliar word when reading a text. To illustrate, consider an invented word like "splunch." If this word is used in a sentence like "Please splunch that ball to me," the reader can assume from syntactic context that "splunch" is a verb. We would not use a noun, adjective, adverb, or preposition with the object "that ball," and the prepositional phrase "to me" further indicates "splunch" represents an action. However, in

97

the sentence, "Please hand that splunch to me," the reader can assume that "splunch" is a noun. Demonstrative adjectives like "that" modify nouns. Also, we hand someone some*thing*—a thing being a noun; we do not hand someone a verb, adjective, or adverb. Some sentences contain further clues. For example, from the sentence, "The princess wore the glittering splunch on her head," the reader can deduce that it is a crown, tiara, or something similar from the syntactic context, without knowing the word.

SYNTAX TO INDICATE DIFFERENT MEANINGS OF SIMILAR SENTENCES

The syntax, or structure, of a sentence affords grammatical cues that aid readers in comprehending the meanings of words, phrases, and sentences in the texts that they read. Seemingly minor differences in how the words or phrases in a sentence are ordered can make major differences in meaning. For example, two sentences can use exactly the same words but have different meanings based on the word order:

- "The man with a broken arm sat in a chair."
- "The man sat in a chair with a broken arm."

While both sentences indicate that a man sat in a chair, differing syntax indicates whether the man's or chair's arm was broken.

DETERMINING MEANING OF PHRASES AND PARAGRAPHS

Like unknown words, the meanings of phrases, paragraphs, and entire works can also be difficult to discern. Each of these can be better understood with added context. However, for larger groups of words, more context is needed. Unclear phrases are similar to unclear words, and the same methods can be used to understand their meaning. However, it is also important to consider how the individual words in the phrase work together. Paragraphs are a bit more complicated. Just as words must be compared to other words in a sentence, paragraphs must be compared to other paragraphs in a composition or a section.

DETERMINING MEANING IN VARIOUS TYPES OF COMPOSITIONS

To understand the meaning of an entire composition, the type of composition must be considered. Expository writing is generally organized so that each paragraph focuses on explaining one idea, or part of an idea, and its relevance. Persuasive writing uses paragraphs for different purposes to organize the parts of the argument. Unclear paragraphs must be read in the context of the paragraphs around them for their meaning to be fully understood. The meaning of full texts can also be unclear at times. The purpose of composition is also important for understanding the meaning of a text. To quickly understand the broad meaning of a text, look to the introductory and concluding paragraphs. Fictional texts are different. Some fictional works have implicit meanings, but some do not. The target audience must be considered for understanding texts that do have an implicit meaning, as most children's fiction will clearly state any lessons or morals. For other fiction, the application of literary theories and criticism may be helpful for understanding the text.

ADDITIONAL RESOURCES FOR DETERMINING WORD MEANING AND USAGE

While these strategies are useful for determining the meaning of unknown words and phrases, sometimes additional resources are needed to properly use the terms in different contexts. Some words have multiple definitions, and some words are inappropriate in particular contexts or modes of writing. The following tools are helpful for understanding all meanings and proper uses for words and phrases.

- **Dictionaries** provide the meaning of a multitude of words in a language. Many dictionaries include additional information about each word, such as its etymology, its synonyms, or variations of the word.

- **Glossaries** are similar to dictionaries, as they provide the meanings of a variety of terms. However, while dictionaries typically feature an extensive list of words and comprise an entire publication, glossaries are often included at the end of a text and only include terms and definitions that are relevant to the text they follow.
- **Spell Checkers** are used to detect spelling errors in typed text. Some spell checkers may also detect the misuse of plural or singular nouns, verb tenses, or capitalization. While spell checkers are a helpful tool, they are not always reliable or attuned to the author's intent, so it is important to review the spell checker's suggestions before accepting them.
- **Style Manuals** are guidelines on the preferred punctuation, format, and grammar usage according to different fields or organizations. For example, the Associated Press Stylebook is a style guide often used for media writing. The guidelines within a style guide are not always applicable across different contexts and usages, as the guidelines often cover grammatical or formatting situations that are not objectively correct or incorrect.

Developmental Literacy and English Language Learning

LITERACY

Literacy is commonly understood as the *ability to read and write*. UNESCO, the United Nations Educational, Scientific, and Cultural Organization, has further defined literacy as the "ability to identify, understand, interpret, create, communicate, compute, and use printed and written materials associated with varying contexts." Under the UNESCO definition, understanding cultural, political, and historical contexts of communities falls under the definition of literacy. While **reading literacy** may be gauged simply by the ability to read a newspaper, **writing literacy** includes spelling, grammar, and sentence structure. To be literate in a foreign language, one would also need to be able to understand a language by listening and be able to speak the language. Some argue that visual representation and numeracy should be included in the requirements one must meet to be considered literate. Computer literacy refers to one's ability to utilize the basic functions of computers and other technologies. Subsets of reading literacy include phonological awareness, decoding, comprehension, and vocabulary.

PHONOLOGICAL AWARENESS

A subskill of literacy, **phonological awareness**, is the ability to perceive sound structures in a spoken word, such as syllables and the individual phonemes within syllables. **Phonemes** are the sounds represented by the letters in the alphabet. The ability to separate, blend, and manipulate sounds is critical to developing reading and spelling skills. Phonological awareness is concerned with not only syllables, but also **onset sounds** (the initial sound in a word, such as /k/ in 'cat') and **rime** (the sounds that follow the onset in a word, such as /at/ in 'cat'). Phonological awareness is an auditory skill that does not necessarily involve print. It should be developed before the student has learned letter to sound correspondences. A student's phonological awareness is an indicator of future reading success.

ACTIVITIES THAT TEACH PHONOLOGICAL AWARENESS

Classroom activities that teach phonological awareness include language play and exposure to a variety of sounds and the contexts of sounds. Activities that teach phonological awareness include:

- Clapping to the sounds of individual words, names, or all words in a sentence
- Practicing saying blended phonemes
- Singing songs that involve phoneme replacement (e.g., The Name Game)
- Reading poems, songs, and nursery rhymes out loud
- Reading patterned and predictable texts out loud
- Listening to environmental sounds or following verbal directions
- Playing games with rhyming chants or fingerplays
- Reading alliterative texts out loud

- Grouping objects by beginning sounds
- Reordering words in a well-known sentence or making silly phrases by deleting words from a well-known sentence (perhaps from a favorite storybook)

TEACHING OF READING THROUGH PHONICS

Phonics is the process of learning to read by learning how spoken language is represented by letters. Students learn to read phonetically by sounding out the **phonemes** in words and then blending them together to produce the correct sounds in words. In other words, the student connects speech sounds with letters or groups of letters and blends the sounds together to determine the pronunciation of an unknown word. Phonics is a method commonly used to teach **decoding and reading**, but it has been challenged by other methods, such as the whole language approach. Despite the complexity of pronunciation and combined sounds in the English language, research shows that phonics is a highly effective way to teach reading. Being able to read or pronounce a word does not mean the student comprehends the meaning of the word, but context aids comprehension. When phonics is used as a foundation for decoding, children eventually learn to recognize words automatically and advance to decoding multisyllable words with practice.

ALPHABETIC PRINCIPLE AND ALPHABET WRITING SYSTEMS

The **alphabetic principle** refers to the use of letters and combinations of letters to represent speech sounds. The way letters are combined and pronounced is guided by a system of rules that establishes relationships between written and spoken words and their letter symbols. Alphabet writing systems are common around the world. Some are **phonological** in that each letter stands for an individual sound and words are spelled just as they sound. However, keep in mind that there are other writing systems as well, such as the Chinese **logographic** system and the Japanese **syllabic** system.

FACTS CHILDREN SHOULD KNOW ABOUT LETTERS

To be appropriately prepared to learn to read and write, a child should learn:

- That each letter is **distinct** in appearance
- What **direction and shape** must be used to write each letter
- That each letter has a **name**, which can be associated with the shape of a letter
- That there are **26** letters in the English alphabet, and letters are grouped in a certain order
- That letters represent **sounds of speech**
- That **words** are composed of letters and have meaning
- That one must be able to **correspond** letters and sounds to read

DEVELOPMENT OF LANGUAGE SKILLS

Children learn language through interacting with others, by experiencing language in daily and relevant context, and through understanding that speaking and listening are necessary for effective communication. Teachers can promote **language development** by intensifying the opportunities a child has to experience and understand language.

Teachers can assist language development by:

- Modeling enriched vocabulary and teaching new words
- Using questions and examples to extend a child's descriptive language skills
- Providing ample response time to encourage children to practice speech
- Asking for clarification to provide students with the opportunity to develop communication skills
- Promoting conversations among children
- Providing feedback to let children know they have been heard and understood, and providing further explanation when needed

RELATIONSHIP BETWEEN ORAL AND WRITTEN LANGUAGE DEVELOPMENT

Oral and written language development occur simultaneously. The acquisition of skills in one area supports the acquisition of skills in the other. However, oral language is not a prerequisite to written language. An immature form of oral language development is babbling, and an immature form of written language development is scribbling. **Oral language development** does not occur naturally, but does occur in a social context. This means it is best to include children in conversations rather than simply talk at them. **Written language development** can occur without direct instruction. In fact, reading and writing do not necessarily need to be taught through formal lessons if the child is exposed to a print-rich environment. A teacher can assist a child's language development by building on what the child already knows, discussing relevant and meaningful events and experiences, teaching vocabulary and literacy skills, and providing opportunities to acquire more complex language.

PRINT-RICH ENVIRONMENT

A teacher can provide a **print-rich environment** in the classroom in a number of ways. These include:

- **Displaying** the following in the classroom:
  o Children's names in print or cursive
  o Children's written work
  o Newspapers and magazines
  o Instructional charts
  o Written schedules
  o Signs and labels
  o Printed songs, poems, and rhymes
- Using **graphic organizers** such as KWL charts or story road maps to:
  o Remind students about what was read and discussed
  o Expand on the lesson topic or theme
  o Show the relationships among books, ideas, and words
- Using **big books** to:
  o Point out features of print, such as specific letters and punctuation
  o Track print from right to left
  o Emphasize the concept of words and the fact that they are used to communicate

BENEFITS OF PRINT AND BOOK AWARENESS

Print and book awareness helps a child understand:

- That there is a **connection** between print and messages contained on signs, labels, and other print forms in the child's environment
- That reading and writing are ways to obtain information and communicate ideas
- That **print** written in English runs from left to right and from top to bottom
- That a book has **parts**, such as a title, a cover, a title page, and a table of contents
- That a book has an **author** and contains a **story**
- That **illustrations** can carry meaning
- That **letters and words** are different
- That **words and sentences** are separated by spaces and punctuation
- That different **text forms** are used for different functions
- That print represents **spoken language**
- How to **hold** a book

DECODING

Decoding is the method or strategy used to make sense of printed words and figure out how to correctly pronounce them. In order to **decode**, a student needs to know the relationships between letters and sounds, including letter patterns; that words are constructed from phonemes and phoneme blends; and that a printed word represents a word that can be spoken. This knowledge will help the student recognize familiar words and make informed guesses about the pronunciation of unfamiliar words. Decoding is not the same as comprehension. It does not require an understanding of the meaning of a word, only a knowledge of how to recognize and pronounce it. Decoding can also refer to the skills a student uses to determine the meaning of a **sentence**. These skills include applying knowledge of vocabulary, sentence structure, and context.

ROLE OF FLUENCY IN LITERACY DEVELOPMENT

Fluency is the goal of literacy development. It is the ability to read accurately and quickly. Evidence of fluency includes the ability to recognize words automatically and group words for comprehension. At this point, the student no longer needs to decode words except for complex, unfamiliar ones. He or she is able to move to the next level and understand the **meaning** of a text. The student should be able to self-check for comprehension and should feel comfortable expressing ideas in writing. Teachers can help students build fluency by continuing to provide:

- Reading experiences and discussions about text that gradually increase in level of difficulty
- Reading practice, both silently and out loud
- Word analysis practice
- Instruction on reading comprehension strategies
- Opportunities to express responses to readings through writing

ROLE OF VOCABULARY IN LITERACY DEVELOPMENT

When students do not know the meaning of words in a text, their comprehension is limited. As a result, the text becomes boring or confusing. The larger a student's **vocabulary** is, the better their reading comprehension will be. A larger vocabulary is also associated with an enhanced ability to **communicate** in speech and writing. It is the teacher's role to help students develop a good working vocabulary. Students learn most of the words they use and understand by listening to the world around them (adults, other students, media, etc.) They also learn from their reading experiences, which include being read to and reading independently. Carefully designed activities can also stimulate vocabulary growth, and should emphasize useful words that students see frequently, important words necessary for understanding text, and difficult words, such as idioms or words with more than one meaning.

TEACHING TECHNIQUES PROMOTING VOCABULARY DEVELOPMENT

A student's **vocabulary** can be developed by:

- Calling upon a student's **prior knowledge** and making comparisons to that knowledge
- **Defining** a word and providing multiple examples of the use of the word in context
- Showing a student how to use **context clues** to discover the meaning of a word
- Providing instruction on **prefixes**, **roots**, and **suffixes** to help students break a word into its parts and decipher its meaning
- Showing students how to use a **dictionary and a thesaurus**
- Asking students to **practice** new vocabulary by using the words in their own writing
- Providing a **print-rich environment** with a word wall
- Studying a group of words related to a **single subject**, such as farm words, transportation words, etc. so that concept development is enhanced

AFFIXES, PREFIXES, AND ROOT WORDS

Affixes are syllables attached to the beginning or end of a word to make a derivative or inflectional form of a word. Both prefixes and suffixes are affixes. A **prefix** is a syllable that appears at the beginning of a word that, in combination with the root or base word, creates a specific meaning. For example, the prefix "mis" means "wrong." When combined with the root word "spelling," the word "misspelling" is created, which means the "wrong spelling." A **root word** is the base of a word to which affixes can be added. For example, the prefix "in" or "pre" can be added to the latin root word "vent" to create "invent" or "prevent," respectively. The suffix "er" can be added to the root word "manage" to create "manager," which means "one who manages." The suffix "able," meaning "capable of," can be added to "manage" to create "managable," which means "capable of being managed."

> **Review Video: Affixes**
> Visit mometrix.com/academy and enter code: 782422

SUFFIXES

A suffix is a syllable that appears at the end of a word that, in combination with the root or base word, creates a specific meaning. There are three types of suffixes:

- **Noun suffixes** – Noun suffixes can change a verb or adjective to a noun. They can denote the act of, state of, quality of, or result of something. For example, "-ment" added to "argue" becomes "argument," which can be understood as "the act of resulting state from arguing." Noun suffixes can also denote the doer, or one who acts. For example, "-eer" added to "auction" becomes "auctioneer," meaning "one who auctions." Other examples include "-hood," "-ness," "-tion," "-ship," and "-ism."
- **Verb suffixes** – These change other words to verbs and denote "to make" or "to perform the act of." For example, "-en" added to "soft" makes "soften," which means "to make soft." Other verb suffixes are "-ate" (perpetuate), "-fy" (dignify), and "-ize" (sterilize).
- **Adjectival suffixes** – These suffixes change other words to adjectives and include suffixes such as "-ful," which means "full of." When added to "care," the word "careful" is formed, which means "full of care." Other examples are "-ish," "-less," and "-able."

> **Review Video: English Root Words**
> Visit mometrix.com/academy and enter code: 896380

STRATEGIES TO IMPROVE READING COMPREHENSION

Teachers can model the strategies students can use on their own to better comprehend a text through a read-aloud. First, the teacher should do a walk-through of the story **illustrations** and ask, "What's happening here?" The teacher should then ask students to **predict** what the story will be about based on what they have seen. As the book is read, the teacher should ask open-ended questions such as, "Why do you think the character did this?" and "How do you think the character feels?" The teacher should also ask students if they can **relate** to the story or have background knowledge of something similar. After the reading, the teacher should ask the students to **retell** the story in their own words to check for comprehension. Possible methods of retelling include performing a puppet show or summarizing the story to a partner.

ROLE OF PRIOR KNOWLEDGE IN DETERMINING APPROPRIATE LITERACY EDUCATION

Even preschool children have some literacy skills, and the extent and type of these skills have implications for instructional approaches. **Comprehension** results from relating two or more pieces of information. One piece comes from the text, and another piece might come from **prior knowledge** (something from a student's long-term memory). For a child, that prior knowledge comes from being read to at home; taking part in other literacy experiences, such as playing computer or word games;

being exposed to a print-rich environment at home; and observing examples of parents' reading habits. Children who have had **extensive literacy experience** are better prepared to further develop their literacy skills in school than children who have not been read to, have few books or magazines in their homes, are seldom exposed to high-level oral or written language activities, and seldom witness adults engaged in reading and writing. Children with a scant literacy background are at a disadvantage. The teacher must not make any assumptions about their prior knowledge, and should use intense, targeted instruction. Otherwise, the student may have trouble improving their reading comprehension.

THEORIES OF LANGUAGE DEVELOPMENT

Four theories of language development are:

- **Learning approach** – This theory assumes that language is first learned by imitating the speech of adults. It is then solidified in school through drills about the rules of language structures.
- **Linguistic approach** – Championed by Noam Chomsky in the 1950s, this theory proposes that the ability to use a language is innate. This is a biological approach rather than one based on cognition or social patterning.
- **Cognitive approach** – Developed in the 1970s and based on the work of Piaget, this theory states that children must develop appropriate cognitive skills before they can acquire language.
- **Sociocognitive approach** – In the 1970s, some researchers proposed that language development is a complex interaction of linguistic, social, and cognitive influences. This theory best explains the lack of language skills among children who are neglected, have uneducated parents, or live in poverty.

CLASSROOM PRACTICES BENEFITING SECOND LANGUAGE ACQUISITION

Since some students may have a limited understanding of English, a teacher should employ the following practices to promote second language acquisition:

- Make all instruction as **understandable** as possible and use simple and repeated terms.
- Relate instruction to the **cultures** of ESL children.
- Increase **interactive activities** and use gestures or nonverbal actions when modeling.
- Provide language and literacy development instruction in **all curriculum areas**.
- Establish **consistent routines** that help children connect words and events.
- Use a **schedule** so children know what will happen next and will not feel lost.
- Integrate ESL children into **group activities** with non-ESL children.
- Appoint bilingual students to act as **student translators**.
- Explain actions as activities happen so that a **word to action relationship** is established.
- Initiate opportunities for ESL children to **experiment** with and practice new language.
- Employ **multisensory learning**.

TEACHING STRATEGIES TO PROMOTE LISTENING SKILLS OF ESL STUDENTS

Listening is a critical skill when learning a new language. Students spend a great deal more time listening than they do speaking, and far less time reading and writing than speaking. One way to encourage ESL students to listen is to talk about topics that are of **interest** to the ESL learner. Otherwise, students may tune out the speaker because they don't want to put in that much effort to learn about a topic they find boring. Another way to encourage ESL students to listen is to talk about content or give examples that are **easy** to understand or are **related** to a topic that is familiar to ESL students. Culturally relevant materials will be more interesting to ESL students, will make them feel more comfortable, and will contain vocabulary that they may already be familiar with.

CONSIDERATIONS RELEVANT TO ESL STUDENTS RELATED TO LEARNING BY LISTENING

Listening is not a passive skill, but an **active** one. Therefore, a teacher needs to make the listening experience as rewarding as possible and provide as many auditory and visual clues as possible. Three ways that the teacher can make the listening experience rewarding for ESL students are:

- Avoid **colloquialisms** and **abbreviated or slang terms** that may be confusing to the ESL listener, unless there is enough time to define them and explain their use.
- Make the spoken English understandable by stopping to **clarify** points, **repeating** new or difficult words, and **defining** words that may not be known.
- Support the spoken word with as many **visuals** as possible. Pictures, diagrams, gestures, facial expressions, and body language can help the ESL learner correctly interpret the spoken language more easily and also leaves an image impression that helps them remember the words.

TOP-DOWN AND BOTTOM-UP PROCESSING

ESL students need to be given opportunities to practice both top-down and bottom-up processing. If they are old enough to understand these concepts, they should be made aware that these are two processes that affect their listening comprehension. In **top-down processing**, the listener refers to **background and global knowledge** to figure out the meaning of a message. For example, when asking an ESL student to perform a task, the steps of the task should be explained and accompanied by a review of the vocabulary terms the student already understands so that the student feels comfortable tackling new steps and new words. The teacher should also allow students to ask questions to verify comprehension. In **bottom-up processing**, the listener figures out the meaning of a message by using "**data**" obtained from what is said. This data includes sounds (stress, rhythm, and intonation), words, and grammatical relationships. All data can be used to make conclusions or interpretations. For example, the listener can develop bottom-up skills by learning how to detect differences in intonation between statements and questions.

LISTENING LESSONS

All students, but especially ESL students, can be taught **listening** through specific training. During listening lessons, the teacher should guide students through three steps:

- **Pre-listening activity** – This establishes the purpose of the lesson and engages students' background knowledge. This activity should ask students to think about and discuss something they already know about the topic. Alternatively, the teacher can provide background information.
- **The listening activity** – This requires the listener to obtain information and then immediately do something with that information. For example, the teacher can review the schedule for the day or the week. The students are being given information about a routine they already know, but need to be able to identify names, tasks, and times.
- **Post-listening activity** – This is an evaluation process that allows students to judge how well they did with the listening task. Other language skills can be included in the activity. For example, this activity could involve asking questions about who will do what according to the classroom schedule (Who is the lunch monitor today?) and could also involve asking students to produce whole sentence replies.

HELPING ESL STUDENTS UNDERSTAND SUBJECT MATTER

SPEAKING

To help ESL students better understand subject matter, the following teaching strategies using spoken English can be used:

- **Read aloud** from a textbook, and then ask ESL students to **verbally summarize** what was read. The teacher should assist by providing new words as needed to give students the opportunity to practice vocabulary and speaking skills. The teacher should then read the passage again to students to verify accuracy and details.
- The teacher could ask ESL students to explain why the subject matter is important to them and where they see it fitting into their lives. This verbalization gives them speaking practice and helps them relate to the subject.
- Whenever small group activities are being conducted, ESL students can be placed with **English-speaking students**. It is best to keep the groups to two or three students so that the ESL student will be motivated by the need to be involved. English-speaking students should be encouraged to include ESL students in the group work.

READING

There are supplemental printed materials that can be used to help ESL students understand subject matter. The following strategies can be used to help ESL students develop English reading skills.

- Make sure all ESL students have a **bilingual dictionary** to use. A thesaurus would also be helpful.
- Try to keep **content area books** written in the ESL students' native languages in the classroom. Students can use them side-by-side with English texts. Textbooks in other languages can be ordered from the school library or obtained from the classroom textbook publisher.
- If a student lacks confidence in his/her ability to read the textbook, the teacher can read a passage to the student and have him or her **verbally summarize** the passage. The teacher should take notes on what the student says and then read them back. These notes can be a substitute, short-form, in-their-own-words textbook that the student can understand.

GENERAL TEACHING STRATEGIES TO HELP ESL STUDENTS

Some strategies can help students develop more than one important skill. They may involve a combination of speaking, listening, and viewing. Others are mainly classroom management aids. General teaching strategies for ESL students include:

- **Partner** English-speaking students with ESL students as study buddies and ask the English-speaking students to share notes.
- Encourage ESL students to ask **questions** whenever they don't understand something. They should be aware that they don't have to be able to interpret every word of text to understand the concept.
- Dictate **key sentences** related to the content area being taught and ask ESL students to write them down. This gives them practice in listening and writing, and also helps them identify what is important.
- **Alternate** difficult and easy tasks so that ESL students can experience academic success.
- Ask ESL students to **label** objects associated with content areas, such as maps, diagrams, parts of a leaf, or parts of a sentence. This gives students writing and reading experience and helps them remember key vocabulary.

Language and Literature

Figurative Language

LITERAL AND FIGURATIVE MEANING

When language is used **literally**, the words mean exactly what they say and nothing more. When language is used **figuratively**, the words mean something beyond their literal meaning. For example, "The weeping willow tree has long, trailing branches and leaves" is a literal description. But "The weeping willow tree looks as if it is bending over and crying" is a figurative description—specifically, a **simile** or stated comparison. Another figurative language form is **metaphor**, or an implied comparison. A good example is the metaphor of a city, state, or city-state as a ship, and its governance as sailing that ship. Ancient Greek lyrical poet Alcaeus is credited with first using this metaphor, and ancient Greek tragedian Aeschylus then used it in *Seven Against Thebes,* and then Plato used it in the *Republic.*

FIGURES OF SPEECH

A figure of speech is a verbal expression whose meaning is figurative rather than literal. For example, the phrase "butterflies in the stomach" does not refer to actual butterflies in a person's stomach. It is a metaphor representing the fluttery feelings experienced when a person is nervous or excited—or when one "falls in love," which does not mean physically falling. "Hitting a sales target" does not mean physically hitting a target with arrows as in archery; it is a metaphor for meeting a sales quota. "Climbing the ladder of success" metaphorically likens advancing in one's career to ascending ladder rungs. Similes, such as "light as a feather" (meaning very light, not a feather's actual weight), and hyperbole, like "I'm starving/freezing/roasting," are also figures of speech. Figures of speech are often used and crafted for emphasis, freshness of expression, or clarity.

> **Review Video: Figure of Speech**
> Visit mometrix.com/academy and enter code: 111295

FIGURATIVE LANGUAGE

Figurative language extends past the literal meanings of words. It offers readers new insight into the people, things, events, and subjects covered in a work of literature. Figurative language also enables readers to feel they are sharing the authors' experiences. It can stimulate the reader's senses, make comparisons that readers find intriguing or even startling, and enable readers to view the world in different ways. When looking for figurative language, it is important to consider the context of the sentence or situation. Phrases that appear out of place or make little sense when read literally are likely instances of figurative language. Once figurative language has been recognized, context is also important to determining the type of figurative language being used and its function. For example, when a comparison is being made, a metaphor or simile is likely being used. This means the comparison may emphasize or create irony through the things being compared. Seven specific types of figurative language include: alliteration, onomatopoeia, personification, imagery, similes, metaphors, and hyperbole.

> **Review Video: Figurative Language**
> Visit mometrix.com/academy and enter code: 584902

ALLITERATION AND ONOMATOPOEIA

Alliteration describes a series of words beginning with the same sounds. **Onomatopoeia** uses words imitating the sounds of things they name or describe. For example, in his poem "Come Down, O Maid," Alfred Tennyson writes of "The moan of doves in immemorial elms, / And murmuring of innumerable bees." The word "moan" sounds like some sounds doves make, "murmuring" represents the sounds of bees buzzing. Onomatopoeia also includes words that are simply meant to represent sounds, such as "meow," "kaboom," and "whoosh."

PERSONIFICATION

Another type of figurative language is **personification**. This is describing a non-human thing, like an animal or an object, as if it were human. The general intent of personification is to describe things in a manner that will be comprehensible to readers. When an author states that a tree *groans* in the wind, he or she does not mean that the tree is emitting a low, pained sound from a mouth. Instead, the author means that the tree is making a noise similar to a human groan. Of course, this personification establishes a tone of sadness or suffering. A different tone would be established if the author said that the tree was *swaying* or *dancing*. Alfred Tennyson's poem "The Eagle" uses all of these types of figurative language: "He clasps the crag with crooked hands." Tennyson used alliteration, repeating /k/ and /kr/ sounds. These hard-sounding consonants reinforce the imagery giving visual and tactile impressions of the eagle.

SIMILES AND METAPHORS

Similes are stated comparisons using "like" or "as." Similes can be used to stimulate readers' imaginations and appeal to their senses. Because a simile includes *like* or *as*, the device creates more space between the description and the thing being described than a metaphor does. If an author says that *a house was like a shoebox*, then the tone is different than the author saying that the house *was* a shoebox. Authors will choose between a metaphor and a simile depending on their intended tone.

Similes also help compare fictional characters to well-known objects or experiences, so the reader can better relate to them. William Wordsworth's poem about "Daffodils" begins, "I wandered lonely as a cloud." This simile compares his loneliness to that of a cloud. It is also personification, giving a cloud the human quality loneliness. In his novel *Lord Jim* (1900), Joseph Conrad writes in Chapter 33, "I would have given anything for the power to soothe her frail soul, tormenting itself in its invincible ignorance like a small bird beating about the cruel wires of a cage." Conrad uses the word "like" to compare the girl's soul to a small bird. His description of the bird beating at the cage shows the similar helplessness of the girl's soul to gain freedom.

A **metaphor** is a type of figurative language in which the writer equates something with another thing that is not particularly similar, instead of using *like* or *as*. For instance, *the bird was an arrow arcing through the sky*. In this sentence, the arrow is serving as a metaphor for the bird. The point of a metaphor is to encourage the reader to consider the item being described in a *different way*. Let's continue with this metaphor for a flying bird. You are asked to envision the bird's flight as being similar to the arc of an arrow. So, you imagine the flight to be swift and bending. Metaphors are a way for the author to describe an item *without being direct and obvious*. This literary device is a lyrical and suggestive way of providing information. Note that the reference for a metaphor will not always be mentioned explicitly by the author. Consider the following description of a forest in winter: *Swaying skeletons reached for the sky and groaned as the wind blew through them.* In this example, the author is using *skeletons* as a metaphor for leafless trees. This metaphor creates a spooky tone while inspiring the reader's imagination.

> **Review Video: Metaphor**
> Visit mometrix.com/academy and enter code: 133295

LITERARY EXAMPLES OF METAPHOR

A **metaphor** is an implied comparison, i.e. it compares something to something else without using "like", "as", or other comparative words. For example, in "The Tyger" (1794), William Blake writes, "Tyger Tyger, burning bright, / In the forests of the night." Blake compares the tiger to a flame not by saying it is like a fire, but by simply describing it as "burning." Henry Wadsworth Longfellow's poem "O Ship of State" (1850) uses an extended metaphor by referring consistently throughout the entire poem to the state, union, or republic as a seagoing vessel, referring to its keel, mast, sail, rope, anchors, and to its braving waves, rocks, gale, tempest, and "false lights on the shore". Within the extended metaphor, Wordsworth uses a specific metaphor: "the anchors of thy hope!"

TED HUGHES' ANIMAL METAPHORS

Ted Hughes frequently used animal metaphors in his poetry. In "The Thought Fox," a model of concise, structured beauty, Hughes characterizes the poet's creative process with succinct, striking imagery of an idea entering his head like a wild fox. Repeating "loneliness" in the first two stanzas emphasizes the poet's lonely work: "Something else is alive / Beside the clock's loneliness." He treats an idea's arrival as separate from himself. Three stanzas detail in vivid images a fox's approach from the outside winter forest at starless midnight —its nose, "Cold, delicately" touching twigs and leaves; "neat" paw prints in snow; "bold" body; brilliant green eyes; and self-contained, focused progress—"Till, with a sudden sharp hot stink of fox," he metaphorically depicts poetic inspiration as the fox's physical entry into "the dark hole of the head." Hughes ends by summarizing his vision of a poet as an interior, passive idea recipient, with the outside world unchanged: "The window is starless still; the clock ticks, / The page is printed."

> **Review Video: Simile**
> Visit mometrix.com/academy and enter code: 642949
>
> **Review Video: Metaphor**
> Visit mometrix.com/academy and enter code: 133295

HYPERBOLE

Hyperbole is excessive exaggeration used for humor or emphasis rather than for literal meaning. For example, in *To Kill a Mockingbird*, Harper Lee wrote, "People moved slowly then. There was no hurry, for there was nowhere to go, nothing to buy and no money to buy it with, nothing to see outside the boundaries of Maycomb County." This was not literally true; Lee exaggerates the scarcity of these things for emphasis. In "Old Times on the Mississippi," Mark Twain wrote, "I... could have hung my hat on my eyes, they stuck out so far." This is not literal, but makes his description vivid and funny. In his poem "As I Walked Out One Evening", W. H. Auden wrote, "I'll love you, dear, I'll love you / Till China and Africa meet, / And the river jumps over the mountain / And the salmon sing in the street." He used things not literally possible to emphasize the duration of his love.

> **Review Video: Hyperbole and Understatement**
> Visit mometrix.com/academy and enter code: 308470

LITERARY IRONY

In literature, irony demonstrates the opposite of what is said or done. The three types of irony are **verbal irony**, **situational irony**, and **dramatic irony**. Verbal irony uses words opposite to the meaning. Sarcasm may use verbal irony. One common example is describing something that is confusing as "clear as mud." For example, in his 1986 movie *Hannah and Her Sisters,* author, director, and actor Woody Allen says to his character's date, "I had a great evening; it was like the Nuremburg Trials." Notice these employ similes. In situational irony, what happens contrasts with what was expected. O. Henry's short story *The Gift of the Magi* uses situational irony: a husband and wife each sacrifice their most prized possession to buy each other a Christmas present. The irony is that she sells her long hair to buy him a watch fob, while he sells his heirloom pocket-watch to buy her the jeweled combs for her hair she had long wanted; in the end, neither of them can use their gifts. In dramatic irony, narrative informs audiences of more than its characters know. For example, in *Romeo and Juliet,* the audience is made aware that Juliet is only asleep, while Romeo believes her to be dead, which then leads to Romeo's death.

> **Review Video: Irony**
> Visit mometrix.com/academy and enter code: 374204

IDIOMS

Idioms create comparisons, and often take the form of similes or metaphors. Idioms are always phrases and are understood to have a meaning that is different from its individual words' literal meaning. For example, "break a leg" is a common idiom that is used to wish someone luck or tell them to perform well. Literally, the phrase "break a leg" means to injure a person's leg, but the phrase takes on a different meaning when used as an idiom. Another example is "call it a day," which means to temporarily stop working on a task, or find a stopping point, rather than literally referring to something as "a day." Many idioms are associated with a region or group. For example, an idiom commonly used in the American South is "'til the cows come home." This phrase is often used to indicate that something will take or may last for a very long time, but not that it will literally last until the cows return to where they reside.

Literary Analysis

LITERARY TERMINOLOGY

In works of prose such as novels, a group of connected sentences covering one main topic is termed a **paragraph**. In works of poetry, a group of verses similarly connected is called a **stanza**. In drama, when early works used verse, these were also divided into stanzas or **couplets**. Drama evolved to use predominantly prose. Overall, whether prose or verse, the conversation in a play is called **dialogue**. Large sections of dialogue spoken by one actor are called **soliloquies** or **monologues**. Dialogue that informs audiences but is unheard by other characters is called an **aside**. Novels and plays share certain common elements, such as **characters**, the people in the story; **plot**, the action of the story; **climax** when action or dramatic tension reaches its highest point; and **denouement**, the resolution following the climax. Sections dividing novels are called **chapters**, while sections of plays are called **acts**. Subsections of plays' acts are called **scenes**. Novel chapters usually do not have subsections. However, some novels do include groups of chapters that form different sections.

LITERARY ANALYSIS

The best literary analysis shows special insight into at least one important aspect of a text. When analyzing literary texts, it can be difficult to find a starting place. Many texts can be analyzed several different ways, often leaving an overwhelming number of options for writers to consider. However, narrowing the focus to a particular element of literature can be helpful when preparing to analyze a text. Symbolism, themes, and motifs are common starting points for literary analysis. These three methods of analysis can lead to a holistic analysis of a text, since they involve elements that are often distributed throughout the text. However, not all texts feature these elements in a way that facilitates a strong analysis, if they are present at all. It is also common to focus on character or plot development for analysis. These elements are compatible with theme, symbolism, and allusion. Setting and imagery, figurative language, and any external contexts can also contribute to analysis or complement one of these other elements. The application of a critical, or literary, theory to a text can also provide a thorough and strong analysis.

SETTING AND TIME FRAME

A literary text has both a setting and time frame. A **setting** is the place in which the story as a whole is set. The **time frame** is the period in which the story is set. This may refer to the historical period the story takes place in or if the story takes place over a single day. Both setting and time frame are relevant to a text's meaning because they help the reader place the story in time and space. An author uses setting and time frame to anchor a text, create a mood, and enhance its meaning. This helps a reader understand why a character acts the way he does, or why certain events in the story are important. The setting impacts the **plot** and character **motivations**, while the time frame helps place the story in **chronological context**.

EXAMPLE

Read the following excerpt from The Adventures of Huckleberry Finn by Mark Twain and analyze the relevance of setting to the text's meaning:

> We said there warn't no home like a raft, after all. Other places do seem so cramped up and smothery, but a raft don't. You feel mighty free and easy and comfortable on a raft.

This excerpt from *The Adventures of Huckleberry Finn* by Mark Twain reveals information about the **setting** of the book. By understanding that the main character, Huckleberry Finn, lives on a raft, the reader can place the story on a river, in this case, the Mississippi River in the South before the Civil War. The information about the setting also gives the reader clues about the **character** of Huck Finn: he clearly values independence and freedom, and he likes the outdoors. The information about the setting in the quote helps the reader to better understand the rest of the text.

THEME

The **theme** of a passage is what the reader learns from the text or the passage. It is the lesson or **moral** contained in the passage. It also is a unifying idea that is used throughout the text; it can take the form of a common setting, idea, symbol, design, or recurring event. A passage can have two or more themes that convey its overall idea. The theme or themes of a passage are often based on **universal themes**. They can frequently be expressed using well-known sayings about life, society, or human nature, such as "Hard work pays off" or "Good triumphs over evil." Themes are not usually stated **explicitly**. The reader must figure them out by carefully reading the passage. Themes are often the reason why passages are written; they give a passage unity and meaning. Themes are created through **plot development**. The events of a story help shape the themes of a passage.

EXAMPLE

Explain why "Take care of what you care about" accurately describes the theme of the following excerpt.

> Luca collected baseball cards, but he wasn't very careful with them. He left them around the house. His dog liked to chew. One day, Luca and his friend Bart were looking at his collection. Then they went outside. When Luca got home, he saw his dog chewing on his cards. They were ruined.

This excerpt tells the story of a boy who is careless with his baseball cards and leaves them lying around. His dog ends up chewing them and ruining them. The lesson is that if you care about something, you need to take care of it. This is the theme, or point, of the story. Some stories have more than one theme, but this is not really true of this excerpt. The reader needs to figure out the theme based on what happens in the story. Sometimes, as in the case of fables, the theme is stated directly in the text. However, this is not usually the case.

CONFLICT

A **conflict** is a problem to be solved. Literary plots typically include one conflict or more. Characters' attempts to resolve conflicts drive the narrative's forward movement. **Conflict resolution** is often the protagonist's primary occupation. Physical conflicts like exploring, wars, and escapes tend to make plots most suspenseful and exciting. Emotional, mental, or moral conflicts tend to make stories more personally gratifying or rewarding for many audiences. Conflicts can be external or internal. A major type of internal conflict is some inner personal battle, or **man versus self**. Major types of external conflicts include **man versus nature**, **man versus man**, and **man versus society**. Readers can identify conflicts in literary plots by identifying the protagonist and antagonist and asking why they conflict, what events develop the conflict, where the climax occurs, and how they identify with the characters.

Read the following paragraph and discuss the type of conflict present:

> Timothy was shocked out of sleep by the appearance of a bear just outside his tent. After panicking for a moment, he remembered some advice he had read in preparation for this trip: he should make noise so the bear would not be startled. As Timothy started to hum and sing, the bear wandered away.

There are three main types of conflict in literature: **man versus man**, **man versus nature**, and **man versus self**. This paragraph is an example of man versus nature. Timothy is in conflict with the bear. Even though no physical conflict like an attack exists, Timothy is pitted against the bear. Timothy uses his knowledge to "defeat" the bear and keep himself safe. The solution to the conflict is that Timothy makes noise, the bear wanders away, and Timothy is safe.

CONFLICT RESOLUTION

The way the conflict is **resolved** depends on the type of conflict. The plot of any book starts with the lead up to the conflict, then the conflict itself, and finally the solution, or **resolution**, to the conflict. In **man-versus-man** conflicts, the conflict is often resolved by two parties coming to some sort of agreement or by one party triumphing over the other party. In **man-versus-nature** conflicts, the conflict is often resolved by man coming to some realization about some aspect of nature. In **man-versus-self** conflicts, the conflict is often resolved by the character growing or coming to an understanding about part of himself.

SYNTAX AND WORD CHOICE

Authors use words and **syntax**, or sentence structure, to make their texts unique, convey their own writing style, and sometimes to make a point or emphasis. They know that word choice and syntax contribute to the reader's understanding of the text as well as to the tone and mood of a text.

ALLUSION

An allusion is an uncited but recognizable reference to something else. Authors use language to make allusions to places, events, artwork, and other books in order to make their own text richer. For example, an author may allude to a very important text in order to make his own text seem more important. Martin Luther King, Jr. started his "I Have a Dream" speech by saying "Five score years ago..." This is a clear allusion to President Abraham Lincoln's "Gettysburg Address" and served to remind people of the significance of the event. An author may allude to a place to ground his text or make a cultural reference to make readers feel included. There are many reasons that authors make allusions.

> **Review Video: Allusion**
> Visit mometrix.com/academy and enter code: 294065

COMIC RELIEF

Comic relief is the use of comedy by an author to break up a dramatic or tragic scene and infuse it with a bit of **lightheartedness**. In William Shakespeare's *Hamlet*, two gravediggers digging the grave for Ophelia share a joke while they work. The death and burial of Ophelia are tragic moments that directly follow each other. Shakespeare uses an instance of comedy to break up the tragedy and give his audience a bit of a break from the tragic drama. Authors sometimes use comic relief so that their work will be less depressing; other times they use it to create irony or contrast between the darkness of the situation and the lightness of the joke. Often, authors will use comedy to parallel what is happening in the tragic scenes.

MOOD AND TONE

Mood is a story's atmosphere, or the feelings the reader gets from reading it. The way authors set the mood in writing is comparable to the way filmmakers use music to set the mood in movies. Instead of music, though, writers judiciously select descriptive words to evoke certain moods. The mood of a work may convey joy, anger, bitterness, hope, gloom, fear, apprehension, or any other emotion the author wants the reader to feel. In addition to vocabulary choices, authors also use figurative expressions, particular sentence structures, and choices of diction that project and reinforce the moods they want to create. Whereas mood is the reader's emotions evoked by reading what is written, **tone** is the emotions and attitudes of the writer that she or he expresses in the writing. Authors use the same literary techniques to establish tone as they do to establish mood. An author may use a humorous tone, an angry or sad tone, a sentimental or unsentimental tone, or something else entirely.

MOOD AND TONE IN THE GREAT GATSBY

To understand the difference between mood and tone, look at this excerpt from F. Scott Fitzgerald's *The Great Gatsby*. In this passage, Nick Caraway, the novel's narrator, is decribing his afforable house, which sits in a neighborhood full of expensive mansions.

> "I lived at West Egg, the—well the less fashionable of the two, though this is a most superficial tag to express the bizarre and not a little sinister contrast betweeen them. My house was at the very tip of the egg, only fifty yard from the Sound, and squeezed between two huge places that rented for twelve or fifteen thousand a season ... My own house was an eyesore, but it was a small eyesore, and it had been overlooked, so I had a view of the water, a partial view of my neighbor's lawn, and the consoling proximity of millionaires—all for eighty dollars a month."

In this description, the mood created for the reader does not match the tone created through the narrator. The mood in this passage is one of disatisfaction and inferiority. Nick compares his home to his neighbors', saying he lives in the "less fashionable" neighborhood and that his house is "overlooked," an "eyesore," and "squeezed between two huge" mansions. He also adds that his placement allows him the "consoling proximity of millionaires." A literal reading of these details leads the reader to have negative feelings toward Nick's house and his economic inferiority to his neighbors, creating the mood.

However, Fitzgerald also conveys an opposing attitude, or tone, through Nick's description. Nick calls the distinction between the neighboorhoods "superficial," showing a suspicion of the value suggested by the neighborhoods' titles, properties, and residents. Nick also undermines his critique of his own home by calling it "a small eyesore" and claiming it has "been overlooked." However, he follows these statements with a description of his surroundings, claiming that he has "a view of the water" and can see some of his wealthy neighbor's property from his home, and a comparison between the properties' rent. While the mental image created for the reader depicts a small house shoved between looming mansions, the tone suggests that Nick enjoys these qualities about his home, or at least finds it charming. He acknowledges its shortcomings, but includes the benefits of his home's unassuming appearance.

> **Review Video: Style, Tone, and Mood**
> Visit mometrix.com/academy and enter code: 416961

CHARACTER DEVELOPMENT

When depicting characters or figures in a written text, authors generally use actions, dialogue, and descriptions as characterization techniques. Characterization can occur in both fiction and nonfiction and is used to show a character or figure's personality, demeanor, and thoughts. This helps create a more engaging experience for the reader by providing a more concrete picture of a character or figure's tendencies and features. Characterizations also gives authors the opportunity to integrate elements such as dialects, activities, attire, and attitudes into their writing.

To understand the meaning of a story, it is vital to understand the characters as the author describes them. We can look for contradictions in what a character thinks, says, and does. We can notice whether the author's observations about a character differ from what other characters in the story say about that character. A character may be dynamic, meaning they change significantly during the story, or static, meaning they remain the same from beginning to end. Characters may be two-dimensional, not fully developed, or may be well developed with characteristics that stand out vividly. Characters may also symbolize universal properties. Additionally, readers can compare and contrast characters to analyze how each one developed.

A well-known example of character development can be found in Charles Dickens's *Great Expectations*. The novel's main character, Pip, is introduced as a young boy, and he is depicted as innocent, kind, and humble. However, as Pip grows up and is confronted with the social hierarchy of Victorian England, he becomes arrogant and rejects his loved ones in pursuit of his own social advancement. Once he achieves his social goals, he realizes the merits of his former lifestyle, and lives with the wisdom he gained in both environments and life stages. Dickens shows Pip's ever-changing character through his interactions with others and his inner thoughts, which evolve as his personal values and personality shift.

> **Review Video: Character Changes**
> Visit mometrix.com/academy and enter code: 408719

DIALOGUE

Effectively written **dialogue** serves at least one, but usually several, purposes. It advances the story and moves the plot, develops the characters, sheds light on the work's theme or meaning, and can, often subtly, account for the passage of time not otherwise indicated. It can alter the direction that the plot is taking, typically by introducing some new conflict or changing existing ones. Dialogue can establish a work's narrative voice and the characters' voices and set the tone of the story or of particular characters. When fictional characters display enlightenment or realization, dialogue can give readers an understanding of what those characters have discovered and how. Dialogue can illuminate the motivations and wishes of the story's characters. By using consistent thoughts and syntax, dialogue can support character development. Skillfully created, it can also represent real-life speech rhythms in written form. Via conflicts and ensuing action, dialogue also provides drama.

DIALOGUE IN FICTION

In fictional works, effectively written dialogue does more than just break up or interrupt sections of narrative. While dialogue may supply exposition for readers, it must nonetheless be believable. Dialogue should be dynamic, not static, and it should not resemble regular prose. Authors should not use dialogue to write clever similes or metaphors, or to inject their own opinions. Nor should they use dialogue at all when narrative would be better. Most importantly, dialogue should not slow the plot movement. Dialogue must seem natural, which means careful construction of phrases rather than actually duplicating natural speech, which does not necessarily translate well to the written word. Finally, all dialogue must be pertinent to the story, rather than just added conversation.

POINT OF VIEW

Another element that impacts a text is the author's point of view. The **point of view** of a text is the perspective from which a passage is told. An author will always have a point of view about a story before he or she draws up a plot line. The author will know what events they want to take place, how they want the characters to interact, and how they want the story to resolve. An author will also have an opinion on the topic or series of events which is presented in the story that is based on their prior experience and beliefs.

The two main points of view that authors use, especially in a work of fiction, are first person and third person. If the narrator of the story is also the main character, or *protagonist*, the text is written in first-person point of view. In first person, the author writes from the perspective of *I*. Third-person point of view is probably the most common that authors use in their passages. Using third person, authors refer to each character by using *he* or *she*. In third-person omniscient, the narrator is not a character in the story and tells the story of all of the characters at the same time.

> **Review Video: Point of View**
> Visit mometrix.com/academy and enter code: 383336

FIRST-PERSON NARRATION

First-person narratives let narrators express inner feelings and thoughts, especially when the narrator is the protagonist as Lemuel Gulliver is in Jonathan Swift's *Gulliver's Travels.* The narrator may be a close friend of the protagonist, like Dr. Watson in Sir Arthur Conan Doyle's *Sherlock Holmes.* Or, the narrator can be less involved with the main characters and plot, like Nick Carraway in F. Scott Fitzgerald's *The Great Gatsby.* When a narrator reports others' narratives, she or he is a "**frame narrator**," like the nameless narrator of Joseph Conrad's *Heart of Darkness* or Mr. Lockwood in Emily Brontë's *Wuthering Heights.* **First-person plural** is unusual but can be effective. Isaac Asimov's *I, Robot*, William Faulkner's *A Rose for Emily*, Maxim Gorky's *Twenty-Six Men and a Girl*, and Jeffrey Eugenides' *The Virgin Suicides* all use first-person plural narration. Author Kurt Vonnegut is the first-person narrator in his semi-autobiographical novel *Timequake.* Also unusual, but effective, is a **first-person omniscient** (rather than the more common third-person omniscient) narrator, like Death in Markus Zusak's *The Book Thief* and the ghost in Alice Sebold's *The Lovely Bones.*

SECOND-PERSON NARRATION

While **second-person** address is very commonplace in popular song lyrics, it is the least used form of narrative voice in literary works. Popular serial books of the 1980s like *Fighting Fantasy* or *Choose Your Own Adventure* employed second-person narratives. In some cases, a narrative combines both second-person and first-person voices, using the pronouns *you* and *I*. This can draw readers into the story, and it can also enable the authors to compare directly "your" and "my" feelings, thoughts, and actions. When the narrator is also a character in the story, as in Edgar Allan Poe's short story "The Tell-Tale Heart" or Jay McInerney's novel *Bright Lights, Big City*, the narrative is better defined as first-person despite its also addressing "you."

THIRD-PERSON NARRATION

Narration in the **third person** is the most prevalent type, as it allows authors the most flexibility. It is so common that readers simply assume without needing to be informed that the narrator is not a character in the story, or involved in its events. **Third-person singular** is used more frequently than **third-person plural**, though some authors have also effectively used plural. However, both singular and plural are most often included in stories according to which characters are being described. The third-person narrator may be either objective or subjective, and either omniscient or limited. **Objective third-person** narration does not include what the characters described are thinking or feeling, while **subjective third-person** narration does. The **third-person omniscient** narrator knows everything about all characters, including their thoughts and emotions, and all related places, times, and events. However, the **third-person limited** narrator may know everything about a particular character, but is limited to that character. In other words, the narrator cannot speak about anything that character does not know.

ALTERNATING-PERSON NARRATION

Although authors more commonly write stories from one point of view, there are also instances wherein they alternate the narrative voice within the same book. For example, they may sometimes use an omniscient third-person narrator and a more intimate first-person narrator at other times. In J. K. Rowling's series of *Harry Potter* novels, she often writes in a third-person limited narrative, but sometimes changes to narration by characters other than the protagonist. George R. R. Martin's series *A Song of Ice and Fire* changes the point of view to coincide with divisions between chapters. The same technique is used by Erin Hunter (a pseudonym for several authors of the *Warriors, Seekers,* and *Survivors* book series). Authors using first-person narrative sometimes switch to third-person to describe significant action scenes, especially those where the narrator was absent or uninvolved, as Barbara Kingsolver does in her novel *The Poisonwood Bible*.

HISTORICAL AND SOCIAL CONTEXT

Fiction that is heavily influenced by a historical or social context cannot be comprehended as the author intended if the reader does not keep this context in mind. Many important elements of the text will be influenced by any context, including symbols, allusions, settings, and plot events. These contexts, as well as the identity of the work's author, can help to inform the reader about the author's concerns and intended meanings. For example, George Orwell published his novel *1984* in the year 1949, soon after the end of World War II. At that time, following the defeat of the Nazis, the Cold War began between the Western Allied nations and the Eastern Soviet Communists. People were therefore concerned about the conflict between the freedoms afforded by Western democracies versus the oppression represented by Communism. Orwell had also previously fought in the Spanish Civil War against a Spanish regime that he and his fellows viewed as oppressive. From this information, readers can infer that Orwell was concerned about oppression by totalitarian governments. This informs *1984*'s story of Winston Smith's rebellion against the oppressive "Big Brother" government, of the fictional dictatorial state of Oceania, and his capture, torture, and ultimate conversion by that government. Some literary theories also seek to use historical and social contexts to reveal deeper meanings and implications in a text.

TEXTUAL EVIDENCE

No literary analysis is complete without textual evidence. Summaries, paraphrases, and quotes are all forms of textual evidence, but direct quotes from the text are the most effective form of evidence. The best textual evidence is relevant, accurate, and clearly supports the writer's claim. This can include pieces of descriptions, dialogue, or exposition that shows the applicability of the analysis to the text. Analysis that is average, or sufficient, shows an understanding of the text; contains supporting textual evidence that is relevant and accurate, if not strong; and shows a specific and clear response. Analysis that partially meets criteria also shows understanding, but the textual evidence is generalized, incomplete, only partly relevant or accurate, or connected only weakly. Inadequate analysis is vague, too general, or incorrect. It may give irrelevant or incomplete textual evidence, or may simply summarize the plot rather than analyzing the work. It is important to incorporate textual evidence from the work being analyzed and any supplemental materials and to provide appropriate attribution for these sources.

Theme and Plot

THEMES IN LITERATURE

When we read parables, their themes are the lessons they aim to teach. When we read fables, the moral of each story is its theme. When we read fictional works, the authors' perspectives regarding life and human behavior are their themes. Unlike in parables and fables, themes in literary fiction are usually not meant to preach or teach the readers a lesson. Hence, themes in fiction are not as explicit as they are in parables or fables. Instead, they are implicit, and the reader only infers them. By analyzing the fictional characters through thinking about their actions and behavior, understanding the setting of the story, and reflecting on how its plot develops, the reader comes to infer the main theme of the work. When writers succeed, they communicate with their readers such that common ground is established between author and audience. While a reader's individual experience may differ in its details from the author's written story, both may share universal underlying truths which allow author and audience to connect.

DETERMINING THEME

In well-crafted literature, theme, structure, and plot are interdependent and inextricable: each element informs and reflects the others. The structure of a work is how it is organized. The theme is the central idea or meaning found in it. The plot is what happens in the story. Titles can also inform us of a work's theme. For instance, the title of Edgar Allan Poe's "The Tell-Tale Heart" informs readers of the story's theme of guilt before they even read about the repeated heartbeat the protagonist hears immediately before and constantly after committing and hiding a murder. Repetitive patterns of events or behaviors also give clues to themes. The same is true of symbols. For example, in F. Scott Fitzgerald's *The Great Gatsby,* for Jay Gatsby the green light at the end of the dock symbolizes Daisy Buchanan and his own dreams for the future. More generally, it is also understood as a symbol of the American Dream, and narrator Nick Carraway explicitly compares it to early settlers' sight of America rising from the ocean.

THEMATIC DEVELOPMENT
THEME IN THE GREAT GATSBY

In *The Great Gatsby*, F. Scott Fitzgerald portrayed 1920s America as greedy, cynical, and rife with moral decay. Jay Gatsby's lavish weekly parties symbolize the reckless excesses of the Jazz Age. The growth of bootlegging and organized crime in reaction to Prohibition is symbolized by the character of Meyer Wolfsheim and by Gatsby's own ill-gotten wealth. Fitzgerald symbolized social divisions using geography. The "old money" aristocrats like the Buchanans lived on East Egg, while the "new money" bourgeois like Gatsby lived on West Egg. Fitzgerald also used weather, as many authors have, to reinforce narrative and emotional tones in the novel. Just as in *Romeo and Juliet*, where William Shakespeare set the confrontation of Tybalt and Mercutio and its deadly consequences on the hottest summer day under a burning sun, in *The Great Gatsby*, Fitzgerald did the same with Tom Wilson's deadly confrontation with Gatsby. Both works are ostensible love stories carrying socially critical themes about the destructiveness of pointless and misguided behaviors—family feuds in the former, pursuit of money in the latter.

> **Review Video: Thematic Development**
> Visit mometrix.com/academy and enter code: 576507

THEME IN LES MISÉRABLES

In Victor Hugo's novel *Les Misérables*, the overall metamorphosis of protagonist Jean Valjean from a cynical ex-convict into a noble benefactor demonstrates Hugo's theme of the importance of love and compassion for others. Hugo also reflects this in more specific plot events. For example, Valjean's love for Cosette sustains him through many difficult periods and trying events. Hugo illustrates how love and compassion for others beget the same in them: Bishop Myriel's kindness to Valjean eventually inspires him to become honest. Years later, Valjean, as M. Madeleine, has rescued Fauchelevent from under a fallen carriage, Fauchelevent returns the compassionate act by giving Valjean sanctuary in the convent. M. Myriel's kindness also ultimately enables Valjean to rescue Cosette from the Thénardiers. Receiving Valjean's father-like love enables Cosette to fall in love with and marry Marius, and the love between Cosette and Marius enables the couple to forgive Valjean for his past crimes when they are revealed.

THEME IN "THE TELL-TALE HEART"

In one of his shortest stories, "The Tell-Tale Heart," Poe used economy of language to emphasize the murderer-narrator's obsessive focus on bare details like the victim's cataract-milky eye, the sound of a heartbeat, and insistence he is sane. The narrator begins by denying he is crazy, even citing his extreme agitation as proof of sanity. Contradiction is then extended: the narrator loves the old man, yet kills him. His motives are irrational—not greed or revenge, but to relieve the victim of his "evil eye." Because "eye" and "I" are homonyms, readers may infer that eye/I symbolizes the old man's identity, contradicting the killer's delusion that he can separate them. The narrator distances himself from the old man by perceiving his eye as separate, and dismembering his dead body. This backfires when he imagines the victim's heartbeat, which is really his own, just before he kills him and frequently afterward. Guilty and paranoid, he gives himself away. Poe predated Freud in exploring the paradox of killing those we love and the concept of projecting our own processes onto others.

THEME IN THE WORKS OF WILLIAM FAULKNER AND CHARLES DICKENS

William Faulkner contrasts the traditions of the antebellum South with the rapid changes of post-Civil War industrialization in his short story "A Rose for Emily." Living inside the isolated world of her house, Emily Grierson denies the reality of modern progress. Contradictorily, she is both a testament to time-honored history and a mysterious, eccentric, unfathomable burden. Faulkner portrays her with deathlike imagery even in life, comparing her to a drowned woman and referring to her skeleton. Emily symbolizes the Old South; as her social status is degraded, so is the antebellum social order. Like Miss Havisham in Charles Dickens' *Great Expectations,* Emily preserves her bridal bedroom, denying change and time's passage. Emily tries to control death through denial, shown in her necrophilia with her father's corpse and her killing of Homer Barron to stop him from leaving her, then also denying his death. Faulkner uses the motif of dust throughout to represent not only the decay of Emily, her house, and Old Southern traditions, but also how her secrets are obscured from others.

THEME IN MOBY-DICK

The great White Whale in *Moby-Dick* plays various roles to different characters. In Captain Ahab's obsessive, monomaniacal quest to kill it, the whale represents all evil, and Ahab believes it his duty and destiny to rid the world of it. Ishmael attempts through multiple scientific disciplines to understand the whale objectively, but fails—it is hidden underwater and mysterious to humans—reinforcing Melville's theme that humans can never know everything; here the whale represents the unknowable. Melville reverses white's usual connotation of purity in Ishmael's dread of white, associated with crashing waves, polar animals, albinos—all frightening and unnatural. White is often viewed as an absence of color, yet white light is the sum total of all colors in the spectrum. In the same way, white can signify both absence of meaning, and totality of meaning incomprehensible to humans. As a creature of nature, the whale also symbolizes how 19th-century white men's exploitative expansionistic actions were destroying the natural environment.

THEME IN *THE OLD MAN AND THE SEA*

Because of the old fisherman Santiago's struggle to capture a giant marlin, some people characterize Ernest Hemingway's *The Old Man and the Sea* as telling of man against nature. However, it can more properly be interpreted as telling of man's role as part of nature. Both man and fish are portrayed as brave, proud, and honorable. In Hemingway's world, all creatures, including humans, must either kill or be killed. Santiago reflects, "man can be destroyed but not defeated," following this principle in his life. As heroes are often created through their own deaths, Hemingway seems to believe that while being destroyed is inevitable, destruction enables living beings to transcend it by fighting bravely with honor and dignity. Hemingway echoes Romantic poet John Keats' contention that only immediately before death can we understand beauty as it is about to be destroyed. He also echoes ancient Greek and Roman myths and the Old Testament with the tragic flaw of overweening pride or overreaching. Like Icarus, Prometheus, and Adam and Eve, the old man "went out too far."

UNIVERSAL THEMES

The Old Testament book of Genesis, the Quran, and the Epic of Gilgamesh all contain flood stories. Versions differ somewhat: Genesis describes a worldwide flood, attributing it to God's decision that mankind, his creation, had become incontrovertibly wicked in spirit and must be destroyed for the world to start anew. The Quran describes the flood as regional, caused by Allah after sending Nuh (notice the similarity in name to Noah) as a messenger to his people to cease their evil. The Quran stipulates that Allah only destroys those who deny or ignore messages from his messengers. Marked similarities also exist: in the Gilgamesh poems Utnapishtim, like Noah, is instructed to build a ship to survive the flood. Both men also send out birds afterward as tests, using doves and a raven, though with different outcomes. Many historians and archeologists believe a Middle Eastern tidal wave was a real basis for these stories. However, their universal themes remain the same: the flood was seen as God's way of wiping out humans whose behavior had become ungodly.

THEME OF OVERREACHING

A popular theme throughout literature is the human trait of **reaching too far** or **presuming** too much. In Greek mythology, Daedalus constructed wings of feathers and wax that men might fly like birds. He permitted his son Icarus to try them, but cautioned the boy not to fly too close to the sun. The impetuous youth (in what psychologist David Elkind later named adolescence's myth of invincibility) ignored this, flying too close to the sun. The wax melted, the wings disintegrated, and Icarus fell into the sea and perished. In the Old Testament, God warned Adam and Eve not to eat fruit from the tree of knowledge of good and evil. Because they ignored this command, they were banished from Eden's eternal perfection, condemning them to mortality and suffering. The Romans were themselves examples of overreaching in their conquest and assimilation of most of the then-known world and ultimate demise. In Christopher Marlowe's *Dr. Faustus* and Johann Wolfgang von Goethe's *Faust,* the protagonist sells his soul to the Devil for unlimited knowledge and success, ultimately leading to his own tragic end.

STORY VS. DISCOURSE

In terms of plot, "story" is the characters, places, and events originating in the author's mind, while "discourse" is how the author arranges and sequences events—which may be chronological or not. Story is imaginary; discourse is words on the page. Discourse allows story to be told in different ways. One element of plot structure is relating events differently from the order in which they occurred. This is easily done with cause-and-effect; for example, in the sentence, "He died following a long illness," we know the illness preceded the death, but the death precedes the illness in words. In Kate Chopin's short story "The Story of an Hour" (1894), she tells some of the events out of chronological order, which has the effect of amplifying the surprise of the ending for the reader. Another element of plot structure is selection. Chopin omits some details, such as Mr. Mallard's trip home; this allows readers to be as surprised at his arrival as Mrs. Mallard is.

PLOT AND MEANING

Novelist E. M. Forster has made the distinction between story as relating a series of events, such as a king dying and then his queen dying, versus plot as establishing motivations for actions and causes for events, such as a king dying and then his queen dying from grief over his death. Thus, plot fulfills the function of helping readers understand cause-and-effect in events and underlying motivations in characters' actions, which in turn helps them understand life. This affects a work's meaning by supporting its ability to explain why things happen, why people do things, and ultimately the meaning of life. Some authors find that while story events convey meaning, they do not tell readers there is any one meaning in life or way of living, but rather are mental experiments with various meanings, enabling readers to explore. Hence stories may not necessarily be constructed to impose one definitive meaning, but rather to find some shape, direction, and meaning within otherwise random events.

CLASSIC ANALYSIS OF PLOT STRUCTURE

In *Poetics,* Aristotle defined plot as "the arrangement of the incidents." He meant not the story, but how it is structured for presentation. In tragedies, Aristotle found results driven by chains of cause and effect preferable to those driven by the protagonist's personality or character. He identified "unity of action" as necessary for a plot's wholeness, meaning its events must be internally connected, not episodic or relying on *deus ex machina* or other external intervention. A plot must have a beginning, middle, and end. Gustav Freytag adapted Aristotle's ideas into his Pyramid (1863). The beginning, today called the exposition, incentive, or inciting moment, emphasizes causes and de-emphasizes effects. Aristotle called the ensuing cause and effect *desis,* or tying up, today called complications which occur during the rising action. These culminate in a crisis or climax, Aristotle's *peripateia.* This occurs at the plot's middle, where cause and effect are both emphasized. The falling action, which Aristotle called the *lusis* or unraveling, is today called the dénouement. The resolution comes at the catastrophe, outcome, or end, when causes are emphasized and effects de-emphasized.

> **Review Video: Plot Line**
> Visit mometrix.com/academy and enter code: 944011

ANALYSIS OF PLOT STRUCTURES THROUGH RECURRING PATTERNS

Authors of fiction select characters, places, and events from their imaginations and arrange them to create a story that will affect their readers. One way to analyze plot structure is to compare and contrast different events in a story. For example, in Kate Chopin's "The Story of an Hour," a very simple but key pattern of repetition is the husband's leaving and then returning. Such patterns fulfill the symmetrical aspect that Aristotle said was required of sound plot structure. In James Baldwin's short story, "Sonny's Blues," the narrator is Sonny's brother. In an encounter with one of Sonny's old friends early in the story, the brother initially disregards his communication. In a subsequent flashback, Baldwin informs us that this was the same way he had treated Sonny. In Nathaniel Hawthorne's "Young Goodman Brown," a pattern is created by the protagonist's recurrent efforts not to go farther into the wood. In Herman Melville's "Bartleby the Scrivener" and in William Faulkner's "Barn Burning," patterns are also created by repetition such as Bartleby's repeated refusals and the history of barn-burning episodes, respectively.

LITERARY THEORIES AND CRITICISM AND INTERPRETATION

Literary theory includes ideas that guide readers through the process of interpreting literature. Literary theory, as a subject, encompasses several specific, focused theories that lead readers to interpret or analyze literature through the context of the theory using the subjects and elements it involves. Some commonly used and discussed literary theories include **postcolonial theory**, **gender and feminist theory**, **structuralism**, **new historicism**, **reader-response theory**, and **sociological criticism**.

- **Postcolonial theory** involves the historical and geographical context of a work and leads readers to consider how colonization informs the plot, characters, setting, and other elements in the work.

- **Gender and feminist theory** invites readers to interpret by looking at its treatment of and suggestions about women and a culture's treatment of women. As with most literary theories, this information can be clearly stated or strongly implied in a work, but it may also be gleaned through looking closely at symbols, characters, and plot elements in a work.
- **Structuralism** uses the structure and organization of a work and the foundations of language to examine how and what a text conveys about the human experience and how those findings connect to common human experiences.
- **New historicism** heavily relies on the cultural and historical context of a work, including when it was written, where the author lives or lived, the culture and history of that location, and other works from the same culture. New historical readings seek to examine these details to expose the ideologies of the location and culture that influenced the work.
- **Reader-response theory** uses the individual reader's response to the text and experience while reading the text to examine the meaning of the reader's relationship with the text and what that relationship suggests about the reader or the factors impacting their experience.
- **Sociological criticism** considers the societies that are relevant to a text. The author's society and any reader's society are important to the text, as sociological criticism seeks to uncover what the text implies or reveals about those societies. This method of criticism can also involve studying the presentation of a society within the text and applying it to the author's society or their other writings.

Language and Communication

DIVERSITY AND SITUATIONAL NATURE OF LANGUAGE

Language is a diverse tool that allows people to communicate. However, language is often impacted and molded by the culture that uses it. This can make it difficult to learn and use a new language, since not all native speakers of the language will use it or interpret it the same way. For example, English is spoken all over America, but Americans in various regions of the country speak using different **dialects**. Other differences in speech include **accents** and **rhythm of speech**. Language is also manipulated by situations. Some terms and phrases have multiple meanings. A word's meaning often depends on the **context** in which the word or phrase is used, meaning that non-native speakers must learn to interpret situations to understand messages.

FACTORS OF LANGUAGE AND COMMUNICATION

INFLUENCES ON LANGUAGE

While dialect and diction are heavily influenced by an individual's culture and the location and history of the place they live, other personal factors can also impact language. A person's ethnicity, religious beliefs or background, and gender can influence the way they use and understand language. **Ethnicity** impacts language by incorporating a group's communication norms into an individual's speech and behavior. These norms may affect a speaker's tone, volume, or pace. These factors may lead others outside of that group to misinterpret the speaker's message, depending on their understanding of how those factors are used in speech. A person's **religious beliefs** can also affect their use of language. Religious beliefs and practices may lead an individual to abstain from using certain terms and may change the context in which a speaker uses specific words, or change their understanding of the word's usage. Additionally, a person may use language differently depending on their gender. **Gender's** influence on communication varies by region and industry. A region or industry's treatment of gender roles often impacts language use among its members. This can lead members of one gender group to be more assertive or submissive or to use different terms and phrases.

CULTURE AND COMMUNICATION

Individuals from different countries and cultures communicate differently. Not only do many people speak different languages, but they also speak using different inflections, volumes, tones, and dialects.

These factors can have a significant impact on communication, even if the communicators speak the same language. In different cultures, certain behaviors are associated with different meanings and implications. When communicators from different cultures have a conversation, these expectations and associations may lead to misunderstanding. For example, Americans are considered to be louder and more demonstrative than people from other countries. Someone from a country where people speak more quietly who is not aware of this characterization may perceive an American's volume or large gestures as an indication of anger, when in reality, the American speaker is calm. The American may similarly perceive the other person as sad or shy due to their quiet voice, when the speaker is actually happy and comfortable in the conversation. Awareness of these factors and effects promotes respect for others and helps speakers understand the reasons for differences in communication, rather than allowing these differences to create division or conflict.

Dialect

LANGUAGE VS. DIALECT

Languages are distinct and structured forms of verbal communication. Languages have cohesive sets of rules and words that are shared between the majority of that language's users. The main identifier of a language is that members of other languages are incapable of communicating fluently with members of another language group. New languages are formed as different dialects grow further apart until the members of each dialect can no longer innately communicate with each other.

Dialects are subsets of languages that do not violate the rules of the language as a whole, but which vary from other dialects in vocabulary usage, grammar forms, pronunciation, and spelling. Two major groupings of dialects are American and British English. Most American English and British English speakers can communicate with relative ease with one another, though the pronunciation, vocabulary (torch vs. flashlight; trunk vs. boot), spelling (meter vs. metre; color vs. colour), and grammar (in American English, collective nouns are always considered singular, but can be singular or plural in British English).

DEVELOPMENT OF DIALECTS OVER TIME

Dialects are formed primarily through the influences of location and time, but can be the result of other elements of **social stratification** as well (economic, ethnic, religious, etc.). As one group of a language's speakers is separated from another, in British and American English speakers for example, the language develops in isolated locations at the same time, resulting in distinct dialects. Language changes continuously over time as new words and phrases are adopted and others are phased out. Eventually, these small changes result culminate into enough grammar and vocabulary changes that the speakers of the distinct dialects cannot easily communicate with one another and the dialects can then be recognized as distinct languages.

USE OF DIALECT IN MEDIA

Literary authors often use dialect when writing dialogue to illustrate the social and geographical backgrounds of specific characters, which supports character development. For example, in *The Adventures of Huckleberry Finn* (1885), Mark Twain's novel is written in the dialect of a young, uneducated, white, Southern character, opening with this sentence: "You don't know about me without you have read a book by the name of The Adventures of Tom Sawyer, but that ain't no matter." Twain uses a different and exaggerated dialect to represent the speech of the African-American slave Jim: "We's safe, Huck, we's safe! Jump up and crack yo' heels. Dat's de good ole Cairo at las', I jis knows it."

In *To Kill a Mockingbird,* author Harper Lee used dialect in the characters' dialogue to portray an uneducated boy in the American South: "Reckon I have. Almost died the first year I come to school and et them pecans—folks say he pizened 'em." Lee also uses many Southern regional expressions, such as "right stove up," "What in the sam holy hill?", "sit a spell," "fess" (meaning "confess"), "jim-dandy," and "hush your fussing." These contribute to Lee's characterization of the people she describes, who live in a small town in Alabama circa the 1930s. In *Wuthering Heights* (1847), Emily Bronte reproduces Britain's 18th-19th-century Yorkshire dialect in the speech of servant Joseph: "Running after t'lads, as usuald!... If I war yah, maister, I'd just slam t'boards i' their faces all on 'em, gentle and simple! Never a day ut yah're off, but yon cat o' Linton comes sneaking hither; and Miss Nelly, shoo's a fine lass!"

DIALECT VS. DICTION

When written as characters' dialogue in literary works, dialect represents the particular pronunciation, grammar, and figurative expressions used by certain groups of people based on their geographic region, social class, and cultural background. For example, when a character says, "There's gold up in them thar hills," the author is using dialect to add to the characterization of that individual. Diction is more related to individual characters than to groups of people. The way in which a specific character speaks, including his or her choice of words, manner of expressing himself or herself, and use of grammar all represent individual types of diction. For example, two characters in the same novel might describe the same action or event using different diction: One says "I'm heading uptown for the evening," and the other says "I'm going out for a night on the town." These convey the same literal meaning, but due to their variations in diction they are expressed in different ways.

> **Review Video: Dialogue, Paradox, and Dialect**
> Visit mometrix.com/academy and enter code: 684341

INFLUENCES ON REGIONAL DIALECT

Linguistic researchers have identified regional variations in vocabulary choices, which have evolved because of differences in local climates and how they influence human behaviors. For example, in the Southern United States, the Linguistic Atlas of the Gulf States (LAGS) Project by Dr. Lee Pederson of Emory University discovered and documented that people living in the northern or Upland section of the Piedmont plateau region call the fungal infection commonly known as athlete's foot "toe itch," but people living in the southern or Lowland section call it "ground itch." The explanation for this difference is that in the north, temperatures are cooler and people wear shoes accordingly, so they associate the itching with the feet in their description, but in the south, temperatures are hotter and people often went barefoot, so they associated the itching with the ground that presumably transmitted the infection.

USING DIALECT IN WRITING

Dialect is most appropriate for informal or creative writing. Using dialectal writing when communicating casually or informally, such as in a text message or a quick email to a peer, is acceptable. However, in academic and professional contexts, writing using indications of dialect is inappropriate and often unacceptable. If the audience includes individuals who have a higher rank than the author, or authority over the author, it is best not to write in a way that suggests a dialect.

World Literature

AMERICAN LITERARY PERIODS
DARK ROMANTICS

In American literature, a group of late Romantic writers are recognized as **Dark Romantics**. These authors' works may be associated with both the Romantic and Gothic movements. These works emphasize nature and emotion, aligning them with Romanticism, and include dark themes and tones, aligning them with Gothic literature. However, these works do not all feature the historically inspired characteristics of Gothic literature, and their morals or outcomes more closely resemble those of Romantic literature. The Dark Romantics include writers such as Edgar Allan Poe, Nathaniel Hawthorne, Emily Dickinson, and Herman Melville.

TRANSCENDENTALISM

Transcendentalism was a smaller movement that occurred alongside the American Romantic movement. The **transcendentalists** shared the Romantic emphasis on emotion and also focused heavily on how a person experiences life through their senses. They extended these sentiments to suggest that through embracing one's senses, an individual could transcend, or experience a state of being above physical humanity. They also extended the Romantic emphasis on subjectivity through their praise of self-sufficiency, as exemplified through Ralph Waldo Emerson's *Self-Reliance*. Emerson was a prominent transcendentalist. His writings included an essay titled *Nature*, which explains a progression from the use of the senses to the achievement of transcendence. Transcendentalist literature includes several essays that discuss the value of the senses and emotions or the process of transcendence. Transcendentalists also wrote poetry that includes the frequent use of imagery, metaphors, and references to nature. These elements reflect the ideas of transcendentalism and create a resemblance to the alleged experience of transcendence. Ralph Waldo Emerson, Henry David Thoreau, and Walt Whitman were all prominent writers in this movement.

COLONIAL AMERICA

The **colonial era** in America was influenced by immigration from England to what is now New England. These immigrants were mainly Puritans who centered their society in New England on their religious beliefs, allowing those beliefs to inform all aspects of their lives. This is apparent in the literature of the time, as much of it includes essays and sermons that discuss religion or the way the Puritans believed one should live and conduct themselves. Colonial literature also includes many poems, and these works also discuss or reference religious ideas and themes. There was not much fiction written in Colonial America, as most of the literature was written to inform or persuade.

ROMANTIC PERIOD

The **American Romantic** movement is also known as the American Renaissance. This movement yielded several notable American writers and works that began characterizing American literature and differentiating it from British literature. This literature, written after the American Revolutionary War and until the end of the Civil War, praised individualism and featured an expression of national pride and patriotism. The transcendentalists' extreme ideas about self-sufficiency and subjectivity reiterated this individualism, and their recommendations about society and its structure furthered the separation of American literature from British literature. While this period shaped the definition of American literature, it is criticized for featuring a narrow view of American politics and social issues at the time, as well as promoting a small group of similar writers.

HARLEM RENAISSANCE

The **Harlem Renaissance** took place in America during the 1920s and 1930s. The changing economy and opportunities led African Americans in the south to seek new lifestyles in other parts of America at the beginning of the 20th century. Many moved to Harlem, a small area in New York City. This group of African Americans yielded highly influential scholarly and artistic works, including poetry, fiction, music, and plays. The Harlem Renaissance marked an opportunity for these intellectuals and artists, who were largely ignored in the aftermath of the Civil War, to use their talents and express themselves through their works. While artists often featured personal expression in their works, the Harlem Renaissance was unique in its volume of culturally expressive works. This cultural expression and the movement's main ideas also contributed to the Civil Rights movement by promoting a spirit of unity among African Americans. The Harlem Renaissance eventually ended in the wake of the stock market crash in 1929. As the Great Depression began, financial support for the arts dwindled, making it difficult for many artists to succeed financially. Some members of the Harlem Renaissance who influenced American literature include Langston Hughes, Zora Neale Hurston, and Paul Robeson.

BRITISH LITERARY PERIODS
NEOCLASSICAL

The **British Neoclassical** period began in the middle of the 17th century and ended in the late 18th century. The latter part of the movement also took place alongside the Enlightenment, a period of scientific discovery and study that influenced many Western cultures. The Enlightenment's concern with intellectual pursuits and improvement increased discussions of introspection, or an individual's analysis of their own behavior, thoughts, and self. These ideas also affected society in England, as they contributed to a general attitude of complacency and a desire to ignore the past. The period saw a slightly increased acceptance of female writers, as their works were viewed as a method of self-reflection and improvement. The changes in the British society allowed several new forms of literature to gain popularity and acceptance, usually for their introspective qualities. Essays, diaries, and letters all displayed the author's thoughts and experience, aligning them with the culture's values. Novels also gained popularity, as many were fictional diaries or epistolary novels. Journalism flourished during the Neoclassical period, leading to the creation of the newspaper. Literary criticism also gained popularity, though it was used to criticize an author and their style rather than examine or analyze the content of the work.

VICTORIAN

The **Victorian Era** in England was influenced by variety of events and ideas, many of which were influenced by the Victorians' economy. The Industrial Revolution in England changed the circumstances of work for the Victorians. The changing industries and lack of labor laws led to several problems and a wide division between Victorian social classes. These factors inspired and saturated much of Victorian literature. Many novels' plots and characters were heavily influenced by social and economic issues, and many poems referenced and criticized specific events that occurred during this period.

While the structure of Victorian society was a major influence on literature, there were other popular topics that appeared in literature. Topics like evolution, psychology, and colonization frequently appeared in Victorian literature, reflecting the concerns and interests of the Victorian culture. The Victorian society was also characterized by a strict moral code that supported the view of women as homemakers and criticized the idea of female writers. Not only did this affect the portrayal of women in literature, but it also led some female novelists, such as the Bronte sisters, to write under a pseudonym and present their works as having been written by a man. Victorian literature also popularized forms of literature, including the novel and the dramatic monologue, a poetic form developed by Robert Browning. Victorian writers include Charles Dickens, Oscar Wilde, Elizabeth Barrett Browning, Emily Bronte, Matthew Arnold, and Thomas Hardy.

WORLD LITERARY CHARACTERISTICS AND PERIODS

While many other nations shared literary movements with America and England, there are numerous literary movements that are unique to other countries and cultures. Some of these literary movements can be understood as variations of movements like Romanticism or modernism, since they occurred at similar times and feature similar elements, but the political and cultural events of each country shaped their version of each movement. Most regions also have some type of mythology, and while different mythologies have similar characters and events, each region's mythology is unique and significant to the region's literature. Another common feature of world literature is colonialism. Many nations are former colonies of European countries, and the effects of colonization are present in modern literature from countries worldwide, making it a key feature of many regions' body of literature.

AFRICAN LITERATURE

Literature from some cultures was not recorded until the 19th century, causing any movements and trends to be informed by ideas told aloud. This is true of African literature, where stories and ideas were spoken and passed down through the generations. Early African poetry was often metaphorical, structured or written to form a paradox, and included a riddle or puzzling statement. Proverbs and didactic tales were also told frequently, reflecting the dominant religions in a given region and time period. These poems and stories also reflect the variety of languages spoken in Africa and the shifts in each language's usage. Early African literature, once people began writing it down, included stories and proverbs that had been passed down, translations of religious texts, and descriptions of the way of life in different African cultures or groups. These cultures and the events specific to each culture produce a unique body of literature that places emphasis on certain topics and ideas. For example, much of the modern literature written in South Africa discusses politics and issues of race, since the country's history is characterized by events and movements that revolved around these topics.

ASIAN LITERATURE

Asian literature features writings from several different countries and languages and has spanned many centuries. Popular forms of writing have come from Asia, such as the haiku. A couple of significant literary movements include The Hungry Generation in South Asia and the Misty Poets in China. The Hungry Generation is a literary movement involving literature written in the Bengali language, spoken mainly in West Bengal and Bangladesh. The literature is characterized by unique and innovative writing, which impacted the use of figurative language in the region. The Hungry Generation also discussed cultural issues, particularly colonization in the region, and many participants were arrested for their work. The Misty Poets in China were characterized by their expressive use of abstractions. Their name, Misty Poets, comes from their writings, which were difficult to interpret due to their use of abstract language and ambiguity. This movement was partly inspired by the Misty Poets' distaste for literary realism, though its influence is detectable within their poetry. Many of the Misty Poets were punished for their poetry, since the poetry of this movement was also politically critical.

LATIN AMERICAN LITERATURE

Latin American literature has several literary movements, many of which occurred near the same time as American and British literary movements and share ideas and trends with their English counterparts. Despite these similarities, each of these movements is distinguishable as its own movement with unique impacts of Latin American literature. By the 17th century, written language was in use in Mexico, and Latin American literary trends and figures had been recognized. During the 18th century, Latin American literature featured a variety of ideas and themes within each form of literature. By the 19th century, literary themes were more unified throughout popular Latin American literature. In the early 19th century, Latin American literature embraced the Romantic movement as it came to an end in England and the United States. Several Latin American countries were also fighting for independence during this time, amplifying the Romantic idea of national pride and identity.

In the wake of the Romantic movement, Latin American literature introduced the unique Modernismo movement, which yielded a large volume of poetry and is characterized by the use of whimsical imagery and discussions of spiritual ideas. Following Modernismo was the Vanguardia movement, which was created to introduce diversity within Latin American literature after modernism permeated the literature of the time. Vanguardia involved writers taking risks in their writing and breaking the mold from typical Latin American literature. In the 20th century, Estridentismo followed the Vanguardia movement, marrying the Vanguardia movement with the European Avant-Garde movement. Other 20th century movements function similarly by adapting literary movements from other regions to suit the themes and trends in Latin American literature, reflect Latin American cultures, and set their literature apart from other cultures.

Literary Periods and Movements

OLD ENGLISH

The English language developed over a long period of time through interactions between different groups in Europe, including the Romans, the Germans, and the Celtics. The Anglo-Saxons, a group that left what is now Germany and settled in England, further established the English language by using what is now called **Old English**. While Old English laid foundations for modern English, its usage fundamentally differs from the way English is used today. For example, Old English relied on inflections to create meaning, placing little importance on the order of the words in the sentence. Its use of verbs and tenses also differs from modern English grammar. The Anglo-Saxons also used kennings, or compound words that functioned as figurative language.

Old English, as a language influenced by several cultures, had dialects from its inception. Differences in usage also came from the division between secular and religious cultures. This division heavily influenced Old English literature, as most of the literature from the time is categorized according to the set of beliefs it reflects. Most of the influential literature of the time includes riddles, poems, or translations of religious texts. Surviving Old English poetry mainly discusses real heroes and battles or provides a narrative about a fictional hero. Many of these fictional poems are considered lays, or lais, which are narrative poems that are structured using couplets of lines containing eight syllables each. The translations were often of passages from the Christian Bible, adaptations of Biblical passages, or copies of Christian hymns. Old English persisted until the 12th century, where it was eventually replaced with Middle English. Influential literature from this period includes *Beowulf*, "The Wanderer," "The Wife's Lament," and "The Seafarer."

MIDDLE ENGLISH

Old English was replaced by **Middle English**, which was used from the 12th century to the 16th century. Old English was not governed by a consistent set of grammatical rules until the Norse people, their language, and its structure influenced the integration of grammar into English, leading to Middle English. Middle English relied less on inflections than Old English, instead creating variations by using affixes and synonyms. The development of grammar was further facilitated by the printing press, which made it easier for writers to comply with grammar rules since the printing of identical copies reduced variation between texts.

Old English's evolution into Middle English can be narrowed down to three stages: Early, Central, and Late Middle English. Early Middle English, though it showed a change in the language, maintained the writing style of Old English. Central Middle English is characterized by the development of dialects within written communication, which is partly due to scribes who translated texts or parts of texts using terms from their own dialect, rather than the source. Late Middle English includes numerous developments that created the foundation for Modern English. *The Canterbury Tales*, "Sir Gawain and the Green Knight," and "Le Morte d'Arthur" are all Middle English texts that are still read and studied today.

THE RENAISSANCE

The **Renaissance** swept through Europe and lasted for multiple centuries, bringing many developments in culture, the arts, education, and philosophy. The Renaissance in England did not begin until the late 15th century. Though ideas and cultures of the past, especially those of the ancient Greeks and Romans, inspired the Renaissance, the period saw innumerable developments in the English language and literature. The Renaissance was characterized by a focus on the humanities, allowing the arts, including literature, to flourish. At the time, drama was the possibly the most popular form of literature, as the popularity of plays and theatrical performances greatly increased. Much of Renaissance literature is still studied today, maintaining its influence on Western literature. Poetry was also popular, and the period saw the development of new forms of poetry, such as the sonnet. Sonnets are often recognized according to one of four styles, each of which was popularized by a Renaissance writer. Lyrical poetry, which discusses emotions and is often written using first-person point of view, was also popular during the Renaissance.

In addition to new forms and literary trends, the Renaissance period also impacted English literature by facilitating discussion over the translation of the Bible. Education at the time often included instruction in Greek and Latin, allowing those with an education to read ancient texts in their original language.

However, this instruction did not reach the majority of the public. The Protestant Reformation encouraged discussions about translating the Bible to make it accessible to more people. This suggestion was challenged by those who doubted the ability of the English language to fully reflect the original text. Eventually, the Bible was translated to English, and William Tyndale's partial translation became especially influential for later translations and the continuing development of the English language. Influential writers of the English Renaissance include William Shakespeare, John Donne, John Milton, Edmund Spenser, and Christopher Marlowe.

GOTHIC

The Gothic literary movement, beginning in the 18th century and persisting through the 19th century, took inspiration from the architecture and cultures of the Late Middle Ages in Europe. The Late Middle Ages saw the popularity of Gothic architecture, most prominently in places of worship. These structures inspired many of the settings in **Gothic literature**, as a large volume of Gothic literature takes place in an impressive location, such as a castle or ornate mansion. Gothic works also are often set in the past, long before the time the story was written. This aligns with prominent themes in Gothic literature, as several pieces are informed by an event that occurred before the story begins or a character who died before the plot's first event.

Another common characteristic of Gothic literature is its eerie, dark, suspenseful tone. Authors of Gothic literature often created this tone by setting their works in secluded and strange locations and incorporating intense, unsettling, or even supernatural events and scenarios into the plot. This tone is also created through the theme of death or mortality that often appears in Gothic literature. These characteristics support the aim of many Gothic writers to create fiction that evokes a certain emotion from the reader or shapes their reading experience. Well-known authors of Gothic literature include Horace Watpole, Ann Radcliffe, Edgar Allan Poe, and Nathaniel Hawthorne. While the Gothic literary movement took place in the 18th and 19th centuries, many works have been published in more recent centuries that have several characteristics of Gothic literature and may be included within the overall Gothic genre.

NATURALISM

Naturalism was an active literary movement in the late 19th century, taking place alongside movements such as realism and modernism. Naturalism's development in America was delayed and appeared in various ways, obscuring the true American naturalist genre. **Naturalism**, like realism, rejected the emotional focus and sentimentality of Romanticism and provided a type of social commentary. However, the naturalist movement stretched the ideas of realism, promoting literature that authentically depicts the life of the common man and criticizing the influence of morality on such literature. Naturalist literature often includes characters who belong to a lower class and experience circumstances beyond their own control and takes place in urban settings. Prominent themes in naturalist literature include nature as an apathetic force, the influence of heredity, and life as something to be endured and survived. One of the most influential naturalist writers is French writer Emile Zola. Influential American Naturalists include Stephen Crane, Hamlin Garland, and Theodore Dreiser.

MODERNISM

The Modernist literary movement was largely influenced by industrialization, which heavily impacted both the Unites States and England, primarily in the 19th century. **Modernism** in literature was characterized by an attempt to turn away from the norms and traditions of literature and use new techniques and methods. Modernist literature was often written in first person and used devices and techniques to reveal problems within society. For the American modernists, these societal changes came from industrialization and the first World War, which effected the general view of human nature and reliability. In England, there were additional factors contributing to this shift. Modernism began during Queen Victoria's reign, which defined the period known as the Victorian Era. The Victorian society was characterized by a strict moral code that permeated England's society at the time. This moral code was

incompatible with the Modernist's desire to turn away from tradition, but the changes that accompanied Victoria's death in 1901 enabled the Modernist movement to grow in England. American Modernist writers include Ezra Pound, William Carlos Williams, and Gertrude Stein. British Modernist writers include Matthew Arnold, William Butler Yeats, T. S. Eliot, and Joseph Conrad.

POSTMODERNISM

Postmodernism grew out of Modernism's reliance on science and universal assertions, but emphasized the individual's subjective perception of reality, as it is often more authentic to an individual's experience than a universally applied statement. Postmodernism asserts that since each person creates their own version of reality, fully and accurately defining reality is futile and impossible. Due to this skepticism, postmodern writers use many concrete details, rather than abstract details, because they can be objectively observed and arc not left up to the individual. The postmodernist literary movement began around the 1960s. The literary movement included a variety of new genres and techniques, reflecting the postmodernist idea that things like art cannot be truly defined or simplified. Notable American writers of the postmodernist movement include Kurt Vonnegut, John Barth, and Thomas Pynchon. British postmodernist writers include John Fowles and Julian Barnes.

Pedagogical Content Knowledge

English Language Arts Pedagogy

CLASSROOM MATERIALS THAT SUPPORT LITERACY ACROSS THE CURRICULUM

In a classroom that supports literacy, the teacher should provide **labels** combining words and pictures on all objects. This continually stimulates students to associate written language with the objects and concepts it represents. Especially to support disabled students, teachers should use their particular interests and needs as a guide for labeling things. Printed directions, signs, calendars, and schedules are materials that students should use regularly in the classroom. These help students realize how language is used in everyday life. When the class is studying a certain topic, theme, or book, the teacher and students can work together to redesign the classroom using printed and written materials that reflect that topic, theme, or book. This enables students to fully experience and "live" the lesson rather than just observing it. All of the materials must be adapted for any students' special needs. For instance, in a class including blind/visually impaired students, labels, signs and other print materials can incorporate Braille words and textured surfaces.

ADDRESSING DIVERSE STUDENT ABILITIES AND NEEDS

Teachers must consider the **diversity** among the skills and needs of their students as they design their classroom learning environments. The teachers should **individualize** the setting and their instruction so that every student is represented. Individualization and instructional differentiation should not only address disabled students' needs; they should also regularly provide suitable opportunities for these students to participate on an ongoing basis in activities that involve literacy and integrate it into all content areas. According to research, a salient need of students with diverse literacy backgrounds is that they often have trouble connecting new information to their existing knowledge. This ability is a critical component of learning. When teachers plan and organize their classrooms to offer literacy activities that are accessible to disabled students—and that immerse them in literacy experiences and give them opportunities to connect new with old information, and spoken with printed language—these students can then access the general education curriculum.

ACTIVITIES FOR STUDENTS WITH DISABILITIES TO DEVELOP LITERACY SKILLS AND PARTICIPATE IN GENERAL CURRICULUM

To participate in the general curriculum, students with disabilities need to understand the **alphabetic principle**, i.e. that printed language represents spoken language; connect print with speech; and be able to relate new information to their prior knowledge. Teachers can support these developments by designing classrooms as literacy-rich settings, immersing special-needs and other students in **accessible literacy activities** across all content areas. For example, students can interact with alphabet-letter magnets, cookie-cutters, and stamps; concrete manipulatives allow students not developmentally ready for exclusively abstract thought to understand concepts using real objects. Discussing daily schedules requires students to read and comprehend printed language, and then use spoken language to demonstrate and apply their understanding. Playing letter/word games like Bingo, Pictionary, Boggle, and Scrabble gives practice with creating and manipulating language, enhancing recognition and cognitive flexibility. Providing photos of peers, teachers, staff, and classroom activities and having students label them helps students connect written language with familiar, meaningful images. Daily communication notebooks help students further integrate literacy into their school days.

IMPLICATIONS OF CULTURAL AND LINGUISTIC DIFFERENCES REGARDING LITERACY DEVELOPMENT

Educational research shows that the **cultural values** of families and/or communities influence children's literacy development, and also that culture is a significant factor to understanding children's home literacy environments. Researchers have also found that cultural purposes, perspectives, and contexts affect how students with disabilities in particular interact with the literacy environments they encounter. They say children's preparation levels entering formal education reflect their families' and communities' values and beliefs about literacy. Cultural attitudes about literacy then influence how schools deliver instruction and literacy experiences. Teachers must assess culturally diverse students' interactions with the environment, and design literacy-rich classrooms, with students' diverse backgrounds in mind. Students learning English (ELL/ESL) enter school either not knowing English or just learning it, lacking exposure to specific vocabulary and literature. Literacy-rich classrooms help them participate in regular curriculum. Teacher should read aloud often to these students, include print in their native language in classrooms, permit mistakes during student attempts to use English, encourage students to reread books repeatedly. and plan activities entailing language use.

DRAWBACKS OF WHOLE-CLASS AND SMALL-GROUP READING, AND FLEXIBLE GROUPING MODEL

A major disadvantage of **whole-class reading** is that students who read above the average class level go unchallenged and can become bored, while students reading below average level are lost. Yet the **small-group method** intended to remedy this also has the drawback that, as traditionally implemented, most time is used for skill instruction, leaving far too little time for students to actually read the text. One solution is a **flexible grouping model**, e.g., Grouping Without Tracking (Paratore, 1990). This model uses a "sandwich" structure: teachers give students shared-reading processes at the beginning and end of the lesson, but provide differentiated instruction to two groups in the middle as they read the text. Teachers give indirect guidance to students who can read more independently, and more direct support to struggling readers. Teachers reunite the groups to lead them in a final discussion. Students with reading difficulties gain reading proficiency and comprehension from direct teacher support, enabling them to contribute better to the whole-class discussion, so all share this experience equally.

JIGSAW APPROACH TO SHARED READING

Students reading below grade level may be able to access and comprehend some texts or portions of them, but have difficulty with harder parts/texts—for example, informational texts with more challenging subject matter and specialized vocabulary. When a text intended for the whole class contains such challenging material, one solution the teacher can use is a **jigsaw approach**. The teacher selects various portions of the text that are less difficult and assigns them to students reading below grade level. Whereas such texts overall might present struggles for these students, they find the easier portions more manageable when they tackle only these parts, as selected and assigned by the teacher, in small groups of students with comparable reading levels. The teacher makes each small student group responsible for comprehension of their assigned portion of text. Then the teacher brings the class back together, having each group report what they read, understood, and learned. The whole class then collaborates to help each other make connections among the learning each group reported.

USING THEMES TO CONNECT TEXTS

Any inclusive classroom will contain students who read at various age/grade levels. As a result, some books used as core texts are going to present difficulties for some of the students, who read below grade level and/or lack background knowledge and vocabulary of the subject. One way a teacher can facilitate all students' comprehension of such texts is to provide **supplementary texts** that allow readers at different levels easier access—texts on the same subject or theme as the more difficult core text. Teachers have students read these more accessible texts independently during small-group reading periods. This makes it easier for students with less reading proficiency to learn the core vocabulary and build their background knowledge. Thus, they are more prepared to tackle the more difficult core text during whole-class shared reading periods. With such preparation, less proficient readers are more likely to become engaged and active participants in the shared reading of a difficult text in the whole-group setting.

ASSIGNING STUDENTS TO SMALL GROUPS FOR GUIDED READING EXERCISES

Expert educators and researchers recommend that when teachers divide classes into small student groups for **guided reading**, they should not be overly concerned with assigning students to exact reading levels. Rather, though they will want to group students whose literacy development is similar and who read around a similar level, they should give more attention to organizing groups according to the students' *areas of need*. For example, a teacher might identify students who share in common a need for help with noticing changes in setting, other students who share difficulties with recognizing and differentiating characters, some students who demonstrate problems with following and/or reproducing events they read in a text in the correct chronological sequence, some students who have trouble identifying and/or articulating the main idea in a text portion, etc. The teacher can create a group of students sharing one of these challenges, announce to the class what this group's focus is, and then invite other students to join this group by choice if they experience the same need.

HELPING TEACHERS PROVIDE MORE EQUITABLE LEARNING OPPORTUNITIES USING WORD COUNTS

Books designed for lower reading levels typically contain fewer words, both per page and overall. Yet students who are reading below their grade levels require not fewer reading opportunities, but more, to practice and improve their reading skills. For example, within one class of second-grade students, the teacher might have one group using a text with over 80 words on just the first page, while another group uses a text with a total of 80 words in the entire book. This difference shows that the teacher will need to use several texts within certain groups to give them equal amounts of reading material and practice as readers of denser/longer texts during group reading times. Teachers can look at the backs of the books they assign during guided reading sessions, and maintain simple logs of their **word counts**. Comparing these word counts among groups can help teachers to equalize the numbers of words that each student group actually works with during small-group guided reading periods.

CONNECTING TEXT SETS FOR SMALL-GROUP GUIDED READING ACROSS DIFFERENT READING DIFFICULTY LEVELS

When teachers select textbooks to teach a unit/lesson on a certain topic, they often compile **text sets**—groups of books all related to the same topic/theme. Because classes usually include students reading at different levels, teachers also often gather books at different reading levels for text sets. When collecting books representing multiple reading levels, the teacher can also intentionally organize the text set so all books are connected. For example, the books might share similar content; similar language, style, and vocabulary words; or similar layouts. Selecting books sharing such a commonality at different reading levels makes it easier for students to draw useful connections between easier and harder texts. It also facilitates students' flexibility in working across multiple reading levels, which builds their skills and confidence for faster progress. Additionally, to prepare some students to read books that teachers felt would prove too difficult otherwise, they can use easier texts with similar themes/language/formats to establish contexts for the harder ones.

ENHANCING STUDENTS' INDEPENDENT READING THROUGH THE READING MATERIAL PROVIDED

In addition to whole-class and small-group reading exercises, students need some time reading **texts of their own choice**, which they can easily read with little or no support, to attain comfort, fluency, and confidence. To ensure more opportunities for practice, with equal time for all students, teachers should provide text sets at multiple reading levels for each content area. Experts suggest 70% of books should be easily accessible, and, in addition to classroom libraries, using rolling carts lets book collections travel among classrooms. Multiple reading levels let more advanced readers peruse a harder text, while less advanced readers read several easier texts; this equalizes the time and words they have for practicing. Because critics find some leveled readers lack variety in gender/race/class/other sociocultural aspects of characters, teachers should build diverse book collections representing all students. Teachers can inform their selections via student interest surveys and familiarity with students' individual identities, personalities, and special interests. Knowing individual students can help match them to texts as effectively as leveled book lists.

ENGAGING STUDENTS IN READING

Experts find excessive attention to **leveling** as a way of matching texts to students can be restrictive, undermining high-quality instruction that balances the needs of the reader with the demands of the text. Teachers must consider that assigning certain texts will cause students to disengage from reading and avoid it rather than engage in it. In the real world, people read many different kinds of materials. Therefore, a teacher has better chances of finding texts that engage students, and that motivate them to read and allow them to perceive themselves as readers, by mindfully selecting **varied text genres** with **varied difficulty**. In classrooms incorporating various student reading levels, this can be the best method to procure classroom acceptability of accessible texts. Teachers can also use **individualized instructional formats**, such as Readers Workshop (Atwell, 1998), which balance issues of difficulty, choice, and engagement; develop reader communities affording more reading experiences with authenticity, meaning, and enjoyment; and form stronger, positive teacher-student relationships via individualized consultations. Teachers should also incorporate **accessible alternative texts** for independent activities.

ALTERNATIVE READING AND WRITING FORMS TO HELP STUDENTS ATTAIN GREATER PROGRESS IN READING

When students read and write outside of school, they choose many alternative forms of reading and writing. To engage these students while they are in school, teachers should think about adding such **alternative materials** to their own instructional programs. For example, teachers might incorporate such media as graphic novels, magazines, newspapers, plays, anthologies of poetry, e-books and other digital/online content, and texts that students have written themselves. Educational experts advise that just because it can be harder to determine the reading levels of such alternative text formats, teachers should not shy away from using them. Because they represent examples of text that people (including students) read in real life, they provide not only excellent practice for students' present and future reading of real-world materials, but also motivation to read and meaningful experiences in reading. Another boon of using these authentic, alternative texts is that they frequently incorporate multiple reading levels, so that nearly every student can read some portions of them.

VIEWING SKILLS

Viewing skills can be sharpened by having students look at a single image, such as a work of art or a cartoon, and simply asking students what they **see**. The teacher can ask what is happening in the image, and then elicit the details that clue the students in to what is happening. Of course, there may be more than one thing happening. The teacher should also question the students about the message of the image, its purpose, its point of view, and its intended audience. The teacher should ask for first impressions, and then provide some background or additional information to see if it changes the way students look at or interpret the image. The conclusion of the lesson should include questions about what students learned from the exercise about the topic, themselves, and others.

BENEFITS

Students are exposed to multiple **images** every day. It is important for them to be able to effectively **interpret** these images. They should be able to make sense of images and the spoken and print language that often accompany them. Learning can be enhanced with images because they allow for quicker connections to prior knowledge than verbal information. Visuals in the classroom can also be

133

motivational, can support verbal information, and can express main points, sometimes resulting in instant recognition.

Some of the common types of images that students see every day include: bulletin boards, computer graphics, diagrams, drawings, illustrations, maps, photographs, posters, book covers, advertisements, websites, multimedia presentations, puppet shows, television, videos, print cartoons, models, paintings, animation, drama or dance performances, films, and online newscasts and magazines.

ACTIVITIES TO STRENGTHEN SKILLS

Activities at school that can be used to strengthen the **viewing skills** of students of varying ages include:

- **Picture book discussions** – Students can develop an appreciation of visual text and the language that goes with it through guided discussions of picture books that focus on the style and color of the images and other details that might capture a child's attention.
- **Gallery walks** – Students can walk around a room or hallway viewing the posted works of other students and hear presentations about the works. They can also view a display prepared by the teacher. Students are expected to take notes as they walk around, have discussions, and perhaps do a follow-up report.
- **Puppet theater and drama presentations** – Students can learn about plots, dialogue, situations, characters, and the craft of performance from viewing puppet or drama presentations, which also stimulate oral communication and strengthen listening skills. Discussions or written responses should follow performances to check for detail acquisition.

CLASSROOM VIEWING CENTER

A **classroom viewing center** should contain magazines, CD-ROMs, books, videos, and individual pictures (photographs or drawings). Students should have a **viewing guide** that explains expectations related to the viewing center (before, during, and after using the center). For younger students, the teacher can ask questions that guide them through the viewing rather than expecting them to read the guidelines and write responses.

- **Before** viewing, students should think about what they already know about the subject and what they want to learn from the viewing.
- **During** the viewing, students should make notes about whatever interests them or is new to them.
- **After** viewing, students could discuss or individually write down what they found to be the most interesting idea or striking image and explain why it caught their attention.

TYPES OF QUESTIONS TO ASK IF VIEWING IS A NARRATIVE

A teacher should make students responsible for gaining information or insight from the **viewing**. Setting expectations increases student attention and critical thinking. As with any viewing, the students should consider what they already know about the topic and what they hope to gain by watching the narrative before viewing it. During the viewing, the students should take notes (perhaps to answer questions provided by the teacher).

After the viewing, students should be able to answer the following questions:

- What was the time period and setting of the story?
- Who were the main characters?
- How effective was the acting?
- What was the problem or goal in the story?
- How was the problem solved or the goal achieved?
- How would you summarize the story?

- What did you learn from the story?
- What did you like or dislike about the story or its presentation?
- Would you recommend this viewing to others?
- How would you rate it?

DIFFICULTIES RELATED TO LEARNING BY LISTENING

It is difficult to learn just by listening because the instruction is presented only in spoken form. Therefore, unless students take notes, there is nothing for them to review. However, an active listener will anticipate finding a **message** in an oral presentation and will listen for it, **interpreting** tone and gestures as the presentation progresses. In group discussions, students are often too busy figuring out what they will say when it is their turn to talk to concentrate on what others are saying. Therefore, they don't learn from others, but instead come away knowing only what they already knew. Students should be required to respond directly to the previous speaker before launching into their own comments. This practice will force students to listen to each other and learn that their own responses will be better because of what can be added by listening to others.

GRAPHIC ORGANIZERS

The purpose of **graphic organizers** is to help students classify ideas and communicate more efficiently and effectively. Graphic organizers are visual outlines or templates that help students grasp key concepts and master subject matter by simplifying them down to basic points. They also help guide students through processes related to any subject area or task. Examples of processes include brainstorming, problem solving, decision making, research and project planning, and studying. Examples of graphic organizers include:

- **Reading** – These can include beginning, middle, and end graphs or event maps.
- **Science** – These can include charts that show what animals need or how to classify living things.
- **Math** – These can include horizontal bar graphs or time lines.
- **Language arts** – These can include alphabet organizers or charts showing the components of the five-paragraph essay.
- **General** – These can include KWL charts or weekly planners.

SPEAKING SKILLS CHILDREN IN ELEMENTARY/INTERMEDIATE SCHOOL SHOULD HAVE

Children of elementary/intermediate school age should be able to:

- Speak at an appropriate volume, tone, and pace that is understandable and appropriate to the audience
- Pronounce most words accurately
- Use complete sentences
- Make eye contact
- Use appropriate gestures with speech
- Exhibit an awareness of audience and adjust content to fit the audience (adjust word choices and style to be appropriate for peers or adults)
- Ask relevant questions
- Respond appropriately when asked questions about information or an opinion, possibly also being able to provide reasons for opinions
- Speak in turn, not interrupt, and include others in conversations
- Provide a summary or report orally
- Participate in small and large group discussions and debates
- Read orally before an audience
- Conduct short interviews
- Provide directions and explanations orally, including explanations of class lessons

VIEWING SKILLS ELEMENTARY/INTERMEDIATE SCHOOL CHILDREN SHOULD HAVE

Children of elementary school age should be developing or have attained the ability to understand the importance of **media** in people's lives. They should understand that television, radio, films, and the Internet have a role in everyday life. They should also be able to use media themselves (printing out material from the Internet or making an audio or video tape, for example). They should also be aware that the purpose of advertising is to sell. Children of intermediate school age should be developing or have attained the ability to **obtain and compare information** from newspapers, television, and the Internet. They should also be able to judge its **reliability and accuracy** to some extent. Children of this age should be able to tell the difference between fictional and non-fictional materials in media. They should also be able to use a variety of media, visuals, and sounds to make a presentation.

LISTENING SKILLS CHILDREN SHOULD DEVELOP THROUGH THEIR ELEMENTARY/INTERMEDIATE SCHOOL YEARS

Through the elementary/intermediate school years, children should develop the following listening skills:

- Follow oral instructions consistently
- Actively listen to peers and teachers
- Avoid creating distracting behavior or being distracted by the behavior of others most of the time
- Respond to listening activities and exhibit the ability to discuss, illustrate, or write about the activity and show knowledge of the content and quality of the listening activity
- Respond to listening activities and exhibit the ability to identify themes, similarities, differences, ideas, forms, and styles of activities
- Respond to a persuasive speaker and exhibit the ability to analyze and evaluate the credibility of the speaker and form an opinion describing whether they agree or disagree with the point made
- Demonstrate appropriate social behavior while part of an audience

STAGES OF WRITING

The **three stages of writing** are drawing, dictating, and writing. During the **drawing stage**, young learners use scribbles or pictures to convey their message. When asked to "read" their drawing, children in the drawing stage will use their picture to tell a story, as if they were mimicking a book being read to them. In the **dictation stage**, learners will tell their thoughts to a literate person, who will in turn write the words for the child. During this stage, the student is aware that the written words on the page represent their thoughts and can sometimes recognize the beginning sounds of the words they are saying, including some sight words. In the third and final stage, the **writing stage**, students are able to write their own thoughts in a way that can be recognized by others. Both beginning and ending sounds are represented in the words, along with some vowels. Students in this stage also understand spacing between words and the idea of creating complete sentences.

NORM-REFERENCED AND CRITERION-REFERENCED ASSESSMENTS

Norm-referenced assessments are used to gauge a student's success by comparing his or her score to a theoretical "average" score achieved by students of the same age or grade level. With a norm-referenced assessment, a student's achievement is decided based on how much better or worse that student scored in comparison to his or her peers. In contrast, **criterion-referenced assessments** are scored based on each student's individual ability to show mastery of specific learning standards. Students are deemed successful if they are able to achieve mastery of concepts that are appropriate for their age or grade level, regardless of how their peers perform.

IRI

The **Informal Reading Inventory (IRI)**, also known as the **Qualitative Reading Inventory (QRI)** is a survey used to assess the instructional needs of individual readers. The IRI is used to determine a reader's grade-level reading, fluency, comprehension, vocabulary, oral reading accuracy, word recognition, word meaning, and reading strategies. The IRI is an ongoing assessment that should be administered several times a year starting from first grade through twelfth grade. Teachers should use the outcomes of these assessments to determine appropriate reading material for individual students and to identify and implement specific needs and strategies for individual learners or groups of learners.

UNIVERSAL SCREENING ASSESSMENTS, DIAGNOSTIC ASSESSMENTS, AND PROGRESS MONITORING

Universal screening assessments are brief surveys given to all students at the beginning of each school year, which are used to determine the mastery of critical skills and concepts. These screenings should be repeated approximately three times a year to ensure that students are performing at age-appropriate levels. **Diagnostic assessments** are used to help educators make sense of universal screening assessment scores. Based on diagnostics, teachers can identify the specific educational gaps of individual students and use that information to modify and differentiate instruction. **Progress monitoring** is used to determine if the educational interventions and strategies put in place (based on the diagnostic testing) are actually working. Struggling students are often monitored more closely to ensure that educational gaps are being filled at an appropriate and sufficient rate.

FORMAL AND INFORMAL ASSESSMENTS

Formal assessments, which include norm-based assessments, criterion-based assessments, intelligence tests, and diagnostic assessments are data driven. These types of assessments are used to determine a student's overall achievement and can be used to compare each student's abilities to his or her peers. Formal assessments are often shared with students and stakeholders to determine whether or not a student is performing at an appropriate level for his or her age or grade level. **Informal assessments**, which include running records, cloze tests, reading inventories, portfolios, and so on are not data driven. Instead, informal assessments use performance-driven tasks to guide instruction and provide informal ratings about each student's individual progress. During these assessments, each student's performance is used to monitor his or her progress and guide future instruction, often in preparation for a formal assessment.

EVALUATING APPROPRIATENESS OF ASSESSMENT INSTRUMENT OR PRACTICE

The two main factors that must be considered when evaluating the appropriateness of assessment instruction and practices are curriculum alignment and cultural bias. **Curriculum alignment** is the act of teaching students the concepts that they will eventually be tested on. To reach proficiency on the standards outlined by state or district mandates, teachers must continuously teach and assess the standards. Avoiding **cultural bias** ensures that all students are given access to all relevant lessons, instruction, and materials. Furthermore, avoiding cultural bias ensures that all students are given a fair opportunity to succeed on any given assessment. This includes accommodating students of certain subgroups with assessment modifications, such as additional testing time, taking the test in his or her native language, and creating types of assessments that are accessible and achievable for students of all backgrounds.

EXAMPLE EVALUATION OF SCORING METHOD

A teacher is assessing a student's ability to identify the main idea of a text. The student correctly identifies the main idea but includes several spelling errors in her written response. The teacher lowers the student's grade, taking points off for misspellings. In this example, the teacher's scoring method is **inappropriate** for the concept being assessed. Although misspellings should be addressed and remedied, the question was designed to assess the student's ability to identify the main idea of the passage. It was not intended to assess the spelling abilities of the student. By lowering the student's score based on misspellings, the teacher is insinuating that the student is unable to correctly identify the main idea of a passage, which is not the case. When assessing a specific skill, it is important that teachers score students based on their ability to complete isolated skills for data to accurately drive future instruction.

PENMANSHIP

Penmanship is a word used to describe a person's *handwriting*. The three main characteristics of penmanship are letter formation, size, and spacing. When teaching penmanship, teachers should start by helping students to correctly form each letter, using arrows to dictate the order and direction in which parts of each letter should be written. Once students have mastered each letter, teachers should focus on letter size or proportion. For example, smaller letters (like c, e, and n) should be half the size of larger letters (such as k, l, or t). Finally, proper spacing should be taught, both between letters and words. Once spacing between words has been mastered, students should begin to work on including punctuation and appropriate spacing between sentences.

IMPORTANCE OF LISTENING AND SPEAKING STRATEGIES

Both listening and speaking strategies are important skills for students in all areas of education. To achieve the highest success, students should be taught how to effectively **speak** and exchange dialogue in large- and small-group settings. In addition, students should be encouraged to question, retell, or reenact the words of others. Equally important, students must learn to actively **listen** and visualize the words of others so that they are able to understand the purpose of what someone else is saying. To check for listening, students should be encouraged to summarize what they have heard and complete graphic organizers outlining important concepts or facts. When given ample opportunity to both speak and listen, students are more likely to excel across all content areas.

DEVELOPING LISTENING AND SPEAKING SKILLS WITH DRAMATIC PLAY

Dramatic play is a type of play in which students are assigned specific roles and encouraged to act those roles out. In dramatic play, students are typically assigned a character but not a script. They are encouraged to take on the feelings and actions of the character they have been assigned and act as that character would act. Dramatic play is an excellent strategy for developing speaking skills as students must clearly identify and express the feelings of their characters. They must speak clearly and loudly enough so that the other actors and the audience can hear what they are saying. In addition, students must actively listen to what the other students in the play are saying to appropriately respond to the actions and words of the other characters in an effort to further develop the story line.

Assessment

RUBRIC FOR ASSESSING STUDENT WRITING

A **rubric** is a checklist used to evaluate what students have learned or accomplished. Teachers can take lesson objectives to form the basis of a rubric. The teacher should explain the rubric to the students before they begin a writing assignment. During their writing exercise, the students can refer to the rubric to guide what and how they write. After the students have completed their writing assignments, the teacher can then apply the rubric to assess their work, checking to see if they have met all of the learning objectives. Students will be less confused and frustrated when teachers have given them well-planned, clearly expressed guidelines. In addition to clearly stating their learning goals, objectives, and expectations for each assignment, teachers should model the kind of performance they expect. Teachers should connect lesson and assignment goals obviously and clearly with student achievement.

SUMMATIVE AND FORMATIVE ASSESSMENTS

Summative assessments evaluate what a student has learned at the end of a lesson, unit, course, or term. A final examination is an example of a summative assessment. **Formative assessments** are ongoing evaluations to demonstrate what a student is in the process of learning and has learned thus far. Formative assessments are not just for evaluation: they are also important for use in the classroom as a teaching tool. As teachers conduct ongoing evaluations via formative assessments, they should use both formal and informal assessment instruments. Teachers should never use the results of only one formal or informal assessment to form permanent student groups. They should only place students into groups after administering, scoring, and interpreting a number of different assessments. Teachers should also create student groups that account for individual differences among the students in every group and should accordingly make these groups sufficiently flexible to accommodate individual student differences.

OBSERVATION

Observational assessment is appropriate for evaluating student progress and the effectiveness of instruction. A teacher can create a checklist of skills, requirements, or competencies that students should attain. The teacher can then observe individuals or student groups and check off the skills or competencies demonstrated. For example, if a teacher has been instructing a class in listening carefully, he or she can compose a checklist with items such as paying attention, refraining from interrupting others, summarizing what ideas the other students have expressed, and asking questions of other students. The teacher can then initiate student discussion and observe, checking off the checklist items he or she observes the students performing. Or, when teaching interview skills, a teacher can make a checklist including confidence, personal appearance, mannerisms, and directly answering interviewer questions. He or she can also observe students participating in mock or real interviews and identify which items the students satisfy.

By observing students as they work on assignments or practice exercises, teachers can obtain valuable information. With kindergarten and first-grade classes, many school districts inform parents of children's progress by filling out "report cards" or inventories. Through experience, long-term teachers typically develop their own methods of making ongoing skills assessments of their students. Books about reading instruction typically include informal reading assessments. Experts recommend that teachers assess student progress in naturalistic ways on a continual basis. They find that teachers and parents continually observing students regarding their status and progress in the physical, cognitive, emotional, and social domains yields the most relevant assessment—particularly with young children. Experts also approve of portfolio assessments and performance assessments for more complete pictures of overall progress than standardized test scores. They also find that writing narrative reports about young children depicts the whole child better than giving them number or letter grades.

OBSERVATIONAL CHECKLISTS

In informal assessment, using **observational checklists** to identify skills attained has an advantage over formal written tests because informal, naturalistic observation enables teachers to record behaviors that traditional written tests cannot include. For example, if teachers want to know whether students can follow all steps of a science experiment in the correct sequence, how many baskets they can make in free throws on the basketball court, or whether they can remember all of the significant parts to include in a speech they write and deliver to the class, they can record these by observing and marking such items on a checklist they have designed in advance—but they could not record any such behaviors through standard "pencil-and-paper" tests. The structure of checklists has the advantage of being consistent, but also the disadvantage of being inflexible. Teachers can remedy the latter by including a place at the end of the checklist to write open-ended comments on their observations of student performance.

RUNNING RECORD

To identify what students are able and unable to do, one informal assessment measure teachers can use is a **running record**. For example, the teacher can listen to a student reading aloud from text such as an essay, a speech, a novel, or a class subject textbook. While listening, the teacher marks a copy of the text to show words the student mispronounces. The teacher draws a line through each word the student skips and draws an arrow under words the student repeats. Teachers may also mark student hesitations at certain words. If the teacher then calculates that the student correctly read 95 percent of the words, the student reads this text at the "Independent" level. If the student correctly reads 90-94 percent of the words, he or she reads this text at the "Instructional" level, indicating satisfactory performance with teacher assistance. Correctly reading 89 percent or fewer words indicates the "Frustration" level, where comprehension may be inadequate. This group of assessment levels is also known as the reading continuum.

ANECDOTAL RECORDS

Anecdotal records can provide good information for formative assessments. For example, when students conduct science experiments or complete class projects, teachers can use anecdotal records to instruct them in writing reports to explain the procedures they followed. When students in group learning activities solve a problem together, teachers can use anecdotal records to document the process used. Such anecdotal documents not only provide the teacher with formative assessment information, but teachers can also use them to give feedback to the group of students. Two disadvantages of using anecdotal records are that they can take more time for teachers to complete than other informal assessments and that they can be hard to use for assigning grades. Two advantages are that anecdotal records can encompass all pertinent information, whereas other assessments may not, and that teachers may use them only for giving students feedback, which eliminates the need to base grades on them.

PORTFOLIO ASSESSMENT

In portfolio assessment, teachers or students create a folder or box and deposit a student's best work products, accumulated over time. In language arts, teachers often collect student writing samples in portfolios for a whole year. Some language arts teachers additionally transmit year-long portfolios to the following year's teacher to aid in student assessment. Teachers can use portfolio assessments in any subject to enable students to assume greater responsibility for planning, organizing, and implementing what they learn. The combined products in the portfolio afford concise depictions of what students have achieved during specific time periods. Portfolios can include handwritten or printed essays, stories, and articles; videos; or computer files of multimedia presentations. Teachers should help students develop guidelines about which materials to place in portfolios, and how to self-assess their own work. The advantages of portfolios over tests include helping students develop self-assessment skills, giving clearer pictures of student progress, and learning from mistakes without the damage of a bad test grade.

RESEARCH-BASED ASSESSMENT TECHNIQUES
ASSESSMENT OF STUDENT LEARNING

To assess student attitudes, educators can create various situations and observe and document their responses, requiring students to choose which behaviors to demonstrate. To assess **cognitive strategies**, teachers can give students learning tasks, require them to select useful strategies for learning new information independently, and expect them to explain and discuss what methods they use for different learning tasks. To assess student **comprehension**, teachers give them topics and ask them to restate and summarize information. Or, teachers may have students apply information in new contexts, such as giving statements with words that are different than those used in the original lesson and asking students to identify their meanings. To assess student **concept understanding**, teachers give students new examples and "non-examples," having students classify these into the right categories. To assess student **creativity**, teachers can give students new problems—including products, presentations, or performances—to study, resolve, or "turn upside down." They can also have students fit solutions and products into specified resources and functions and give them situations that require novel responses or approaches.

ASSESSMENT OF DIFFERENT STUDENT OUTCOMES

To assess students' **critical thinking**, teachers can ask students to evaluate outcomes or information and have them perform research and analysis. To assess student **insight**, teachers should give students opportunities to engage in inquiry and discovery activities, and offer situations for them to manipulate. To assess student **metacognition**, teachers should give a variety of problems or situations to address, and assign students to identify different kinds of thinking strategies for analysis and evaluation of their own thought processes. To assess **multiple intelligences** (cf. Gardner), teachers should give students learning experiences in each of the modalities they target, like verbal, musical, and physical. They should offer students choices of several different modalities. They should also require students to perform in the modalities selected. To assess **motor skills**, teachers must supply resources and situations in which students can perform the skills while the teachers evaluate, using checklists. To assess **problem-solving**, teachers ask students to choose appropriate strategies to solve different problem situations including simple, complex, structured, and unstructured.

ASSESSMENT OF PROCEDURAL KNOWLEDGE, SCIENTIFIC INQUIRY, THINKING SKILLS, AND VERBAL KNOWLEDGE

To assess student **knowledge of principles**, **rules**, **and procedures**, teachers supply situations that require students to correctly apply these to everyday problems. Students are asked to state principles, rules, and procedures, and choose which apply to various scenarios. To assess student **scientific inquiry skills**, teachers give problems or situations that require students to speculate, inquire, and formulate hypotheses. Teachers should also give hands-on activities to conduct research and draw conclusions. To assess student **thinking skills**, teachers can ask students to give summaries of different kinds of thinking strategies. Teachers can provide situations in which students must select the best thinking strategies to apply. Teachers assign students to observe examples of open-mindedness versus closed-mindedness, accurate versus inaccurate, and responsible versus irresponsible applications of thinking methods. Teachers can design scenarios requiring student persistence for analyzing and discovering answers, as well as application of thinking strategies in real-life circumstances. To assess **verbal knowledge**, teachers require information recall, restatement, and comprehension.

TEACHING STRATEGIES TO ADDRESS STUDENT AND FAMILY DIVERSITY

Teachers must recognize that each student is unique. When a teacher respects individual student differences, he or she communicates this attitude to the class. Research finds that cultural differences influence human behavior, and thus play a part in classrooms. Acknowledgement of cultural differences helps to prevent student isolation. To educate students from diverse backgrounds, teachers need to understand a student's culture and individual characteristics—as well as any existing disabilities. Teacher and school involvement with students' families promotes student success during and after school. This requires educators to avoid ethnocentric approaches. Diverse families may need instruction in the school culture of collaboration and communication. Schools also must initially meet family needs physically, socially, and economically to enable involvement, requiring school knowledge of supportive community programs. Communications must be translated for families speaking different languages. Educators need willingness to interact outside of school hours and grounds. They can also recruit parent liaisons with similar cultural backgrounds. Teachers should open parent communications with positive feedback about children.

Inclusive educational programs require meaningful, effective collaboration of educators, students, and families. Teachers must not only meet student and family needs, but they must also communicate their own needs effectively and be willing to find solutions through team-based approaches. Collaboration allows outcomes that individuals cannot achieve alone. Researchers have discovered that despite the challenges of cooperation among staff members, the more teachers interact with each other, the more educational change can be achieved successfully. Understanding of cultural communication differences, respectful disagreement, respect for confidentiality, willingness to compromise, responsible communication of opinions and emotions (such as using "I" statements), tolerance for others' various perspectives, and careful listening to others are communication skills needed for effective communication and collaboration. Some educators advocate multicultural awareness days involving all school personnel, families, and community members when each school year starts. Culturally responsive standards-based instruction (CRSBI) incorporates caring, communication, and curriculum. Educators must also foster positive student-teacher relationships, and assure positive role models for every student.

CREATING SAFE EDUCATIONAL ENVIRONMENTS

Teachers need to establish and sustain classroom environments for students in which they feel nurtured and know that the teacher is open to hearing their feelings, thoughts, and ideas. Teachers are responsible for developing respect for individual differences and openness to discussions in their classrooms. They may need to explain the difference between fairness and equality. For example, students who need eyeglasses cannot be deprived of them, but neither should all students be made to wear them. Teachers can use such examples to illustrate to students that fairness does not mean everybody gets the same treatment: while every student deserves help, that help will differ for different students. Teachers must create student-teacher relationships of mutual trust, and ensure that all students know the teachers care about them, both academically and personally. Teacher beliefs, attitudes, and performance expectations, and how they communicate these, establish this knowledge. Teachers must know student and family languages, communication styles, and home literacy practices and build on these in their classrooms.

OSAT Practice Test

SELECTED RESPONSE PRACTICE QUESTIONS

Questions 1-3 refer to the following excerpts:

> Had we but world enough, and time,
> This coyness, lady, were no crime.
> We would sit down, and think which way
> To walk, and pass our long love's day.
> But at my back I always hear
> Time's winged chariot hurrying near;
> And yonder all before us lie
> Deserts of vast eternity.

1. Who is the author of this poem?

    a. John Donne
    b. Andrew Marvell
    c. George Herbert
    d. Henry Vaughan

2. This poem reflects a thematic tradition known as which of the following?

    a. Carpe diem
    b. Classicism
    c. Cinquain
    d. Conceit

3. What is the meter of the couplets in this poem?

    a. Pentameter
    b. Heptameter
    c. Hexameter
    d. Tetrameter

Questions 4-7 are based on the following excerpt:

> riverrun, past Eve and Adam's, from swerve of shore to bend of bay, brings us by a commodious vicus of recirculation back to Howth Castle and Environs.

4. This is the opening sentence of...

    a. *Ulysses.*
    b. *Finnegans Wake.*
    c. *Adventures in the Skin Trade.*
    d. *A Portrait of the Artist as a Young Man.*

5. In the excerpted sentence, the word "vicus" represents all of the following except:

    a. Vicinity
    b. Vico Way
    c. Giambattista Vico
    d. Vicarage

6. Why does this opening sentence begin with an uncapitalized word?
a. This is to make it stand out to the reader.
b. It is the continuation of the author's previous novel.
c. It forms the completion of the novel's unfinished last sentence.
d. A typesetting error in the original edition was preserved in perpetuity.

7. The author of the excerpted work is famous for using a literary technique known as...
a. Stream-of-consciousness.
b. The unreliable narrator.
c. First-person narration.
d. The author surrogate.

Questions 8-10 refer to the following excerpt:

> Call the roller of big cigars,
> The muscular one, and bid him whip
> In kitchen cups concupiscent curds.
> Let the wenches dawdle in such dress
> As they are used to wear, and let the boys
> Bring flowers in last month's newspapers.
> Let be be finale of seem.
> The only emperor is the emperor of ice-cream.

8. The excerpted poem was written in...
a. The 17th century.
b. The 18th century.
c. The 19th century.
d. The 20th century.

9. Which literary device is shown in the third line of the excerpted stanza?
a. Alliteration
b. Hyperbole
c. Onomatopoeia
d. Metonymy

10. The line "Let be be finale of seem" can be interpreted as reflecting a concept from which of the following?
a. Ovid's *Metamorphoses*
b. Dante's *Divine Comedy*
c. Plato's *Dialogues*
d. Homer's *Iliad*

Questions 11-13 refer to the following excerpt:

> I AM assured by our Merchants, that a Boy or a Girl before twelve Years old, is no saleable Commodity; and even when they come to this Age, they will not yield above [an amount of money] at most, on the Exchange; which cannot turn to Account...to the Parents...; the Charge of Nutriment and Rags, having been at least four Times that Value.
>
> I SHALL now therefore humbly propose my own Thoughts; which I hope will not be liable to the least Objection.

I HAVE been assured by a very knowing *American* of my Acquaintance in *London;* that a young healthy Child, well nursed, is, at a Year old, a most delicious, nourishing, and wholesome Food; whether *Stewed, Roasted, Baked,* or *Boiled;* and, I make no doubt, that it will equally serve in a *Fricasie,* or *Ragoust.*

11. The literary form used in the excerpted piece is...
   a. Persuasion.
   b. Satire.
   c. Exposition.
   d. Bathos.

12. The excerpted work was published in which century?
   a. 20th
   b. 19th
   c. 18th
   d. 17th

13. The author of the excerpted piece also wrote which of the following?
   a. *The Canterbury Tales*
   b. *The Faerie Queene*
   c. *Paradise Lost*
   d. *Gulliver's Travels*

Questions 14-17 refer to the following poem:

The Thought-Fox

I imagine this midnight moment's forest:
Something else is alive
Beside the clock's loneliness
And this blank page where my fingers move.
Through the window I see no star:
Something more near
Though deeper within darkness
Is entering the loneliness:
Cold, delicately as the dark snow
A fox's nose touches twig, leaf;
Two eyes serve a movement, that now
And again now, and now, and now
Sets neat prints into the snow
Between trees, and warily a lame
Shadow lags by stump and in hollow
Of a body that is bold to come
Across clearings, an eye,
A widening deepening greenness,
Brilliantly, concentratedly,
Coming about its own business
Till, with a sudden sharp hot stink of fox,
It enters the dark hole of the head.
The window is starless still; the clock ticks,
The page is printed.

From Ted Hughes: Selected Poems 1957-1967. Copyright © 1972 by Ted Hughes, Harper & Row Publishers, Inc.

14. The primary literary device used by the poet here is...

  a. Foreshadowing.
  b. Irony.
  c. Cliché.
  d. Metaphor.

15. Which of these does the poem really describe?

  a. The process of a fox's natural actions
  b. The process of being inspired by nature
  c. The process of being inspired to write
  d. The process of being attacked by a fox

16. Which of the following best characterizes how this poem portrays the creative process?

  a. The poet exercises tight control of a thought.
  b. The poet is a passive recipient of the thought.
  c. The poet carefully guides the thought to him.
  d. The poet imagines a fox to help him to write.

17. In which of the following forms is this poem written?

  a. In free verse
  b. Rhymed and metered
  c. Unrhymed and metered
  d. Rhymed and unmetered

Questions 18-20 refer to the following excerpts:

I knew I should be grateful to Mrs. Guinea, only I couldn't feel a thing. If Mrs. Guinea had given me a ticket to Europe, or a round-the-world cruise, it wouldn't have made one scrap of difference to me, because wherever I sat—on the deck of a ship or at a street café in Paris or Bangkok—I would be sitting under the same glass bell jar, stewing in my own sour air.

I sank back in the gray, plush seat and closed my eyes. The air of the bell jar wadded round me and I couldn't stir.

[Following a successful shock treatment:]

All the heat and fear had purged itself. I felt surprisingly at peace. The bell jar hung, suspended, a few feet above my head. I was open to the circulating air.

"We'll take up where we left off, Esther," she [my mother] had said, with her sweet, martyr's smile. "We'll act as if all this were a bad dream."

A bad dream.

To the person in the bell jar, blank and stopped as a dead baby, the world itself is the bad dream.

Valerie's last, cheerful cry had been "So long! Be seeing you."

"Not if I know it," I thought.

But I wasn't sure. I wasn't sure at all. How did I know that someday—at college, in Europe, somewhere, anywhere—the bell jar, with its stifling distortions, wouldn't descend again?

From *The Bell Jar* by Sylvia Plath, copyright © 1971 by Harper & Row, Publishers, Inc.

18. The bell jar the author refers to is an example of which literary device?

a. A simile
b. An allusion
c. A metaphor
d. Personification

19. In this book, Plath uses a bell jar to symbolize...

a. The strictures of reality.
b. Her own mental illness.
c. A case of writer's block.
d. A disorder of breathing.

20. Which of the following statements is accurate about Sylvia Plath?

a. *The Bell Jar* was her last in a long series of novels, all of them successful.
b. She ultimately recovered, lived a long life, and wrote many more novels.
c. Plath wrote only a few poems, but *The Bell Jar* was the first of her books.
d. She wrote *The Bell Jar* about her initial breakdown almost a decade later.

21. William Shakespeare wrote during which historical and literary period?

a. Medieval
b. Renaissance
c. Restoration
d. Enlightenment

22. Which of the following was the author of *The Pilgrim's Progress*?

a. John Bunyan
b. William Congreve
c. Daniel Defoe
d. Samuel Butler

Questions 23-24 are based on the following excerpt:

> Come live with me and be my love,
> And we will all the pleasures prove
> That valleys, groves, hills, and fields,
> Woods, or steepy mountain yields.

23. This is the first stanza of a poem written by...

a. Andrew Marvell.
b. Christopher Marlowe.
c. Sir Walter Raleigh.
d. William Shakespeare.

24. The rhyme scheme of this stanza is...

    a. ABAB.

    b. ABBA.

    c. AABB.

    d. ABCD.

25. The legend of Faust has been treated in literature by all of the following except:

    a. Christopher Marlowe

    b. Johann Wolfgang von Goethe

    c. Thomas Mann

    d. Dylan Thomas

26. Of the following works by Alexander Pope, which of the following is a didactic poem?

    a. "An Essay on Criticism"

    b. "The Rape of the Lock"

    c. "The Universal Prayer"

    d. "The Dunciad"

Questions 27-29 refer to the following excerpts:

Excerpt 1:

[First stanza:] I wake to sleep, and take my waking slow.
I feel my fate in what I cannot fear.
I learn by going where I have to go.
[Last stanza:] This shaking keeps me steady. I should know.
What falls away is always. And is near.
I wake to sleep, and take my waking slow.
I learn by going where I have to go.

From *The Waking* by Theodore Roethke, in *Roethke: Collected Poems,* Doubleday & Company, Inc. copyright © 1937-1966 by Beatrice Roethke as Administratrix of the Estate of Theodore Roethke; copyright © 1932-1961 by Theodore Roethke.

Excerpt 2:

[First stanza:] I shut my eyes and all the world drops dead;
I lift my lids and all is born again.
(I think I made you up inside my head.)
[Last stanza:] I should have loved a thunderbird instead;
At least when spring comes they roar back again.
I shut my eyes and all the world drops dead.
(I think I made you up inside my head.)

From *Mad Girl's Love Song* by Sylvia Plath, copyright © 1954 by Sylvia Plath, in A Biographical Note, in *The Bell Jar,* Copyright © 1971 by Harper & Row, Publishers. *Mad Girl's Love Song* first appeared in *Mademoiselle,* August 1953 issue.

Excerpt 3:

[First stanza:] Do not go gentle into that good night,
Old age should burn and rave at close of day;
Rage, rage against the dying of the light.
[Last stanza:] And you, my father, there on the sad height,
Curse, bless, me now with your fierce tears, I pray.
Do not go gentle into that good night.

Rage, rage against the dying of the light.

27. Which is true of all three excerpted poems?

    a.   They are all ballads.
    b.   They are all sonnets.
    c.   They are all villanelles.
    d.   They are all different forms.

28. Which of the excerpted poems focus on the nature of reality vs. the imagination?

    a.   The second and third
    b.   The first and second
    c.   The first and third
    d.   The first, second, and third

29. Which of the excerpted poems deal(s) directly with the subject of death?

    a.   The third
    b.   The second and third
    c.   The first and third
    d.   The first, second, and third

Questions 30-35 refer to the following poem:

I like to see it lap the Miles —
And lick the Valleys up —
And stop to feed itself at Tanks —
And then — prodigious step
Around a pile of Mountains —
And supercilious peer
In Shanties — by the sides of Roads –
And then a Quarry pare
To fit its Ribs
And crawl between
Complaining all the while
In horrid — hooting stanza —
Then chase itself down Hill —
And neigh like Boanerges —
Then — punctual as a Star
Stop — docile and omnipotent
At its own stable door —

30. This poem describes which of the following?

    a.   An aristocratic thoroughbred horse
    b.   The recently invented railroad train
    c.   An incredible mythological monster
    d.   The subject cannot be determined

31. This poem was written around the time of...

    a. The American Revolution.
    b. The French Revolution.
    c. The War of 1812.
    d. The Civil War.

32. An amazing feat in this poem is that the structure of the subject described is mirrored in the poem's...

    a. Vocabulary.
    b. Rhythms.
    c. Syntax.
    d. Tone.

33. The adjectives "docile and omnipotent" in the penultimate line were chosen because they are...

    a. Synonymous.
    b. Nonsensical.
    c. Mechanical.
    d. Contrasting.

34. What is the source of the phrase "And neigh like Boanerges" in the last stanza?

    a. A Greek myth about a creature that inhabits Hades (the underworld)
    b. A New Testament reference to a fiery, strong-voiced preacher/orator
    c. An Old Testament reference to a wrathful prophet seeking vengeance
    d. A Roman name for a mythological animal that lived within a labyrinth

35. This poet famously used dashes for _____ and capitals for _____.

    a. Punctuation; honor
    b. Separation; names
    c. Prosody; emphasis
    d. Continuity; names

Questions 36-38 refer to the following poem:

> Because I could not stop for Death —
> He kindly stopped for me —
> The Carriage held but just Ourselves —
> And Immortality.
>
> We slowly drove — He knew no haste
> And I had put away
> My labor and my leisure too,
> For His Civility —
>
> We passed the School, where Children strove
> At Recess — in the Ring —
> We passed the Fields of Gazing Grain —
> We passed the Setting Sun —
>
> Or rather — He passed Us —
> The Dews drew quivering and chill —

For only Gossamer, my Gown —
My Tippet — only Tulle —

We paused before a House that seemed
A Swelling of the Ground —
The Roof was scarcely visible —
The Cornice — in the Ground —

Since then — 'tis Centuries — and yet
Feels shorter than the Day
I first surmised the Horses' Heads
Were toward Eternity —

36. The descriptions of Death, of the "Fields of Gazing Grain," and of the setting sun all employ which literary device?

   a.   Analogy
   b.   Hyperbole
   c.   Alliteration
   d.   Personification

37. Irrespective of its topic, the tone of this poem would best be described as...

   a.   Serious, grave, and portentously dark
   b.   Detached, alienated, and numb of feeling
   c.   Lighthearted, humorous, and gently ironic
   d.   Frantic, agitated, and with a frenzy of fear

38. What is described in the fifth stanza?

   a.   A home
   b.   A grave
   c.   A church
   d.   A school

39. A distinguishing feature of the form known as haiku is...

   a.   5/7/5 syllables per line
   b.   An ABA rhyme scheme
   c.   Perfectly regular meter
   d.   Lengthy epic narratives

40. Which of the following accurately identifies *The Diary of a Young Girl* by Anne Frank?

   a.   A fictional novel of a 1920s American debutante's diary
   b.   A non-fictional Dutch journal influenced by World War II
   c.   A long, episodic poem depicting childhood schizophrenia
   d.   A British record documenting a sociological diary project

41. This passage is taken from which of the following?

> When I got to camp I warn't feeling very brash, there warn't much sand in my craw; but I says, this ain't no time to be fooling around. So I got all my traps into my canoe again so as to have them out of sight, and I put out the fire and scattered the ashes around to look like an old last-year's camp, and then clumb a tree.

    a. *The Mysterious Stranger*
    b. *The Adventures of Tom Sawyer*
    c. *The Adventures of Huckleberry Finn*
    d. *The Prince and the Pauper*

42. Which of the following statements is most accurate regarding the characters of Drouet and Hurstwood in Theodore Dreiser's novel *Sister Carrie*?

    a. Drouet has the awareness to be decent, but he lacks the morality.
    b. Hurstwood has the morality, but not the awareness, for decency.
    c. Only one of these characters is representative of the middle class.
    d. Drouet is morally decent but unaware; Hurstwood is the opposite.

Questions 43- 45 refer to the following excerpt:

> I bequeath myself to the dirt to grow from the grass I love,
> If you want me again look for me under your boot-soles.

43. What is the title of the poem from which this is taken?

    a. "To You"
    b. "Thou Reader"
    c. "Song of Myself"
    d. "One's-Self I Sing"

44. Which of the following is the best interpretation of the excerpted lines?

    a. The poet means that he will be dead and buried in the future.
    b. The poet means he is one with and an integral part of nature.
    c. The poet means the person addressed is above him in station.
    d. The poet means the recipient stepped on/walked all over him.

45. The excerpted work was published in which century?

    a. 18th
    b. 19th
    c. 20th
    d. 21st

Questions 46-50 refer to the following excerpts:

> I should have been a pair of ragged claws
> Scuttling across the floors of silent seas.
> Shall I part my hair behind? Do I dare to eat a peach?
> I shall wear white flannel trousers, and walk upon the beach.
> I have heard the mermaids singing, each to each.
> I do not think that they will sing to me.
> We have lingered in the chambers of the sea
> By sea-girls wreathed with seaweed red and brown
> Till human voices wake us, and we drown.

46. What is the title of the work from which these excerpts are taken?
   a. "The Waste Land"
   b. "The Love Song of J. Alfred Prufrock"
   c. "Notes Toward the Definition of Culture"
   d. "The Hollow Men"

47. The second excerpt is speaking about...
   a. Indecision.
   b. A vacation.
   c. Mortality.
   d. Drowning.

48. Which of the following is/are the best interpretation(s) of the meaning in the first excerpt?
   a. The speaker's existence is as significant as the life of a crab.
   b. The speaker loves the sea and wishes he could live under it.
   c. The scavenger can create beauty by reconstructing garbage.
   d. The answers choices in (A) and (C) are valid interpretations.

49. Why does the speaker say, "I do not think that they will sing to me"?
   a. Because he feels the despair of existence.
   b. Because he is becoming deaf with old age.
   c. Because he knows mermaids are not real.
   d. Because he is on the beach, not in the sea.

50. Which of the following is the best interpretation of the final line?
   a. Mermaids protect us from drowning; humans ruin it.
   b. The dream of art is ruined by the intrusion of reality.
   c. Dreaming of mermaids is part of death by drowning.
   d. Mermaids bewitch us from knowing that we drown.

51. Which of Chaucer's *Canterbury Tales* is an example of the literary form known as the fabliau?
   a. "The Physician's Tale"
   b. "The Wife of Bath's Tale"
   c. "The Miller's Tale"
   d. "The Pardoner's Tale"

52. Which of the following pairs are NOT both written in the form of frame tales?
   a. *The Canterbury Tales* by Geoffrey Chaucer and *The Decameron* by Giovanni Bocaccio
   b. The *Mahabharata* by Veda Vyasa and *The Parlement of Foules* by Geoffrey Chaucer
   c. *Frankenstein* by Mary W. Shelley and *Wuthering Heights* by Emily Brontë
   d. *The Great Gatsby* by F. Scott Fitzgerald and *To the Lighthouse* by Virginia Woolf

53. Which of the following works was the first ever published in vernacular Italian?
   a. *De re publica (On the Republic)* by Marcus Tullius Cicero
   b. *Il Decameron (The Decameron)* by Giovanni Bocaccio
   c. *La Divina Commedia (The Divine Comedy)* by Dante Alighieri
   d. *Il Nome della Rosa (The Name of the Rose)* by Umberto Eco

Questions 54-56 are based on the following poem:

Leda and the Swan

A sudden blow: the great wings beating still
Above the staggering girl, her thighs caressed
By the dark webs, her nape caught in his bill,
He holds her helpless breast upon his breast.
How can those terrified vague fingers push
The feathered glory from her loosening thighs?
And how can body, laid in that white rush,
But feel the strange heart beating where it lies?
A shudder in the loins engenders there
The broken wall, the burning roof and tower
And Agamemnon dead.
Being so caught up,
So mastered by the brute blood of the air,
Did she put on his knowledge with his power
Before the indifferent beak could let her drop?

William Butler Yeats, 1923

54. "The broken wall, the burning roof and tower/And Agamemnon dead" refer to...
   a. The Punic Wars.
   b. The Trojan War.
   c. The Peloponnesian War.
   d. A murder but no war.

55. In what form is this poem?
   a. A sonnet
   b. Villanelle
   c. Free verse
   d. A sestina

56. The poet's final question best suggests which of the following ideas?
   a. Humans get godlike knowledge and power from the gods.
   b. Human knowledge and power are necessarily incomplete.
   c. Humans in ancient Greece interacted differently with gods.
   d. Humans interacting with gods got power, not knowledge.

57. In the Three Cueing Systems model of word recognition in reading instruction, which system most relates to how words are assembled into meaningful language?
   a. Phonological
   b. Semantic
   c. Syntactic
   d. Pragmatic

58. In the word-recognition model of the Three Cueing Systems used in teaching reading, which of the following is most associated with the meanings of words?
   a. Using pragmatic cues
   b. Phonological system
   c. The syntactic system
   d. The semantic system

59. In the model known in reading instruction as the Three Cueing Systems, which of these relate most to how sounds are used to communicate meaning?

a. Syntactic cues
b. Semantic cues
c. Phonological cues
d. Pragmatic cues

60. In reading instruction, the Three Cueing Systems is one model used. Which of the following represents a valid reading strategy that is NOT a system in the Three Cueing Systems model?

a. Syntactic cues
b. Pragmatic cues
c. Semantic cues
d. Phonological cues

61. Which of the following statements does NOT describe how or why students should be taught to activate their prior knowledge while reading?

a. Teachers should discuss and model connections with existing knowledge to prepare students by helping them consider what they already know about the subject of the text.
b. Students can make better sense of the text by considering how it fits with what they already know.
c. Teachers can lead discussions helping students focus on how the connections they made between the text and their previous knowledge informed their understanding of the text, and on how the text helped them build on their foundations of existing knowledge.
d. Students can limit their understanding of a text to how it fits with what they already know.

62. Which choice most appropriately fills the blanks in this statement? "Teaching children which thinking strategies are used by _____ and helping them use those strategies _____ creates the core of teaching reading." (*Mosaic of Thought,* Keene and Zimmerman, 1997)

a. Reading teachers; in different ways
b. Beginning students; with assistance
c. Proficient readers; independently
d. Published writers; more creatively

63. Scholars have identified three kinds of major connections that students make when reading: connecting text to self, text to the world, and text to text. Which of the following student statements best reflect(s) the connection of text to the world?

a. "These mythic gods have more power, but feel and act like humans."
b. "This novel is set during a period I learned about in my history class."
c. "I can relate to how the main character felt about being controlled."
d. All three statements equally reflect connection of text to the world.

64. When students are taught to use effective reading comprehension strategies, they not only achieve deeper understanding, but they also learn to think about how they think when reading. This is known as...

a. Schemata.
b. Scaffolding.
c. Metacognition.
d. Metamorphosis.

65. Activity settings (Tharp and Gallimore, 1988) are aspects of the sociocultural context that affect how students learn and read. Of five activity settings, one is participant identity, or who the students are. Of the other four, which is most related to motivation?

    a. When the activity is done
    b. Why the activity is done
    c. Where the activity is done
    d. How the activity is done

66. Some experts maintain that teaching reading comprehension entails not only the application of skills, but also the process of actively constructing meaning. This process they describe as *interactive, strategic,* and *adaptable*. Which of the following best defines the *interactive* aspect of this process?

    a. The process involves the text, the reader, and the context in which reading occurs.
    b. The process involves readers using a variety of strategies in constructing meaning.
    c. The process involves readers changing their strategies to read different text types.
    d. The process involves changing strategies according to different reasons for reading.

67. In first-language (L1) and second-language (L2) acquisition, which of the following is true about developmental stages?

    a. L2 learners do not undergo the first stage called the Silent Period as L1 learners do.
    b. L2 learners undergo all stages, but are urged to skip the first stage more than L1s.
    c. L2 learners do not undergo the second stage of Formulaic Speech as L1 learners do.
    d. L2 learners undergo the third stage of Structural and Semantic Simplifications later.

68. Which statement is most accurate about social contexts of L1 and L2 acquisition?

    a. Both L1 and L2 learning can occur in equally varied natural and educational contexts.
    b. L1s are only learned in natural contexts, while L2s are learned in educational contexts.
    c. Variations in L2 proficiency can result from the different contexts of learning the L2s.
    d. L2s are not a speaker's natural language and so are never learned in natural contexts.

69. Which of the following is unique to second-language learning?

    a. Zone of proximal development
    b. The critical period hypothesis
    c. Marked/unmarked features
    d. The process of fossilization

70. An ESL student whose L1 is Chinese tends to omit plural endings and articles before nouns. Of the following, which is the best explanation for these errors?

    a. The student has not yet learned these English grammatical forms.
    b. Omission avoids having to choose among irregular English forms.
    c. Incompatible nature and rules of the L1 are transferring to the L2.
    d. The student does not understand how the L1 and L2 forms relate.

71. Which of the following is the most accurate characterization of dialects?

    a. They are non-standard versions of any language.
    b. They are often seen as less socially acceptable.
    c. They include linguistic features that are incorrect.
    d. They indicate poor/incomplete language learning.

72. Of the following, which statement is correct regarding Standard English?
   a. The formal Standard English applies to written language.
   b. Standard English is universal in English-speaking nations.
   c. Speech communities use the Standard English of writing.
   d. The Standard English construct does not include dialects.

73. The Great Vowel Shift occurred during which time span?
   a. 10th to 13th centuries
   b. 12th to 15th centuries
   c. 15th to 18th centuries
   d. 16th to 19th centuries

74. The Great Vowel Shift caused the pronunciation of long vowels in English to shift:
   a. Farther back in the mouth.
   b. Higher in the mouth.
   c. Lower in the mouth.
   d. Farther to the front of the mouth.

75. Of the following authors, whose English existed *during* the Great Vowel Shift?
   a. William Shakespeare
   b. Geoffrey Chaucer
   c. Emily Dickinson
   d. The Pearl Poet

76. Linguists generally analyze the Great Vowel Shift as having transpired in _____ steps.
   a. Ten
   b. Eight
   c. Six
   d. Four

77. Which of the following areas has NOT been affected in the long term by the Great Vowel Shift?
   a. Written spelling
   b. Teaching reading
   c. Text comprehension
   d. The quality of texts written before the GVS

78. The source of the silent *b* in the English word *debt* was originally...
   a. A Middle English word.
   b. A voiced Old English *b.*
   c. From Latin etymology.
   d. From Greek etymology.

79. We are familiar with the modern English meanings of the word "disaster." But in the 16th century, this word meant...
   a. Catastrophe.
   b. Star-crossed.
   c. A misfortune.
   d. Unflowerlike.

80. The English word "salary" has a 2,000-year-old etymology to a word meaning...

a. Salt.
b. Celery.
c. Money.
d. Earnings.

81. Which of the following is an example of a portmanteau?

a. Fax
b. Brunch
c. Babysitter
d. Saxophone

82. The English language word "quark" is an example of the result of which linguistic process?

a. Blending
b. Conversion
c. Neologisms
d. Onomatopoeia

83. The following sentence is which of the following sentence types?

The questions in this test can give you an idea of what kinds of questions you might find on the actual test; however, they are not duplicates of the actual test questions, which cover the same subject material but may differ in form and content.

a. Simple
b. Complex
c. Compound
d. Compound-complex

84. A patient dies in surgery and the reporting doctor describes the death as a "negative patient outcome." This is *best* identified as an example of...

a. Jargon.
b. Ambiguity.
c. Euphemism.
d. Connotation.

85. Which of the following is NOT typically categorized as a prewriting process?

a. Planning
b. Reflection
c. Visualization
d. Brainstorming

86. Which of the following correctly represents the sequence of stages or steps in the writing process?

a. Prewriting, drafting, revising, editing, publishing
b. Prewriting, drafting, editing, publishing, revising
c. Prewriting, editing, drafting, revising, publishing
d. Prewriting, drafting, editing, revising, publishing

87. Research has found that which of the following occur for students during revision and rewriting?
   a. Students only correct their mechanical errors in revisions.
   b. Students often incorporate new ideas when they rewrite.
   c. Students retain their original writing goals during revision.
   d. Students' planning in prewriting is unaffected in rewriting.

88. Which of the following have researchers learned about children's writing?
   a. Children's writing reflects as much knowledge as they have on any given topic.
   b. Children stop writing when they have run out of things they want to articulate.
   c. Children stop writing when they cannot adequately articulate their knowledge.
   d. Children's writing commonly covers more than they actually know about a topic.

89. Arthur writes a paper. One classmate identifies ideas and words that resonated with her when she read it. Another describes how reading the paper changed his thinking. A third asks Arthur some questions about what he meant by certain statements in the paper. A fourth suggests that a portion of the paper needs more supporting information. This description is most typical of...
   a. A portfolio assessment.
   b. A holistic scoring.
   c. A scoring rubric.
   d. A peer review.

90. Which of the following is the best definition of Information Literacy?
   a. It is the set of skills required for reading and comprehending different information.
   b. It is the cognitive skill set necessary to amass a comprehensive base of knowledge.
   c. It is the skill set required for the finding, retrieval, analysis, and use of information.
   d. It is the set of skills necessary for effectively communicating information to others.

91. What is the primary reason the early 21st century has been referred to as the Information Age?
   a. Because educational and governmental agencies require greater information
   b. Because there are more sources and outputs of information than ever before
   c. Because students can now learn all they need to know in four years of college
   d. Because college students today are much more interested in new information

92. Of the following statements, which adheres to Information Literacy standards?
   a. Students accessing information must critically evaluate it and its sources before using it.
   b. Students accessing information can ascertain how much of it they need after they find it.
   c. Students accessing information efficiently sacrifice broader scope and incidental learning.
   d. Students accessing information ethically must eschew using it to attain specific purposes.

93. Which of the following typically combines signal phrases and parenthetical references for documenting sources in literature?
   a. An MLA list of the works cited
   b. MLA in-text citations in a paper
   c. Adding MLA information notes
   d. All APA citations

94. According to MLA guidelines for writing research papers, which of the following is correct regarding citations of web sources if you do not quickly see the author's name?
a. Assume the author is not named, as this is a common occurrence on the Web.
b. Do not name an agency or corporation as author if it is the sponsor of the source.
c. Author names are often on websites, but need additional looking to discover.
d. It is not permissible to cite the book or article title in lieu of an author's name.

95. When making in-text citations in a research paper, which of the following reflects MLA guidelines for citing Web sources with regard to page numbers?
a. If a Web source does not include pagination, you are advised to avoid citing that source.
b. If page numbers appear on a printout from a website, include these numbers in citations.
c. In-text citations of online sources in research papers should never include page numbers.
d. If the Web source is a PDF file, it is recommended to cite page numbers in your citations.

96. The MLA guidelines for citing multiple authors of the same source in the in-text citations of a research paper are to use the first author's name and "et al" for the other(s) in the case of
a. more than one author.
b. two or three authors.
c. three or more authors.
d. four or more authors.

97. A movie review is one example of what type and purpose of writing?
a. Narration
b. Description
c. Persuasion
d. Exposition

98. Of the following writing types and purposes, which can often be the hardest to write?
a. Expository
b. Persuasive
c. Descriptive
d. Narrative

99. Which of the following do *The Adventures of Huckleberry Finn* by Mark Twain, *The Diary of a Young Girl* by Anne Frank, and "The Fall of the House of Usher" by Edgar Allan Poe have in common?
a. They are all examples of the narrative type and purpose of writing.
b. They are all examples of a purely descriptive writing type/purpose.
c. They are all examples of works of primarily expository writing type.
d. They are all examples of writing of the persuasive type and purpose.

100. When you have a writing assignment, which of the following is true about your audience?
a. You need not identify the audience because it is the teacher who gave the assignment.
b. You should consider how your readers are likely to use what you write.
c. You should know your writing purpose more than a reader's purposes.
d. You are overthinking to wonder about readers' likely attitude/reaction.

101. Which statement is correct regarding the relationship of your audience profile to the decisions you make in writing?

   a. How much time you spend on research is unrelated to your audience.
   b. Your audience does not influence how much information you include.
   c. The writing style, tone and wording you use depend on your audience.
   d. How you organize information depends on structure, not on audience.

102. Which of the following statements is most accurate about writing the introduction to an essay?

   a. The introduction should use the technique of starting essays with dictionary definitions.
   b. The introduction should leave the most attention-getting material for later in the work.
   c. The introduction should move from the focused and specific to the broad and general.
   d. The introduction should move from the broad and general to the focused and specific.

103. When writing an essay, which part of the introduction should come first?

   a. Your thesis statement for the essay
   b. Background on the essay's purpose
   c. Something original to engage reader attention
   d. A "road map" of how you will present the thesis

104. Which of the following is true about effective ways to open the introduction of an essay?

   a. You should summarize your position with your own words, not with a quote.
   b. Citing a surprising statistic related to the topic can grab readers' attention.
   c. Opening with a story or anecdote is counter to the purposes of an essay or paper.
   d. Asking rhetorical questions to open an essay or paper will only frustrate readers.

105. Which of the following is the *worst* way to view the conclusion of an essay?

   a. As a means of including all material that would not fit elsewhere
   b. As a means of reiterating the thesis you stated in the introduction
   c. As a means of synthesizing and/or summarizing your main points
   d. As a means of clarifying the context of your discussion/argument

106. In writing, _____ is the overall written expression of the writer's attitude, and _____ is the individual way in which the writer expresses the former.

   a. Voice; tone
   b. Tone; voice
   c. Style; tone
   d. Voice; style

107. _____ is the overall choice of language you make for your writing; _____ refers to the words that you use when writing within or about a specific discipline.

   a. Vocabulary; diction
   b. Vocabulary; jargon
   c. Diction; vocabulary
   d. Style; vocabulary

108. Which of the following is most accurate regarding writing style?

   a. The kind of diction you use does not affect style.
   b. Add style later in the writing process to give personality.
   c. Style is unrelated to your control of your content.
   d. Your purpose for writing guides your style.

109. When considering strategies for writing assignments, it helps to know the cognitive (or learning) objectives your teacher intends for an assignment. If the assignment asks you to "describe," "explain," "summarize," "restate," "classify," or "review" some material you read, what is the cognitive objective?

    a.   Knowledge recall
    b.   Application
    c.   Comprehension
    d.   Evaluation

110. Your writing assignment asks you to "organize," "plan," "formulate," "assemble," "compose," "construct," and/or "arrange" some material. Which of the following cognitive (learning) objectives is the teacher aiming to meet with this assignment?

    a.   Analysis
    b.   Synthesis
    c.   Evaluation
    d.   Application

111. Which of the following processes used in writing is the most complex?

    a.   Evaluation
    b.   Application
    c.   Comprehension
    d.   Knowledge recall

112. Of the following learning and writing processes, which strategy is associated with synthesis in college-level writing?

    a.   Comparing and contrasting
    b.   Explaining cause and effect
    c.   Giving support to an opinion
    d.   Analysis

113. Which of the following writing strategies is (or are) among the most commonly used forms of synthesis in college-level writing?

    a.   Explaining cause and effect
    b.   Comparing and contrasting
    c.   Proposing a solution
    d.   Using persuasion

114. Among writing projects that can develop from research, which of the following discourse aims is represented by a white paper, an opinion survey, an annotated bibliography, and a problem solution?

    a.   Expressive
    b.   Exploratory
    c.   Informative
    d.   Persuasive

115. "This treatise developed from an initial idea about the way a plant develops from a seed." The preceding sentence is an example of which literary device and argument method?

    a.   Analogy
    b.   Allegory
    c.   Allusion
    d.   Antithesis

116. In the famous balcony scene of William Shakespeare's *Romeo and Juliet,* Romeo says:

> But soft! What light through yonder window breaks?
> It is the east, and Juliet is the sun.
> Arise, fair sun, and kill the envious moon,
> Who is already sick and pale with grief,
> That thou her maid art far more fair than she:
> Be not her maid, since she is envious;
> Her vestal livery is but sick and green
> And none but fools do wear it; cast it off.

The literary device Shakespeare used here is also used in all *except* which of the following?

a. T. S. Eliot's description of the fog in "The Love Song of J. Alfred Prufrock" (1915)
b. Robert Frost's entire poem "The Road Not Taken" (1916)
c. Carl Sandburg's whole short poem "Fog" (1916)
d. All of these use the same device as Shakespeare

117. Of the following sentences, which one appeals to emotion?

a. It is dangerous to use a cell phone while driving because you steer one-handed.
b. Statistics of accident risk show that cell-phone use while driving is dangerous.
c. It is really stupid to use a cell phone when you drive because it is so dangerous.
d. Many state laws ban cell-phone use when driving due to data on more accidents.

118. Which of the following gives an example of a fallacy of inconsistency?

a. "There are exceptions to all general statements."
b. "Please pass me; my parents will be upset if I fail."
c. "He is guilty; there is no evidence that he is innocent."
d. "Have you stopped cheating on your assignments?"

119. In the 1984 comedy movie *All of Me,* a character from another country, who has no experience with either telephones or flush toilets, flushes a toilet and then a phone rings. He flushes again and the phone rings again. After this occurs several times, the character concludes that pulling the toilet's flush handle causes the ringing. This is an example of which type of cognitive bias?

a. An above-average effect
b. A clustering illusion
c. A confirmation bias
d. A framing bias

120. Archie says, "Asian people are all terrible drivers." The *most precise* definition of this statement is...

a. A stereotype.
b. An inference.
c. An assumption.
d. A generalization.

Answer Key and Explanations

1. B: The author of the excerpted poem, "To His Coy Mistress," is Andrew Marvell. Marvell, Donne (A), Herbert (C), and Vaughan (D) were all members of a group of mainly 17th-century poets known as the Metaphysical Poets for their common time period, themes, content, and style.

2. A: Carpe diem is Latin for "seize the day." This tradition reflects the theme that time flies and that life is fleeting, and thus we should take advantage of the present moment. The tradition of classicism (B) reflects ancient Greek and Roman ideals of beauty and principles of form and discipline (as opposed to Romanticism's principles of emotional impact), as reflected in the works of Alexander Pope and John Dryden. The cinquain (C) is a five-line type of poem in which line 1 is a one-word title, line 2 contains two words describing the title, line 3 has three words telling the action, line 4 contains four words expressing the feeling, and line 5 reverts back to one word that recalls the title. The conceit (D) type of poetry uses a metaphor, simile, or image comparing two very dissimilar things, such as Shakespeare's Sonnet # 18, "Shall I compare thee to a summer's day?"

3. D: Tetrameter means four beats per line, which is the meter of the rhymed couplets in this poem. Pentameter (A) means five beats per line. Heptameter (B) means seven beats per line. Hexameter (C) means six beats per line. Also, beats are only the stressed syllables, not total syllables.

4. B: This is the opening sentence of James Joyce's last novel, *Finnegans Wake* (1939). He published *Ulysses* (A) previously, in 1922; and *A Portrait of the Artist as a Young Man* (D) even earlier, in 1916. *Adventures in the Skin Trade* (C) was not written by Joyce but by Dylan Thomas (1938).

5. D: Joyce used the word "vicus" because it means "vicinity" (A) or "lane" in Latin; to refer to Vico Way (B), the name of the shore road running alongside of Dublin Bay; and to allude to Giambattista Vico (C), an Italian philosopher (1688-1744) who espoused the cyclic theory of history, a theme in Joyce's novel.

6. C: The lower-case initial letter of the first word was not an error (D). It did not continue Joyce's previous novel (B). And he did not use it to make the opening stand out as different to the reader (A). Rather, it is uncapitalized to show that it completes the book's last sentence fragment, "A way a lone a last a loved a long the—." By writing the end of the book to be completed and continued only by the beginning, Joyce embodied the cyclical nature of history and of the novel within its sentence structure.

7. A: Joyce is famous for using stream-of-consciousness in his novels, as in *Ulysses* and *Finnegans Wake*. The unreliable narrator (B) is a technique used often in murder mysteries, as by Edgar Allan Poe in "The Tell-Tale Heart," "The Cask of Amontillado," and many other stories and by Agatha Christie in *The Murder of Roger Ackroyd*. Joyce is not famous for using it. He used third-person narration and often included soliloquies, but is not famous for using first-person narration (C). An example of the author surrogate (D) is Socrates in Plato's works; Joyce is not known for using this technique.

8. D: "The Emperor of Ice-Cream" was written by Wallace Stevens in 1922. The style of the excerpted stanza is typical of modern poetry and does not reflect the conventions of 17th-century (A), 18th-century (B), or 19th-century (C) poems.

9. A: "In kitchen cups concupiscent curds" makes use of alliteration, the repetition of the same initial sound and/or letter in adjoining or nearby words—in this case, the sound /k/ from the letter "c." Hyperbole (B) is the device of exaggeration. Onomatopoeia (C) is the device of words sounding like what they mean (for example, "the clang of the bell" or "the gun went bang"). Metonymy (D) is the device of referring to a noun by an associated thing (such as using "the White House" to mean the U.S. government, or "Hollywood" to mean the American film and television industry).

10. C: Plato's *Dialogues* expound the philosophy of Socrates, including the concept that the mortal life of humanity and the world of the human senses and perception are an illusion, while the eternal life of the divine and the world of the ideal are reality, rather than vice versa. Stevens refers to this concept with "Let be be finale of seem"—meaning that "seem" is what we perceive, and is followed by "be," which is the reality found after life—as the first stanza's boys bringing flowers is continued in the second (final) stanza with references to shrouding a dead woman's body. A main theme in option (A) is the creation of the world; an allegorical journey through Hell, Purgatory, and Heaven in choice (B); and, in option (D), a journey home from war, which is also an allegory for every man's life journey.

11. B: The author, Jonathan Swift, wrote the excerpted piece, "A Modest Proposal," as a satire. He was not literally suggesting that children be cooked and eaten, but lampooning the way the British looked down on the Irish with his "proposal" as an ironic example of a "solution" to the poverty and overpopulation in Ireland. Persuasion (A) is a form of argument to sway the reader rather than make fun of something. Exposition (C) is also a straightforward method of giving information. Bathos (D) is a literary mood of overstated emotion that moves suddenly from the sublime to the ridiculous or pedestrian to create an anticlimactic effect.

12. C: "A Modest Proposal" was published in 1729, i.e., the 18th century. It does not have the modern style of the 20th (A) century. The bulk of Swift's work was published in the 1700s, with several pieces published in the late 1690s (D)—but not this one. Swift died in 1745 and even *A Journal to Stella,* published posthumously, was published in 1766, so the 19th century (B) is incorrect.

13. D: Jonathan Swift, author of the excerpted satirical essay "A Modest Proposal," also wrote *Gulliver's Travels* (1726, 1735), a novel satirizing human behavior and parodying the travel genre. *The Canterbury Tales* (A) were written by Geoffrey Chaucer in the 14th century. *The Faerie Queene* (B) was written by Edmund Spenser in the 16th century. *Paradise Lost* (C) was written by John Milton in the 17th century.

14. D: Hughes uses (extended) metaphor by describing the concrete presence of a fox to represent the abstract concept of a poet's inspiration. From beyond the blank window, starless sky, and dark forest, the fox, as a totem for the writer's imagination, approaches from without to inspire, its pawprints in the snow symbolizing print appearing on the blank page. Foreshadowing (A) is the literary device of hinting earlier in a work at something that will become more apparent later. Irony (B) is the device of creating a discrepancy between what is expected and what really occurs (verbal, dramatic, or situational irony). Hughes's work is notable for NOT including any overused expressions known as clichés (C).

15. C: The poem describes how the poet is inspired to write, using the fox to embody the thought that enters the poet's mind (hence the title "The Thought-Fox"). The fox's natural actions (A) are thus symbolic rather than literal. The poet is not inspired by nature (B); in this poem, he uses an element of nature (the fox) to represent the thought that he receives and writes. The fox's entering "the head" is not a literal attack (D) but a symbolic representation of having or getting that thought.

16. B: The poet's passivity and lack of control over the thought, or content, of his writing can be interpreted from Hughes's separation of the thought, which does not arise from within his head, but approaches symbolically in the form of a fox from outside of his head, his body, and even his house. This separation is emphasized by the description of the Thought-Fox as "Coming about its own business." The poet as passive recipient is further shown in the last stanza, where the fox "enters the dark hole of the head." This passivity is further reflected in the last line, "The page is printed," as Hughes uses passive voice to represent the writing process, rather than saying that he himself prints the page.

17. A: This poem is written in free verse, meaning it has no regular rhyme scheme (options B and D) or metrical pattern (choices B and C). There is some partial rhyming, as in the sight rhyme of "snow" and "now" in stanza 3; the near rhymes of "star" with "near" in stanza 2 and "lame" with "come" in stanza 3; the rhymes of "darkness" and "loneliness" in stanza 2, "snow" and "hollow" in stanza 4, and "greenness" with "business" in stanza 5; and the off rhyme of "fox" with "ticks" in the last stanza. However, these are not regular, like the repeated rhymes of an established rhyme scheme. There is also no regular meter or number of beats per line. Hence the overall form of this poem is free verse.

18. C: The bell jar is a metaphor, an implied comparison between two things. A simile (A) is an overtly stated comparison; it would be a simile if she had written, "It was *like* a bell jar." An allusion (B) is an implied, indirect, or incidental reference, usually to a real or fictional person, place, or event. Personification (D) or anthropomorphism is attributing human characteristics to non-human animals or things.

19. B: The bell jar is Plath's metaphor for her mental illness. She describes feeling confined, not by reality (A), but by her own depression and its attendant alienated feelings and distorted perceptions. Writer's block (C) was not the bell jar but a symptom of it (her illness), as when she wrote about fearing she would never be able to write again. Moreover, though Plath did experience inability to write at times and her fear was genuine, she also produced many great poems as well as this novel during and in spite of her illness. Her references to "stewing in my own sour air," being unable to stir with the "air of the bell jar wadded round me," closed off from the "circulating air," being "blank and stopped as a dead baby," and "the bell jar, with its stifling distortions," do not signify any literal breathing disorder (D), but rather a metaphorical lack of the fresh air of reality and sanity.

20. D: Sylvia Plath underwent a serious breakdown and hospitalization in 1953; she wrote about this experience in *The Bell Jar* around 1961 (published in England in 1963 and America in 1971.) *The Bell Jar* was Plath's only novel (A). Plath wrote many poems, not a few (C). She did not recover to live a long life or write more novels (B); she committed suicide in 1963, a month after *The Bell Jar*'s London publication. (There is some evidence she intended to have the suicide attempt discovered and be rescued from it. She recounts a number of suicide attempts in *The Bell Jar,* which were either discovered in time or she found she could not complete.) While she wrote other prose pieces early in her career, *The Bell Jar* was, she wrote, "my world… as seen through the distorting lens of a bell jar." Before her death at age 30, she had intended to write a second novel about "that same world as seen through the eyes of health."

21. B: Shakespeare (1564-1616) wrote during the Renaissance. The Medieval (A) era (also known as the Middle Ages) was earlier, ending before the 16th century (circa 1485), and included authors like Geoffrey Chaucer, Dante Alighieri, the Pearl Poet and author of *Sir Gawain and the Green Knight,* and Sir Thomas Malory. The Restoration (C) period followed the Renaissance, circa 1660-1700, and included authors like John Dryden, who wrote poetry, satire, and criticism. The Enlightenment (D) occurred from 1700-1785, and included the authors Jonathan Swift, Alexander Pope, Dr. Samuel Johnson and James Boswell.

22. A: John Bunyan (1628-1688) was the author of *The Pilgrim's Progress*, a religious allegory. William Congreve (B) (1670-1729) wrote *The Way of the World,* originally a play not successful on the theatre stage, but subsequently highly regarded as a literary exemplar of the comedy of manners. Daniel Defoe (C) (circa 1660-1731) is known for *Robinson Crusoe* and other adventure novels. Samuel Butler (D) (1612-1680), one of the Augustan poets, wrote the burlesque poem "Hudibras."

23. B: This is the first stanza of "The Passionate Shepherd to His Love" by Christopher Marlowe (1564-1593). Andrew Marvell (A) also included poems on pastoral themes in his oeuvre, including "The Garden"; however, he lived later (1621-1678) than Marlowe and was one of the Metaphysical Poets. Sir Walter Raleigh (C) was more contemporary (1552-1618) with Marlowe and wrote "The Nymph's Reply to the Shepherd," among others. William Shakespeare (D) was a contemporary (1564-1616) of Raleigh and Marlowe and also included pastoral themes in his songs and sonnets, including "Shall I compare thee to a summer's day?"

24. C: The rhyme scheme of this stanza, and the rest of the poem, is AABB: The second line rhymes with the first, and the fourth line rhymes with the third. This use of rhyming couplets was popular in the poetry of the time.

25. D: The legend of Faust, who sold his soul to the devil in exchange for knowledge (echoing Adam and Eve's fall from grace in Eden caused by their desire for knowledge), has been popular throughout the various literary eras. Marlowe (A) wrote *Dr. Faustus* near the end of the 1500s. Goethe (B) wrote his German dramatic masterpiece *Faust* in the 19th century. Mann (C), also German, wrote the novel *Doktor Faustus* in the 20th century.

26. A: None of the above. These are all titles of poems written by Pope. "An Essay on Criticism" (A) is a didactic poem discussing literary theory, modeled after the style, language, and tone of the ancient Roman poet Horace. "The Rape of the Lock" (B) is a satirical poem, like "The Dunciad" and many others; Pope became famous for his satires. "The Universal Prayer" (C) is also a poem from Pope's *Moral Essays,* stating his beliefs. Pope wrote in a variety of styles on diverse subjects, including romantic, philosophical, political, pastoral, and others as well as satires, but all of his works were poetry.

27. C: The poems excerpted are all villanelles (D). The villanelle has nineteen lines with five tercets (three-line stanzas) and an ending quatrain (four-line stanza). The first and third line of the first stanza are alternately quoted in the last line of each subsequent stanza and both lines are repeated as a refrain at the end of the last stanza. Villanelles typically have ABA rhyme schemes. The quoted excerpts are not in ballad (A) form, which often uses quatrains, and rhymes either all alternating lines or second and fourth lines. (A famous example is "The Rime of the Ancient Mariner" by Samuel Taylor Coleridge.) Sonnet (B) form also differs from villanelle form. The Petrarchan sonnet has 14 lines, with a major shift in thinking or *volta* between the octave and sestet. The Shakespearean sonnet's 14 lines are three quatrains with ABAB/CDCD/EFEF rhymes and ending with a pivotal GG couplet. Sonnets also lack the repetition characteristic of villanelles.

28. B: The first poem excerpted, "The Waking" by Theodore Roethke, is a meditation on the nature of waking reality vs. dreaming imagination and which is which; life vs. death, mortality vs. immortality, process/journey vs. product/destination, world vs. self; the constancy of change; and the inability to control or even understand the mysteries of life, nature, and eternity. The second poem excerpted, "Mad Girl's Love Song" by Sylvia Plath (options A and B), also contemplates the nature of reality vs. imagination via the existentialist argument that we construct and destroy our own realities, and nothing objective exists beyond these. The third excerpted poem, "Do not go gentle into that good night" by Dylan Thomas (options A and C), focuses instead on how the dying should approach death.

29. A: Dylan Thomas' "Do not go gentle into that good night," addressed to his dying father, expresses the idea that death should be approached with spirited resistance rather than serene acceptance. The second poem, Sylvia Plath's "Mad Girl's Love Song," despite its use of the words "drops dead" and "born again," is not dealing with death but rather with the existentialist idea that reality is only what we perceive, imagine, or create and does not exist objectively outside of our own constructs. The first poem, Theodore Roethke's "The Waking," explores the nature of both reality vs. dreaming and life vs. death, but does not deal directly with the subject of death as Thomas' poem does.

30. B: This poem was written around 1862, during the Industrial Revolution when the railroad had recently been invented. (The poet's father was one of the owners of a local railroad.) The poet describes this "iron horse" by appropriately using the extended metaphor of a horse, but is not describing an actual horse (A) or a mythic monster (C). Thus it is not true that the subject of the poem cannot be determined (D).

31. D: This poem was written circa 1862. The American Revolution (A) was 1775-1783, the French Revolution (B) was 1789-1799, and the War of 1812 (C) was 1812-1815. The Civil War (D) was 1861-1865. Therefore, this poem was written during the Civil War period.

32. C: The poet performs an amazing structural feat in reflecting the composition of a railroad train in the composition of the poem's single, 17-line sentence. The first two words "I like" are the only subject and predicate; everything after the object "it" is a series of verbs complementing that object: "lap," "lick," "stop," "step," "peer," "pare," "crawl," "chase," "neigh," and "stop." This syntax mirrors the engine (subject and predicate) pulling the train behind it. The train's structure is not as specifically mirrored in vocabulary (A). The poem's rhythms (B) are typical of this poet, who very often wrote in iambic lines of alternating tetrameter and trimeter. The tone (D), a childlike kind of enthusiasm, is deliberately used to suggest its role as a powerful toy, satirizing the "progress" of the modern invention.

33. D: The poet, Emily Dickinson, chose these words because they both contrast with one another and typify characteristics of domesticated horses, thus carrying out her horse metaphor for the "iron horse" of the railroad train. In this sense, they are not contradictory: horses have great physical power, are larger than humans and could easily kill a human, but domesticated horses, when treated well, are also typically obedient and gentle with humans. Thus these words are contrasting rather than synonyms (A). They are not nonsense words (B). While they describe a mechanical object, they are not mechanical (C) words.

34. B: Dickinson compares the train's whistle, first metaphorically to a horse's neigh, and then in the simile "like Boanerges," the last name/nickname given by Jesus to disciples James and John, sons of Zebedee, in Mark 3:17. This name has since come to mean a fiery and/or vociferous preacher or orator, especially one with a powerful voice. One creature inhabiting Hades in Greek myth (A) was Cerberus, the three-headed guardian dog. A mythological animal in a labyrinth (D) was the Minotaur, slain by Theseus. This was a Greek myth, not a Roman one. (Like most Greek culture, it was later appropriated by the Romans.) One Old Testament prophet who was angry at opponents and prayed for vengeance (C) was Jeremiah.

35. C: Dickinson habitually used dashes as a kind of musical mechanism to establish the prosody of her poems and habitually capitalized the initials of certain words to lend them additional emphasis. The dashes were not simply punctuation (A); she used other punctuation marks conventionally in places, and the dashes were more a rhythmic device. She did not capitalize to honor (A) the capitalized words. The dashes were not to separate words (B) and the capitals were not used only with names (B, D). The dashes added control to her prosody rather than providing continuity (D).

36. D: The author of this poem, Emily Dickinson, uses personification by attributing human qualities to nonhuman entities, a practice also known as anthropomorphism. She describes how Death "kindly stopped for me" and "knew no haste." She also describes the grain as "gazing," and notes that the setting sun "passed Us," using pronouns ("He") and human actions ("stopped," "drove," "knew," "gazing," "passed," "paused") to describe nonhumans. Analogy (A) is a comparison of different things, like saying that the human heart is like a pump. Hyperbole (B) is exaggeration. Alliteration (C) is repetition of sounds in adjacent or close words. Although "gazing grain" and "setting sun" both use brief alliteration in the poem, the descriptions of Death do not.

37. C: While the topic of this poem is death, it is treated with a lighthearted tone, finding humor in death with a gentle kind of irony. The diction, word choice, rhythms, and conclusion do not convey gravity, portent or darkness (A). The descriptive details of the journey to Eternity, slow yet seemingly over within a day in retrospect, do not convey detachment, alienation, or numbness (B). The deliberate, placid narrative has no frantic, agitated, frenzied, or fearful (D) qualities. Rather, the poet seems to welcome "Immortality" even as she quietly observes Death's "kindly" character and "Civility"—examples of the aforementioned gentle irony regarding death's inevitability, in that even if we cannot "stop for Death," death will still stop for us.

38. B: The fifth stanza about "a House that seemed/A Swelling of the Ground" is an oblique description of a grave. Its cornice is "in the Ground" and the roof is "scarcely visible," indicating that this "House" was underground. This is not a literal description of a home (A) or a church (C). A school (D) with children at recess is literally described as one of the aspects of life they pass in their journey, in the third stanza. The fifth stanza's description of a grave is in keeping with the whole poem's light, gentle, indirect, yet spiritually accepting treatment of death.

39. A: The haiku, originating in Japanese poetry and since adopted in English-language poetry, is a short poem of only three lines, often with 17 syllables, with the first and third lines having five syllables and the second line having seven syllables. (In Japanese there are many other rules, which become very complicated.) Haiku are typically unrhymed, so they do not have a rhyme scheme (B). Similarly, they do not employ any regular meter (C). Because haiku are typically 17 syllables or fewer, they do not involve long narratives (D).

40. B: This book was the actual diary kept by Anne Frank, a Dutch Jewish teenager whose family and others spent two years hiding in another family's attic before being sent to concentration camps by Nazis during World War II. Frank, 14-15 years old at the time, was intelligent and wrote articulately, depicting both the everyday details and the unusual difficulties of life in hiding and constant fear. The book is invaluable today, not only for its personal perspective on history and details of first-hand experiences with war and Nazism, but also as a testament to a young girl's unshakeable faith in human nature, even in the face of horrible inhumanity: she wrote near the end of her entries (July 15, 1944, only weeks before being arrested by Nazis) in one of the book's most often-quoted passages, "I still believe, in spite of everything, that people are truly good at heart."

41. C: All answer choices are novels by Mark Twain. However, while *The Mysterious Stranger* (A) is also a first-person narrative written in the literate language of its narrator, while *The Adventures of Huckleberry Finn* is written in its narrator's uneducated and Southern regional dialect. *The Adventures of Huckleberry Finn* followed and referred to *The Adventures of Tom Sawyer* (B), which is a third-person narrative rather than in first person. *The Prince and the Pauper* (D) is also a third-person narrative. The use of a first-person narrative in dialect differentiates the correct choice from the others. (*Tom Sawyer* contains similar dialects as *Huckleberry Finn,* but only in dialogue spoken by characters, not in the actual narration, which is third-person and not narrated by a character.) Also, the subject matter of the excerpt does not fit choices A or D.

42. D: In *Sister Carrie* (1900), Drouet is basically a decent person but is deficient in the intelligence or awareness for moral behavior. Therefore, choice A is incorrect. Hurstwood, by contrast, has the intelligence to understand moral behavior, and his awareness allows him to reject his family's superficial values. However, the moral deficiencies of his own character allow him to behave immorally. Therefore, option B is incorrect. In their attitudes toward women, both characters represent the middle class of the time; therefore, choice C is incorrect.

43. C: All choices are titles of poems by the same author, Walt Whitman, and all are published in the volume *Leaves of Grass.* This particular excerpt is taken from "Song of Myself," Whitman's longest and perhaps most famous poem.

44. B: Whitman's masterpiece is his celebration ("singing") of a mystical experience revealing, among other themes, his unity with the universe and nature. This is reflected in the title, *Leaves of Grass,* that he gave his collection of poems including "Song of Myself." The meaning of the excerpt is not simply literal (A). It is also not a metaphor for social classes or roles (C), and it does not refer to mistreatment in a personal relationship (D).

45. B: *Leaves of Grass*, the book of poems containing "Song of Myself," was first published in 1855, and Whitman continued to make revisions over 36 years, releasing subsequent editions through 1891. Hence all editions were published in the 19th century.

46. B: These excerpts are from "The Love Song of J. Alfred Prufrock" by T. S. Eliot. The other choices are also by Eliot. "Prufrock" was one of his earliest poems (published in *Poetry* magazine in 1915 and in a collection, *Prufrock and Other Observations*, in 1917). "The Waste Land" (A), often considered his masterwork, was published in 1922. While these two share several similar themes, "The Waste Land" is far longer and is not written as a dramatic monologue. "Notes Toward the Definition of Culture" (C) is by Eliot, but it is an essay, not a poem. Eliot published his poem "The Hollow Men" (D) in 1925.

47. C: The persona in the poem is speaking about his mortality. His rhetorical questions about parting his hair and eating a peach do not indicate indecision (A) but rather allude to conditions of old age (balding and diarrhea), and the imagery of his dress and the beach allude to retirement—not a vacation (B). This excerpt does not mention drowning (D). (The third excerpt does, but is not literal.)

48. D: Options (A) and (C) both express meanings that can be interpreted from this verse. The speaker compares his existence to that of a crab to show his own sense of unimportance, which is consistent with other parts of the poem expressing his sense of low status (e.g., "No! I am not Prince Hamlet, nor was meant to be... Almost, at times, the Fool"). Moreover, the poet has chosen the image of a crab not only to fit with the poem's other sea imagery, but also because it is a scavenger. Eliot's essay "Tradition and the Individual Talent" suggests that art can rescue the bleakness of modern life by creating beauty from its refuse. The imagery ("ragged," "scuttling," "silent") reinforces this bleak view rather than expressing a simple, literal wish (B).

49. A: This line is an expression of the despair felt by the speaker, characterizing the poet's view of modern life as broken, fragmented, and both alienating and isolating to the individual. While the speaker often mourns his aging throughout the poem ("I grow old... I grow old"), the statement about the mermaids is not literal as in options B and D. The mermaids represent the beautiful dream of the world of art; the speaker feels he cannot be included in or belong to it, even though he can perceive it. He is not saying the mermaids are not real (C) as in the previous line, he has said, "I have heard the mermaids singing." But they only sing to one another ("each to each"), not to him.

50. B: Hearing the mermaids singing to each other is part of Eliot's imagery, symbolizing the beauty found in art and in the beautiful dreams that both inspire it and are created by it. Prufrock's hearing them singing can also symbolize his glimpses of eternity, immortality, the ideal, and/or Paradise—things that art can portray or even achieve, but which he despairs of experiencing. His hearing them singing to each other but thinking they will not sing to him emphasizes his feelings of isolation and futility, which reflect Eliot's desolate view of the modern condition. The meaning is not primarily literal as in options A, C and D.

51. C: The fabliau is a humorous story including an incident that is nearly always indecent. In "The Miller's Tale," the cuckolded husband hangs his rear end out of the window and flatulates into the face of his wife's lover. "The Reeve's Tale," "The Shipman's Tale," "The Summoner's Tale," and others are additional instances of fabliau in *The Canterbury Tales.* "The Physician's Tale" (A) is an example of the literary form of the classical legend. "The Wife of Bath's Tale" (B), an Arthurian story, is an example of one version of the literary form of the romance. "The Pardoner's Tale" (D) is an example of the literary form of the *exemplum*, a type of instructional anecdote or story often used by preachers in sermons to illustrate moral points or principles.

52. D: *The Great Gatsby* by F. Scott Fitzgerald (1925) and *To the Lighthouse* by Virginia Woolf (1927) are both novels, but neither is a frame tale (a story or stories set within a story). Chaucer's *Canterbury Tales* is a 14th-century work that is rather famous for, among other things, being a frame tale containing multiple stories. Bocaccio's *Decameron* is likewise a 14th-century frame tale containing 100 tales. Each story-within-a-story is told by a different character in both *The Canterbury Tales* and *The Decameron* (A). Vyasa's Sanskrit epic the *Mahabharata* (circa 4th century) and Chaucer's 14th-century *The Parlement of Foules (Parliament of Fowls)* also use the frame tale structure—the former for historical, geographical, religious, and moral instruction and the latter framed in the form of a dream. The Gothic-Romantic novel *Frankenstein* (1818) by Mary W. Shelley and the Victorian novel *Wuthering Heights* by Emily Brontë (1847) also use the narrative structure of the frame tale (C).

53. C: Dante wrote his *Divine Comedy* between 1308 and 1321, consisting of three *canticas* (songs or chants): *Inferno* (Hell), *Purgatorio* (Purgatory) and *Paradiso* (Heaven). It was the first work ever published in vernacular Italian, the everyday language actually spoken by the people. Previously, all publications in Italy were issued in Latin, the language of the Roman Catholic Church. This was also true in other countries dominated by the Roman Empire; throughout the Middle Ages, as vernacular languages developed, books began to be published in the local languages. Cicero wrote *De re publica* (*On the Republic*) (A) between 54 and 51 BCE, an ancient Roman work published in Latin. Bocaccio finished writing *Il Decameron* (*The Decameron*) (B) around 1351-1353, after Dante's *Divine Comedy*. Umberto Eco's *Il nome della rosa* (*The Name of the Rose*) (D) is a novel published in modern Italian in 1980.

54. B: In this line, Yeats refers to the Trojan War, which has been indirectly attributed to the rape of Leda by the god Zeus in the form of a swan. This union produced the war-gods Castor and Polydeuces and also Helen of Troy and Clytemnestra. Helen's elopement with Paris triggered the Trojan War, a conflict powered by the war-gods. In the war, Agamemnon killed Clytemnestra's first husband and infant and took Clytemnestra as his wife. After his 10-year absence in the war, Clytemnestra killed Agamemnon. As such, this part of Yeats's poem refers to both a murder *and* a war (D). The Trojan War occurred roughly around the 11th-12th century BCE. The Peloponnesian War (C) between Athens and Sparta occurred from 431-404 BCE, ending the Golden Age of Greece. The Punic Wars (A) between Rome and Carthage occurred from 264-246 BCE, establishing Roman dominance. Hence these both occurred far later than the Trojan War.

55. A: This poem is a sonnet. Specifically, it is the Petrarchan (Italian) sonnet form, composed of an octave (eight lines) and a sestet (six lines), with the transition from former to latter signaling a major change. (The Shakespearean or English sonnet is composed of three quatrains followed by a couplet.) The third line of the sestet is broken for emphasis. It is not a villanelle (B), which has 19 lines rather than the sonnet's 14 and uses a convention of repetition. This poem uses rhyme schemes of ABAB repeated in the octave and ABC repeated in the sestet, and is in iambic pentameter, hence it is not free verse (C). It is not a sestina (D), which dates back to 12th-century Provençal troubadours and has 39 lines rather than 14.

56. B: Yeats' question at the end of the poem best suggests the poignancy of the human condition, which is necessarily incomplete as we do not and cannot have the power or knowledge of the divine. Yeats asks whether, but does not state that, Leda "put on his knowledge with his power" (A). While certainly ancient Greece portrayed humans interacting differently with divinity than modern Western culture does (C), this is not Yeats's point. He uses this mythological event as a device for telescoping sex and history, showing how it generated ("engenders there") forces dominating the Western world, and musing about what Leda might have experienced in the moment. Line 13, "...his knowledge with his power" does not indicate she gained the latter but not the former (D). It asks if she "put on" the two together.

57. C: The Syntactic Cueing System is that set of cues available in the syntax. Syntax is the sentence structure and word order of language. The Phonological (A) Cueing System is that set of cues available in the phonological structure of language. Phonological structure is the language's speech sounds and the letters representing them. The Semantic (B) Cueing System is that set of cues available in the semantics. Semantics are the meaning (and meanings) of words and the morphemes (smallest units of meaning) that comprise words. The Three Cueing Systems model does not include a Pragmatic (C) system. However, it recognizes, as all linguists and reading instructors do, that pragmatic cues involve reader understanding of their reasons for reading and of how text structures operate. (In linguistics, pragmatics is the study of how language is used for social communication.)

58. D: Semantics refers to the meanings of words and language. The semantic system in the Three Cueing Systems model is the set of cues (including words, phrases, sentences, discourse, and complete text) that readers can use to recognize words based on meanings. Pragmatic cues (A) are based on reader purposes for reading and reader understanding of text structure. The phonological system (B) consists of cues related to the phonemic (or sound) structure of language. The syntactic system (C) consists of cues related to the sentence structure and word order of language.

59. C: Phonological cues are based on the speech sounds in words and their alphabetic representations in print. Readers can identify words by knowing sound-to-letter correspondences. Syntactic cues (A) are based on how words are arranged and ordered to create meaningful phrases, clauses and sentences. Semantic cues (B) are based on the meanings of morphemes and words and how they combine to create additional meanings. Pragmatic cues (D) are based on the readers' purposes for reading and their understanding of how textual structures function in the texts that they read.

60. B: Pragmatics is the study of how language is used socially for communication. In reading instruction, pragmatic cues relaté to the reader's purposes for reading and the reader's understanding of the workings of textual structures. Although pragmatic cues are valid and important, the Three Cueing Systems model does not include a pragmatic "system." The three cueing systems named in this theory are the phonological system of sound cues (D), the Semantic system of meaning cues (C), and the Syntactic system of sentence-structure cues (A).

61. D: Reading instructors should teach students to activate their prior knowledge because it will improve their reading comprehension. Before reading, teachers should discuss and model connections with existing knowledge to prepare students by helping them consider what they already know about the subject of the text. While they read, students can make better sense of the text by considering how it fits with what they already know. After reading, teachers can lead discussions helping students focus on how the connections they made between the text and their previous knowledge informed their understanding of the text, and on how the text helped them build on their foundations of existing knowledge.

62. C: Certain cognitive strategies used by good readers have been identified through research. Teaching children these strategies and helping them apply these until they can do so independently are found to support mastery of reading comprehension. Good readers who use such successful strategies are not necessarily reading teachers, and it is not necessary for students to find different ways (A) to apply them. Such strategies are less likely to be used by beginning students, and always applying them with assistance (B) without ever graduating to independent application is less effective. These strategies are used by all proficient readers, not just published writers (D). Finally, creativity is important to many kinds of writing, but not necessary to understand what one reads.

63. A: The student making this observation is connecting reading of a mythological text (presumably Greek or Roman) s/he reads to the world—in this instance, to human nature—by noting that despite greater powers, the gods' emotional reactions and behaviors are like those of humans. The student statement in option B reflects a connection of text to text—fiction (a novel) to historical accounts of a period (for example, see Dickens's *A Tale of Two Cities*). The student statement in option C reflects a connection of text to self: the student can relate to the feelings of a character in the text. Because each choice reflects a different one of the three kinds of student connections named, option D is incorrect.

64. C: Thinking about thinking, or understanding our own cognitive processes, is known as metacognition. Explicitly teaching effective reading comprehension strategies does more than deepen student understanding of reading: it also promotes the higher-order, abstract cognitive skill of metacognition. Schemata (A) (plural; singular is *schema*) is Piaget's term for mental constructs we form to understand the world. Piaget said we either assimilate new information into an existing schema or alter an existing schema to accommodate the new knowledge. Reading instruction experts may refer to experience or background knowledge as schemata because students undergo this cognitive process when they fit what they read to their existing knowledge/experience. Scaffolding (B), a term coined by Jerome Bruner, refers to the temporary support given to students as needed while they learn, which is gradually reduced as they become more independent. Reading instruction experts may also describe students' connections of text to prior experience as scaffolding. Metamorphosis (D) is a term meaning a transformation—literally in biology as with caterpillars into butterflies, or figuratively, as in Franz Kafka's *The Metamorphosis,* wherein protagonist Gregor Samsa becomes a cockroach.

65. B: Why the students participate in a reading/learning activity refers to the motivation for the activity. However, the timing, purpose, location, and method of the learning activity do all influence learning differently according to the cultural, social, and economic factors involved in each specific situation.

66. A: The process of actively constructing meaning from reading is interactive, in that it involves the text itself, the person reading it, and the setting in which the reading is done: the reader interacts with the text, and the text interacts with the reader by affecting him/her; the context of reading interacts with the text and the reader by affecting them both; and the reader interacts with the reading context as well as with the text. Choice B is a better definition of the *strategic* aspect of the process. Options C and D are better definitions of the *adaptable* aspect of the process.

67. B: Researchers find that learners of both their native language (L1) and a second language (L2) go through all three developmental stages, which means that choices A and C are both incorrect. However, learners of a second language are often urged by teachers and others to skip the Silent Period, whereas young children acquiring their native languages are not similarly expected to speak immediately. L2 learners are not likely to undergo the third stage later (D) but sooner than or at a similar time as L1 learners, due either to having not yet learned all linguistic forms of the L2 or to being unable to access all of the L2's forms as they produce language.

68. C: L2s can be learned in a number of educational contexts, such as being segregated from the L1, formally taught via the medium of the L1, through submersion, or within the language classroom but not used to communicate outside it, among many others. They can also be taught/learned in several natural contexts: as the majority language to members of ethnic minority groups, as the official language of a country where learners are non-natives, or for international communication purposes separate from the L1 or official language. Therefore, it is not accurate that L2s are never learned in natural contexts (B and D). Unlike L2s, L1s are always first acquired in natural contexts, meaning choice A is inaccurate.

69. D: The process of fossilization occurs when some of the incorrect forms a learner of a second language has developed are not corrected over time, but become permanently fixed. (When a learner's L2 contains many such fossilized forms, it is termed an interlanguage.) Vygotsky's Zone of Proximal Development (A), in which a learner can accomplish tasks with assistance that s/he could not yet achieve independently, applies to the acquisition of both first and second languages. The hypothesis that there is a critical period for learning language (B) has also been applied to both L1 and L2 acquisition. In the same way, proponents of linguistic universals—both the typological universals proposed by Greenberg and the Universal Grammar described by Chomsky—find that in both first- and second-language learning, marked (language-specific) features do not transfer and are harder to learn, while unmarked (universal across most languages) features conform to general linguistic principles and are easier to learn. Fossilization is the only choice that occurs exclusively in second-language acquisition.

70. C: Omitting articles (for example, *a/an, the, these*) and plural endings (*–s*), which is common among Chinese ESL students, is not because they have not yet learned the English forms (A) or words for these. Nor are these omissions a way to avoid having to choose the correct form among various English irregularities (C). Nor are these errors due to the student's lack of understanding of the relationship between the Chinese and English versions of the forms (D). Rather, Chinese does not include articles or plural endings the way English does, so the student has no frame of reference or comparison. Therefore, the student's ESL pattern of absent articles and plurals reflects the nature and rules of the L1, which have transferred to the L2 but are incompatible with it.

71. B: As linguists have long pointed out, dialects are NOT non-standard versions of a language (A). In linguistics, dialects are *differing* varieties of any language, but these may be vernacular (nonstandard) OR standard versions of a language. They are often considered less socially acceptable, especially in educational, occupational and professional settings, than whichever standard version is most accepted. The linguistic features of dialects are not incorrect (C), but simply different. Their use does not indicate poor or incomplete language learning (D).

72. A: The formal version of Standard English is reflected in dictionaries and grammar books and applied in written language. In speech, Standard English is NOT universal (B): it differs in pronunciation between the regions of North America and between native English speakers in England, Ireland, Australia, India, and other English-speaking areas. Speech communities use a more flexible variety of *informal* Standard English rather than the Standard English of writing (C). The construct of Standard English actually includes a range of dialects (D) because formal Standard English is used in writing and not speech, which by nature dictates a less formal, more flexible version.

73. C: The Great Vowel shift was a huge shift in the phonemics of English pronunciation that occurred from the 15th to 18th centuries in all places where English was spoken and written.

74. B: During the Great Vowel shift, the location of the tongue in the mouth where the long vowels in English were produced eventually shifted to a higher position, altering the sounds of their pronunciation. For example, the letter "e," pronounced /e/ (the sound spelled as "-ay" by Modern English speakers) in Chaucer's day (as it is still pronounced in Romance languages), gradually changed to be pronounced /i/ (the sound spelled as "ee" in Modern English). The tongue's movement back (A), down (C), or front (D) in the mouth would produce respectively different phonemes.

75. A: Shakespeare lived from circa 1564-1616 and wrote most of his known plays and poems between 1589 and 1613, or in the late 16th and early 17th centuries. The Great Vowel Shift occurred from the 15th to 18th centuries. Thus, Shakespeare wrote his Elizabethan English during this major language change. Geoffrey Chaucer (B) lived from circa 1343-1400 and wrote his known works between roughly 1369 and 1399. Therefore, his Middle English was the form that existed *before* the Great Vowel Shift took place. Emily Dickinson (C) wrote her poetry during the 19th century, *after* the Great Vowel Shift. The Pearl Poet (D), author of the *Pearl* poem, *Sir Gawain and the Green Knight,* and other works was a contemporary of Chaucer, meaning his works were also written *before* the Great Vowel Shift.

76. B: Linguists generally analyze the Great Vowel Shift as having consisted of eight steps: Step 1 = /i/ and /u/ → /ƏI/ and /ƏU/; Step 2 = /e/ and /o/ →/i/ and /u/; Step 3 = /a/ →/æ/; Step 4 = /ɛ/ → /e/, /ɔ/ → /o/; Step 5 = /æ/ → /ɛ/; Step 6 = /e/ → /i/; Step 7 = /ɛ/ →/e/; and Step 8 = / ƏI/ and / ƏU/ → /aI/ and /aU/. Step 1 involved downward shifts, Step 3 a forward shift, and Step 8 downward shifts. However, the overall effect of the Great Vowel Shift across all of its steps was an upward shift in the placement of the tongue in the mouth in the pronunciation of all long English vowels.

77. D: The Great Vowel Shift ultimately changed the pronunciation of the long vowels in English completely. Consequently, it has affected orthographic conventions and rules (A), instruction in reading (B), and how easily the modern readers of English texts can comprehend literature written before the

GVS (C), as in the works of Chaucer and others. The sources of difficulty (in addition to changes in vocabulary and usage) for modern readers include not only the earlier spellings, but also the pronunciations that affected those spellings, as well as rhymes.

78. C: The etymology, or origin, of the English word *debt* is the Latin word *debitum*. It came into English during the Middle English form of the language. Therefore, this word was not originally a Middle English word (A) but a Latin word. Because it came from Latin into Middle English, it did not exist as an Old English word with a voiced *b* (B) as Old English preceded Middle English. The origin of this word was not Greek (D) but Latin. NOTE: Early scribes and printers, described by some as "inkhorn scholars," introduced many silent letters to English spellings to indicate their Latin or Greek roots, as in this case.

79. B: In Old Italian, the word *disastro* meant unfavorable in one's stars. It was commonplace to attribute bad fortune to the influences of the stars in the Medieval and Renaissance eras. The Old Italian word came into English in the late 1500s as "disaster" and was used by Shakespeare (cf. *King Lear*). The word's Latin root is *astrum*, meaning "star," and the Latin prefix *dis-*, meaning "apart" and signifying negation. *Catastrophe* (A) and *misfortune* (C) are both Modern English meanings of the word "disaster," whereas the "ill-starred" meaning used in Elizabethan times has now become archaic or obsolete. The root means "star," not the aster flower (D).

80. A: The Latin word *sal* meant "salt." According to the famous ancient historian Pliny the Elder, "in Rome, a soldier was paid in salt," as it was a means of preserving food in the days before refrigeration and was thus a very valuable commodity. The Latin term *salarium*, from the root *sal*, originally meant the salt paid to soldiers but eventually became generalized to mean any kind of payment. (The expression "worth your salt" also derives from this origin.) "Salary" may sound similar to "celery" (B), but their roots and meanings are not the same. While salt eventually referred to any kind of payment including money or other kinds, it never originally meant *money* (C). "Earnings" (D) is a Modern English synonym for "salary" rather than the original meaning of its root word.

81. B: The word "brunch" is a blend of "breakfast" and "lunch". Blends of two or more words are known as portmanteau words. (*Portmanteau* is a French word meaning a suitcase.) "Fax" (A) is an example of clipping, or shortening a word, from its original "facsimile." "Babysitter" (C) is an example of compounding, or combining two or more words into one. "Saxophone" (D) is an example of proper noun transfer: A Belgian family that built musical instruments had the last name of Sax, and this wind instrument was named after them. These represent some of the ways that new words have entered—and still do enter—the English language.

82. C: Neologisms (from *neo-* meaning "new"), also known as "creative coinages," are new words sometimes invented by people which then become parts of our vocabulary. The word "quark" was first coined by the great Irish author James Joyce; he used it in his last novel, *Finnegans Wake*. The physicist Murray Gell-Mann then chose this word from Joyce's work to name the model of elementary particles he proposed (also proposed concurrently and independently by physicist George Zweig) in 1964. Blending (A) is another way new words come into our language; for example, "moped" is a blend of the respective first syllables of "motor" and "pedal." Conversion (B), also called functional shift, changes a word's part of speech. For example, the common nouns "network," "microwave," and "fax," along with the proper noun "Google" have all been converted to verbs in modern usage. Onomatopoeia (D) means words that imitate associated sounds, such as "meow" and "click."

83. D: This is an example of a compound-complex sentence. A simple (A) sentence contains a subject and a verb and expresses a complete thought. Its subject and/or verb may be compound (e.g., "John and Mary" as subject and "comes and goes" as verb). A complex (B) sentence contains an independent clause and one or more dependent clauses. The independent and dependent clauses are joined by a subordinating conjunction or a relative pronoun. A compound (C) sentence contains two independent clauses—two simple sentences—connected by a coordinating conjunction. A compound-complex (also called complex-compound) sentence, as its name implies, combines both compound and complex sentences: it combines more than one independent clause with at least one dependent clause. In the example sentence given, the first two clauses, joined by "however," are independent, and the clause modifying "actual test questions," beginning with "which cover," is a relative, dependent clause.

84. C: A euphemism is an expression used instead of more literal words to make a harsh expression sound softer, to make an impolite description sound more polite, or to make a description less polite (such as saying "bit the dust" instead of "died" in a formal setting). Jargon (A) is the specialized terminology of a specific field or group. This example, however, is NOT medical jargon; a better example might be "expired" or "deceased." Ambiguity (B) means unclear and/or open to multiple interpretations. A better example of ambiguity in this scenario might be, "The surgery did not obtain all of the desired outcomes." This can mean a greater number of things than that the patient died. A connotation (D) is a suggested meaning associated with the literal meaning of a word. For example, "The surgery was abortive" does not state that the patient died, but if the surgery was meant to save the patient's life, the adjective "abortive," meaning unsuccessful or failing to obtain the desired result, could connote that the patient died.

85. B: Typically, after students write something, teachers may ask them to reflect on what they wrote, which would mean that this is NOT a prewriting activity. In writing exercises, teachers will typically ask students to plan (A) what they will write in order to clearly define their main topic and organize their work. Many teachers find it helps students to visualize (C) what they are reading and/or want to write about, and make drawings of what they visualize as preparation for writing. Brainstorming (D) is another common prewriting activity designed to generate multiple ideas from which students can select.

86. A: After prewriting (planning, visualizing, brainstorming), the correct sequence of steps in the writing process are drafting, in which the writer takes the material generated during prewriting work and makes it into sentences and paragraphs; revising, where the writer explores to improve the quality of the writing; editing, in which the writer examines his or her writing for factual and mechanical (grammar, spelling, punctuation) errors and correcting them; and publishing, when the writer finally shares what he or she has written with others who will read it and give feedback.

87. B: Researchers have found that the writing processes both form a hierarchy and are observably recursive in nature. Moreover, they find that when students continually revise their writing, they are able to consider new ideas and to incorporate these ideas into their work. Thus they do not merely correct mechanical errors when revising (A), they also add to the content and quality of their writing. Furthermore, research shows that writers, including students, not only revise their actual writing, during rewrites, they also reconsider their original writing goals rather than always retaining them (C), and they revisit their prewriting plans rather than leaving these unaffected (D).

88. C: Researchers have found that children know a great deal more about a given topic than what their writing usually reflects. Therefore, options A and D are incorrect. Furthermore, researchers have concluded that when children stop writing, they do not do so because they have run out of things to write about the topic (B), but rather because they have not yet developed the means to articulate their knowledge adequately. Educational experts find that these research findings inform writing instruction in that the process of continually rewriting helps children to access and articulate more of the knowledge they actually have.

89. D: This description is most typical of the process of peer review. Classmates read a peer's paper and then identify values in it, describe it, ask questions about it, and suggest points for revision. These are types of helpful feedback identified by experts on writing and collaborative writing. The other choices, however, are not typically collaborative. For a portfolio assessment (A), the teacher collects finished work products from a student over time, eventually assembling a portfolio of work. This affords a more authentic assessment using richer, more multidimensional, and more visual and tactile products for assessment instead of using only standardized test scores for assessment. Holistic scoring (B) is a method of scoring a piece of writing for overall quality (evaluating general elements such as focus, organization, support, and conventions) rather than being overly concerned with any individual aspect of writing. A scoring rubric (C) is a guide that gives examples of the levels of typical characteristics in a piece of writing that correspond to each available score (for example, scores from 1-5).

90. C: According to the Association of College and Research Libraries, Information Literacy is the set of skills that an individual must have for finding, retrieving, analyzing, and using information. It is required not just for reading and understanding information (A). Information Literacy does not mean learning and retaining a lot of information (B), or only sharing it with others (D), but rather knowing how to find information one does not already have and how to evaluate that information critically for its quality and apply it judiciously to meet one's purposes.

91. B: The early 21st century has been dubbed the Information Age primarily because, with widespread Internet use and other innovations in electronic communications and publishing, there are more sources of information and greater output of available information than ever before. While some agencies might require more information (A), this is only possible because such information is more readily available now. Professionals in higher education and research find that with this new explosion of information, college students cannot possibly gain enough information literacy by just reading texts and writing research papers, and cannot learn all they need to know in four years (C). This period is also not called the Information Age due to an increased student interest in acquiring information (D), but due to the increased access to information.

92. A: It is a standard of Information Literacy (IL) that students must use their own critical thinking skills to evaluate the quality of the information and its sources before they use it. Another standard is that the student should ascertain how much information s/he needs for his/her purposes first, deciding this after uncovering excessive information is inefficient (B). An additional IL standard is to access necessary information in an efficient and effective way. However, none of these standards include the idea that students will lose incidental learning or broadness of scope by doing so (C). IL standards include the principle that students *should* use the information they find in ways that are effective for attaining their specific purposes (D).

93. B: The MLA (Modern Language Association) system for documenting literary sources defines in-line citations in a paper as combining signal phrases, which usually include the author's name and introduce information from a source via a fact, summary, paraphrase, or quotation; parenthetical references following the material cited, frequently at the end of the sentence; and, except for web sources that are unpaginated, page number(s). MLA defines a list of works cited (A) as an alphabetized list found at the end of a research paper that gives the information sources referenced in the paper, including each source's publication information, quotations, summaries, and paraphrases. Guidelines for preparing the list of works cited are provided in the *MLA Handbook*. MLA information notes (C) are an optional addition to the MLA parenthetical documentation system. These notes can be used to add important material without interrupting the paper's flow, and/or to supply comments about sources or make references to multiple sources. They may be endnotes or footnotes. Because only one of the answers is correct, Option D is not possible.

94. C: On the Internet, the name of an author is usually provided but may not be visible at first glance. Web sources frequently include the author's name on another page of the same site, such as the website's home page, or in a tiny font at the very end of the web page, rather than in a more conspicuous location. In such cases, students doing online research may have to search more thoroughly than usual to find the author's name. Therefore, they should not immediately assume the author is not named (A). Also, many Web sources are sponsored by government agencies or private corporations and do not give individual author names. In these cases, the research paper *should* cite the agency or corporation name as author (B). Finally, it is much more common for online sources to omit an author's name than it is in print sources. In these cases, it is both permitted and advised by the MLA to cite the article or book title instead (D).

95. D: When online sources you are citing in your research paper are in PDFs and other file formats that have stable pagination, the MLA advises including the page number in the research paper's in-text citation because these numbers are valid and do not change. If a Web source has no pagination, as often happens, the MLA does NOT advise avoiding the citation (A), it advises simply making the citation without a page number because there is not one available. Unlike in PDFs (above), when citing a source from a printout, the MLA advises NOT including page numbers even if you see them because the same page numbers are not always found in all printouts (B). It is not true that in-text citations should never include page numbers (C).

96. D: The MLA guidelines for citing multiple authors of the same work in in-text citations (for both print and online sources) dictate using the first author's name plus "et al" for the other authors when there are four or more authors. If there are two (options A and B) or three (options B and C) authors, the guidelines say to name each author, either in a signal phrase [for example, "Smith and Jones note that... (45)" or "Smith, Jones, and Gray have noted... (45)"] or in a parenthetical reference ["(Smith, Jones, and Gray 45)."].

97. C: Persuasive writing has the purpose of expressing the writer's opinion and/or of convincing the reader of something. A movie review is one example of this writing purpose and type. Other examples include advertisements, editorials, book and music reviews, and literary essays. Narration (A) is a type of writing for telling stories. Description (B) is a type of writing for creating a picture using words that evoke imagery for the reader. Exposition (D) is a type of writing for informing and/or explaining.

98. B: Persuasive writing tries to convince readers to agree with the author's opinion or position regarding a topic. To convince others, writers must have sufficient knowledge about the topic, logical thinking skills, strong beliefs about the topic, and enough technical skill for making logical points, supporting one's opinions, and swaying the reader's emotions. Expository (A) writing aims to give information and/or explanations. It requires sufficient knowledge, practicality, and the technical skill for writing clarity, but it is not as hard as persuasion because it seeks not to convince the reader of anything, only to inform or explain. Descriptive (C) writing seeks to paint verbal pictures that make the described things real to readers through sensory details. This requires imagination and strong creative writing skills, but is not as difficult as persuading the reader to agree with the author's viewpoint. Narrative (D) writing tells a story and can be the easiest, as storytelling and enjoying stories are natural for most people.

99. A: *The Adventures of Huckleberry Finn* by Mark Twain is a fictional novel. *The Diary of a Young Girl* by Anne Frank is a non-fictional journal. "The Fall of the House of Usher" by Edgar Allan Poe is a fictional short story in the horror genre. Novels, personal narratives like diaries/journals, and short stories, as well as biographies and anecdotes are all types of narrative. Narration tells a story, often (but not always) advances chronologically, and has a beginning, middle, and end. Descriptive writing (B) paints a word picture using sensory imagery to make an event, scene, thing, or person more real to the imagination of the reader. Other than character sketches, picture captions, and some kinds of advertising, most writing is not completely descriptive: narrative works typically include descriptive parts. Exposition (C) is found in news stories, encyclopedias, research papers, informational essays, and instruction manuals rather than fiction or journals. Persuasion (D) is more characteristic of editorials, reviews, ads, and literary essays than novels, short stories or diaries.

100. B: For any writing assignment, you should first target an audience, perform an audience analysis, and develop an audience profile to determine what you should include in and omit from your writing. Even though the assigning teacher may be the only one to read your writing, you should not assume s/he is your main audience (A) because the teacher may expect you to write for other readers. In addition to first knowing your purpose for writing before beginning, you should also consider what purpose your writing will meet for your readers (C) and how they are likely to use it. Considering your audience's attitude toward what you will write and their likely reactions are also important to shaping your writing and is NOT overthinking (D).

101. C: The kind of audience for your writing, as well as your purpose, will determine what style, tone, and wording you choose. Knowing your audience will enable you to select writing strategies, style and tone, and specific word choices that will be most understandable and appealing to your readers. Knowing the type of audience will also dictate how much time to spend on research (A). Some readers will expect more supporting evidence, while others will be bored or overwhelmed by it. Similarly, you will want to include more or less information depending on who will be reading what you write (B). And while the structure of your piece does inform how you organize your information, you should also vary your organization according to who will read it (D).

102. D: It is best to begin an essay or paper with a broader, more general introduction to the topic, and move to a more focused and specific point regarding the topic—not vice versa (C)—by the end of the introduction. This point is your thesis statement. Writing experts advise *against* the technique of beginning an essay with a dictionary definition (A) because it has been so overused that it has become ineffective and uninteresting. To engage the reader's interest in your topic, it is best to begin with some very attention-getting material rather than leaving it for later (B).

103. C: The first part of the introduction to an essay or paper should be some original, fresh material that will engage the attention of readers enough so they are interested in continuing to read. Following this should be the transitional portion of the introduction, which gives some pertinent background information about the piece's particular purpose (B). This informs the reader of your reason for focusing on your paper or essay's specific topic. The transitional portion moves the piece to the third part of the introduction: the thesis statement (A), which is a clear expression of the main point you are trying to make in your essay or paper. An optional part of the introduction is an explanation of how you will defend your thesis, giving readers a general idea of how your essay or paper's various points will be organized. This is sometimes described as a "road map" (D).

104. B: One recommended technique for beginning an essay is to cite a surprising statistic related to your essay's topic. This will get the readers' attention, while also giving some information about the topic to be discussed in the rest of the piece. Another effective technique is to begin with an interesting quotation that summarizes your position. This adds interest, support, and power; it is not true that you should use only your own words instead of quoting another's (A). It is also untrue that opening with a story or anecdote is contrary to the purposes of an essay or paper (C); when you have some personal interest in your topic, this technique is useful for emotionally engaging the readers in the subject matter. It is not true that asking rhetorical questions will only frustrate readers (D): this is a technique that helps readers imagine being in different situations so they can consider your topic in new ways.

105. A: While students may sometimes regard the conclusion of their essay or paper as simply the last paragraph that includes all the pieces that they could not fit into earlier parts of the piece, this is an inadequate treatment of the conclusion. Because the conclusion is the last thing the audience reads, they are more likely to remember it. Also, the conclusion is an excellent opportunity to reinforce your main point, remind readers of the importance of your topic, and prod readers to consider the effects of the topic in their own lives and/or in the world at large. A good conclusion should restate your original thesis statement (B), pull together and/or summarize the main points you made (C), and make clear(er) your discussion's or argument's context (D).

106. B: Tone is the writer's overall way of expressing his or her attitude. Voice is who the reader hears speaking in the writing, the individual way the writer uses to express his or her tone—not vice versa (A).

Style (options C and D) is the effect a writer creates through language, mechanics, and attitude or the sound (formal or informal) or impressions (seriousness, levity, grace, fluency) of the writing.

107. C: Diction refers to your overall choice of language for your writing, while vocabulary refers to the specific words in a discipline that you use when writing in or about that discipline—not vice versa (A). Jargon (B) is very specialized terminology used in a discipline that is not readily understood by readers outside of that discipline. It is hence less accessible than the vocabulary of the discipline, and only used in writing intended only for those who are already familiar with it. Style refers to the writer's effect through language and technique (D).

108. D: Knowing your purpose for writing means knowing what you want to achieve with the content of your writing, and thus what writing style to use. Your choice of words and how formal or informal your writing is—your diction—*does* affect your style (A). Diction and tone should be consistent in your writing style, and should reflect vocabulary and writing patterns that suit your writing purpose best. Style is not added later to give writing personality (B). It develops from your purpose for writing, or what you want to accomplish with your writing. Style *is* directly related to your control of the content (C) of your writing.

109. C: The verbs quoted all refer to interpreting information in your own words. This task targets the cognitive objective of comprehension. Tasks targeting knowledge recall (A) would ask you to name, label, list, define, repeat, memorize, order, or arrange the material. Tasks targeting application (B) would ask you to calculate, solve, practice, operate, sketch, use, prepare, illustrate, or apply the material. Tasks targeting evaluation (D) would ask you to judge, appraise, evaluate, conclude, predict, score, or compare the material.

110. B: The verbs quoted all refer to taking pieces or parts of information or knowledge and bringing them together to create a whole, and to building relationships among the parts to fit new or different circumstances. Analysis (A) is the opposite of synthesis—breaking information down into its component parts and demonstrating the relationships among those parts. An assignment for analysis would ask you to compare, distinguish, test, categorize, examine, contrast, or analyze information. Evaluation (C) is making judgments based on given criteria, confirming or supporting certain preferences, and persuading the reader. An assignment targeting evaluation would use words like evaluate, predict, appraise, conclude, score, judge, or compare. Application (D) is using knowledge in new contexts. The assignment would ask you to apply, prepare, practice, use, operate, sketch, calculate, solve, or illustrate.

111. A: Evaluation is the most complex of the thinking/writing strategies listed in these choices because it commonly incorporates the other thinking strategies. Knowledge recall (D) requires showing mastery of information learned. Comprehension (C) requires showing understanding of the information learned. Application (B) requires taking the information learned and using it in new or different circumstances. These processes are not as complex as evaluating (or making critical judgments about) the information learned. Analysis and synthesis are also more complex than knowledge recall, comprehension, and application, though less so than evaluation.

112. C: Comparing and contrasting, explaining cause and effect relationships, and analyzing are the most commonly used forms of analysis in college-level writing. Supporting an opinion (C) you have stated in your writing is one of the most commonly used forms of *synthesis*, not analysis, in college-level writing.

113. C: Proposing a solution to some problem or situation is one of the most commonly used forms of synthesis strategies in college-level writing. The other most commonly used synthesis writing strategy is stating an opinion and supporting it with evidence. Explaining cause and effect (A) and comparing and contrasting (B) are two of the most commonly used *analysis* (not synthesis) writing strategies. Using persuasion (D) to convince the reader is typically combined with the other strategies named to add credibility and acceptance to the position stated by the writer.

114. B: A white paper, opinion survey, annotated bibliography, and problem solution are all examples of the exploratory discourse aim. So are definitions, diagnoses, marketing analyses, feasibility studies, and literature (*not* literary) reviews. The expressive (A) discourse aim is reflected in vision statements, mission statements, proposals, constitutions, legislative bills, etc. Examples of writing reflecting the informative (C) discourse aim include news and magazine articles, reports, and encyclopedia articles. Examples of writing reflecting the persuasive (D) discourse aim include political speeches; editorials; ad campaigns; and works of artistic, social, or political criticism.

115. A: This sentence is an analogy, which compares similarities between two concepts to establish a relationship. Analogy can enhance comprehension of a new concept via comparison to an older/more familiar concept. Allegory (B) uses symbolism to represent a more abstract concept with a more concrete concept. Allusion (C) is a passing reference to a specific work/place/person/event. For example, saying "Susan loves to help and care for other people so much that her friends call her Mother Teresa" is an allusion to a famous person for effectiveness. Antithesis (D) juxtaposes words/phrases/sentences with opposite meanings, balancing these to add insight. A good example is Neil Armstrong's statement during the moon landing: "That's one small step for man, one giant leap for mankind."

116. D: All these choices use the literary device of an extended metaphor, as does the quoted Shakespeare passage wherein Romeo describes Juliet as the sun. In option A, Eliot describes the fog as a cat ("...rubs its back... rubs its muzzle... licked its tongue... Let fall upon its back the soot... curled once about the house, and fell asleep.") Similarly, Carl Sandburg's (1916) poem "Fog" (C) describes the fog that "comes on little cat feet." In option B, Frost uses the extended metaphor of two roads that "diverged in a wood" to describe the journey of life.

117. C: This sentence appeals to the reader's emotions by stating simply that it is dangerous and "really stupid" to use a cell phone while driving; it does not provide any evidence or logic to support the statement. Steering one-handed makes driving more dangerous is a logical, common-sense argument. Supporting evidence such as statistics of greater accident risk is an appeal to logic. Citing the fact that many state laws ban cell phone use while driving supports the idea that it is dangerous, and also refers to data on more accidents from doing so, also appealing to logic rather than emotion.

118. A: A fallacy of inconsistency exists in a statement that contradicts itself or defeats itself. Saying there are exceptions to all general statements is itself a general statement; therefore, according to the content, this statement must also have an exception, implying there are NOT exceptions to all general statements. Option B is an example of a fallacy of irrelevance: passing or failing is determined by course performance, so asking to pass because parents will be upset if one fails is an irrelevant reason for appealing to a teacher for a passing grade. Option C is an example of a fallacy of insufficiency: a statement is made with insufficient supporting evidence. A lack of evidence of innocence is not enough to prove one is guilty because there could also be an equal lack of evidence of guilt. Option D is an example of a fallacy of inappropriate presumption: asking someone if s/he has stopped cheating presumes that s/he has cheated in the past. The person being asked this question cannot answer either "yes" or "no" without confirming that s/he has indeed been cheating. If the person being asked has not been cheating, then the person asking the question is making a false assumption.

119. B: A clustering illusion is a cognitive bias of attributing cause and effect and patterns to unrelated or random events. The character described considers the phone's ringing an effect caused by flushing the toilet, when in reality the two are unrelated. It was mere coincidence that the first ring occurred after he flushed; subsequent rings always occur at preset time intervals, and his repeated flushes simply coincided with these. The above-average effect (A) is the cognitive bias of overestimating our own abilities. The confirmation bias (C) is our tendency to focus on information confirming our pre-existing beliefs while overlooking conflicting information. In comparing ourselves with other people, we notice others' errors more and our own errors less. The framing bias (D) is being influenced by how information is framed rather than the facts. For example, whether a doctor presents the success or failure rate of an operation can influence the patient's decision to undergo it, even if both rates reflect identical data.

120. A: The statement reflects a stereotype. A stereotype is an assumption or generalization made about everybody in an identified group. Assumptions (C) can be made about many things, not just about the members of a certain group. Generalizations (D) also apply to a great many subjects, not just to the characteristics of a specific group of people. An inference (B) is a conclusion based on available evidence rather than on an overt statement of fact. For example, if Archie said, "That man is Asian, so he must be a terrible driver," he would be making an inference based on his stereotype of Asian people. Therefore, stereotype is the most precise definition of the statement.

Thank You

We at Mometrix would like to extend our heartfelt thanks to you, our friend and patron, for allowing us to play a part in your journey. It is a privilege to serve people from all walks of life who are unified in their commitment to building the best future they can for themselves.

The preparation you devote to these important testing milestones may be the most valuable educational opportunity you have for making a real difference in your life. We encourage you to put your heart into it—that feeling of succeeding, overcoming, and yes, conquering will be well worth the hours you've invested.

We want to hear your story, your struggles and your successes, and if you see any opportunities for us to improve our materials so we can help others even more effectively in the future, please share that with us as well. **The team at Mometrix would be absolutely thrilled to hear from you!** So please, send us an email (support@mometrix.com) and let's stay in touch.

> **If you'd like some additional help, check out these other resources we offer for your exam: http://MometrixFlashcards.com/OSAT**

Additional Bonus Material

Due to our efforts to try to keep this book to a manageable length, we've created a link that will give you access to all of your additional bonus material.

Please visit http://www.mometrix.com/bonus948/osateng107 to access the information.